"Cheryl Pierson was an old-fashioned girl . . . she did not drink or smoke or parade around in strange revealing clothes. She had never been in trouble or shown even the most remote signs of delinquency. Cheryl still slept with a teddy bear at night. She had never been to a discotheque. She believed in God. She still was unclear how babies were born. She had never tried marijuana. The most important thing in her life was her family . . ."

*This was the girl who paid a classmate $400 to murder her father—and whom society could judge only by breaking—*

# A DEADLY SILENCE
## The Ordeal of Cheryl Pierson: A Case of Incest and Murder

"A fine book . . . the author, a reporter who covered the story for *The New York Times*, is an unusually artful weaver, and a wise one [as she] tells the story of the Pierson family of Magnolia Drive in Selden, Long Island."
—*The New York Times Book Review*

"Skillful, thoughtful, thorough, powerful!"
—*Kirkus Reviews*

DENA KLEIMAN is an award-winning reporter for *The New York Times*. She lives in New York City.

# A
# DEADLY
# SILENCE

## The Ordeal
## of Cheryl Pierson:
## A Case of Incest
## and Murder

Dena Kleiman

A SIGNET BOOK

**NEW AMERICAN LIBRARY**

A DIVISION OF PENGUIN BOOKS USA INC.

# ACKNOWLEDGMENTS

I am grateful to Ken Emerson, who first gave me the assignment to write a story about Cheryl Pierson for *The New York Times Magazine,* as well as the many other editors at the *Times* who guided my subsequent reporting. I am particularly indebted to Dennis Stern and John Darnton for their encouragement and patience during the time I worked on the book, as well as Peter Millones, who as my editor for many years taught me the skills necessary to take on a project of this magnitude. A special thank you is in order as well to George W. Judson, who oversaw my daily coverage of the Pierson case and whose instincts and judgment were always right. Finally I will forever be grateful to Arthur Gelb and A.M. Rosenthal, who opened up the joys of being reporter to me fifteen years ago by offering me a job.

There are many whose names appear over the course of this book whom I can never sufficiently thank for opening up their homes to me and with great care and candor entrusting me with the very painful intimacies of this tragedy. I would also like to thank K. James McCready, Ed Jablonski, Martin Efman, Paul Gianelli, Dr. Kathleen Oitzinger, and Dr. Jean Goodwin, who so generously gave of their time.

This book would never have been written were it not for Andy Wolk and Dr. Hannah Zackson Wolk, who were never too busy to listen or to cheer me on and are the best friends anyone could have. I also appreciate the time so generously given by my friends

Faith Rosenfeld, David G. Richenthal, Micheline Kleiman, Michael Kaufman, Sandra Salmans, Susan P. Stickells, and Frances Jackson.

Finally I would like to thank Esther Newberg, my agent, for her infectious enthusiasm and unwavering encouragement, and Ann Godoff, my editor, whose intelligence, judgment, and grace I will always appreciate.

To Abe, Henrietta, Gloria,
Micheline and Harry

Yes, I loved him. I loved him when he was my father; when we used to go motorcycle riding and I rode on the back. When he came to my games, I felt good my father was coming to my games. That was something that a father and daughter should do. That's the one thing I miss.

—Cheryl Pierson
*July 1986*

# 1

James Pierson always slept with the bedroom door open; the thick, heavy door that separated his room from the rest of the house. It was not a large house. One could stand at one end and easily hear what was going on in the other. Pierson was the kind of man who liked to do that—to sit in his bedroom and listen to the chatter of the television running in the den; the hum of the Mixmaster in the kitchen as his wife whipped up something sweet for dinner, the squeals of the children at war over some lost toy. No, keeping the door open when he slept at night had nothing to do with being able to hear what was going on in other parts of the house. It was a statement of the way James Pierson said he believed a family should live.

"No secrets," Pierson would say. "I don't want secrets in this house. We're a family. We live here together."

So the bedroom door was open that early icy morning Pierson put on his dungarees and walked down the hall of his brown shingled house on Long Island. Like so many other homes of its kind, it had aluminum siding on the roof he had installed himself, a prayer over the door in the kitchen, a collection of miniature porcelains in the curio cabinet that were thick with dust no matter how many times his wife wiped them clean. He was not a religious man, but Scotch-taped to the window of the front door was a picture of the Pope. A portrait of Jesus Christ hung over the dresser in the master bedroom. The carpeting beneath the grandfather clock in the hall was plush wall to wall.

Pierson was an electrician by training; a large, burly man with bushy red eyebrows and a freckled, boyish face. He wore his hair short and brushed to one side in a way that comically emphasized his ears. No longer the lithe athlete who hoped one day to pitch for the Yankees, his six-foot frame now carried a large belly. But it was his hands that were most like the man himself. Massive. Rough. A counterpoint to anything dainty. There was an ungainliness to Pierson. Particularly now.

Pierson walked into the bedroom of his younger daughter, JoAnn, eight years old. Under the covers, she was almost invisible in that room of hers crammed with the latest of teddy bears and Barbie dolls; the quarters of a child who in other ways had done without. Ever since her mother died Pierson had filled the child's room with anything and everything she asked as if material possessions could possibly fill the void left behind by his wife. He had said it himself. He was awkward with daughters. It was hard enough to be a father to his twenty-year-old son, his namesake, the one he had hoped would make the family proud. But now with the death of his wife, he had more on his hands than he was prepared to handle.

"See you later, Peach," Pierson said, kissing the child on her forehead. He lay the blanket over the young girl's shoulders. She smiled and gave her father a hug. He stood in the doorway and waved.

Pierson now made his way into the bedroom of his other daughter, Cheryl, sixteen years old. She had overslept the day before and been late to school. He wanted to make sure she would not be late again.

"Are you awake?" he asked.

"Uh uh," she grunted, raising her head.

"Now don't fall back asleep." She nodded.

Pierson made his way along the blue shag carpet in the living room and plucked his plaid hunting jacket

and tan down vest from one of the dining room chairs.
Then he opened the door off the kitchen, the way he
always did on weekday mornings. The pavement was
slick, the sky ominous, the outline of his work truck
in the rear yard still fuzzy in the darkness.

There is no way James Pierson could have spotted
the slender young man hidden behind the tree in his
driveway. How stunned Pierson would have been to see
him there: this scrawny young man just sixteen years
old, with braces still on his teeth and not even the trace
of a beard. Pierson turned toward his work truck in the
rear yard, his car keys ready in his right hand.

No one heard the shots. But seconds later on this
quiet stretch of single family homes with their frost-
covered swing sets and above ground pools, James
Pierson, a forty-two-year-old electrician and father of
three, lay dead while the young man who pulled the
trigger got away.

James Pierson and this slender young man met on
that cold February morning for only a matter of seconds. But what brought them together was a powerful
secret that would haunt their families and the quiet
community in which they lived for years to come.

James Pierson's fortieth birthday party was held at the
Knights of Columbus Hall just across from the local
bowling alley. The date was January 7, 1984—by design three days after his actual birthday so it would be
a surprise. His son, James, then seventeen years old,
lured him there by telling his father he wanted to show
him a car. Pierson loved finding a bargain in cars. Old
cars. Fast cars, the faster the better. And Pierson loved
driving them fast, dodging in and out of lanes at 120
miles per hour. Anyone who had ever been a passenger
in a car with James Pierson knew that about him and
that it was a mistake to ask him to slow down.

On that particular night the car in question was a
'56 Chevy; the kind Pierson had driven as a teenager—
a red convertible with dice hanging from the rearview

mirror. The ruse had been his wife, Cathleen's, idea. Kenny Zimlinghaus, his friend and partner, hired the band, and a group of friends pitched in and hired a belly dancer.

Pierson and his son pulled into the catering hall. The lights dimmed. The door swung open. Everyone yelled "surprise" and for the first time anyone could remember, James Pierson, a man who prided himself on control, was visibly shocked—so stunned his frying-pan face went red, he turned away and temporarily had to leave the room. Pierson was never much good at showing his emotions. He was a man's man—the kind that slapped friends too hard on the back and was better at showing his anger than expressing gratitude or sorrow. It was not that he was a man without emotion. He was as sentimental as they came. Downright corny at times, but always guarded. The idea that a stranger would see him cry was probably the most repulsive thought he could imagine.

It was a grand celebration made all the more bitter-sweet by its excess festivity. The balloons. The champagne. The strobe lighting. The loud music. Pierson was addicted to tunes from the fifties, and his wife had made sure the band knew "The Lion Sleeps Tonight," a favorite song. It was Cathleen who had planned the party, but just about everyone in the room wondered if it would be her last. They whispered among themselves about how thin she had become; how swollen her face, how difficult it was on her, how sad for the children. Strangely, Pierson was the only one who failed to notice or truly accept how bad his wife's condition was. He dragged her to doctors. He ranted and raved. But all along he was convinced she would survive.

"Jimmy felt she was going to live forever," recalled Jack Wern, a close friend who was there that night. "He didn't want to believe she was going to die."

Almost everyone who was important to James Pierson was at his fortieth birthday party, and if there was one frozen image of a high point in his life, it might well have been there.

Although his wife was still ill, Pierson's three children seemed to be developing well. James was graduating with high marks that June from Newfield High School. At thirteen, Cheryl was growing into a poised young lady and the model daughter. Everyone knew how proud the Piersons were of Cheryl. How she went to the hospital with her father, helped him shop for groceries, took care of her younger sister, and cooked the family's meals. The little one, JoAnn, six, was probably the most intelligent and charming.

Pierson had become a wealthy man. No one quite knew how. There was the foreman's job he had at Lister Electric. There was the cable television business he was running on the side. There were the real estate deals from time to time. But these days he had more money than he knew what to do with. He had just bought his wife a Lincoln Continental with the license plate CATHLEEN. He had just totally redecorated a new house and bragged to friends he had more money than he thought he would ever need.

"Well, I made it to forty," he declared that night, lifting his glass, his face aglow with pleasure. He hugged his three children and took his wife into his arms for a dance. He was an intensely private man, the kind who preferred, indeed enjoyed, hearing the problems of others. "You have a problem? Come to Jimmy," he would say with his deep, dimpled smile. He always had trouble when others wanted to be generous to him. He was a loud and difficult man with a foul mouth and a crude sense of humor. But he had lots of friends, friends from many walks of life who were intrigued with his offbeat, at times childlike, sense of humor.

"He was so happy at that party," recalled Kenny Zimlinghaus, his business partner and closest friend. "It was such an exciting time. Business was booming.

The kids were doing great. He was so excited about the new house.''

The new house was at 293 Magnolia Drive. It was the house his wife's parents used to live in. Pierson had renovated it and expanded it to nearly twice its original size. People would come and admire the interior; the separate wing of bedrooms set off from the rest of the house by a long hall, the combination safe built into a closet wall, the detailed security system with its flashing green light that allowed Pierson to lie in bed and know exactly where someone was walking at any precise moment.

Just two years later, it was the house where James Pierson would die.

It was Cheryl who discovered her father. She would later say that when she heard the door slam she glanced at the clock radio and it read exactly 6:20 A.M. The school bus wasn't going to be there for another hour, so she briefly put her head back on the pillow until Noel, the family's aging toy poodle, began barking and tugging at her socks in the mad frenzy that Cheryl had come to know meant it was time for the dog to go out. A demure brunette with deepset dark eyes and a dainty button nose, Cheryl's looks were well scrubbed and all American. She wore her hair permed and down to her shoulders with bangs that always seemed to get in her eyes. She was a pretty girl with delicate features and a quick laugh that often got her in trouble. Co-captain of her high school's junior varsity cheerleading team, she was an outgoing, self-confident teenager with an easy sense of humor.

Cheryl would recall that she moved slowly out of bed that morning. She was wearing a pink-flowered nightgown and knee socks. Her bedroom was one removed from her father's, and she shared the bathroom in the hall with her younger sister, JoAnn. She stopped at the bathroom for a moment and then went to the door. Through the frost-covered glass she gazed out at the frigid morning; the sky was an ominous slate. She was thinking she would have to make sure her younger sister wore boots and her new down jacket, when all of a sudden, she would later say, a strange image caught her eye. It was the form of her father lying face down in the driveway.

"Dad," she shrieked. She raced to her room and threw a sweatsuit over her nightgown and in only her knee socks ran out onto the icy driveway. His ankles were turned out like those of a broken doll.

"Dad, are you hurt?" she cried out in the still morning air.

When her father did not reply, she would later tell police, Cheryl ran across the driveway to the home of her neighbors, Michael and Alberta Kosser.

Magnolia Drive is a main thoroughfare in Selden. It is lined with modest but comfortable homes, virtually all populated with children. But at this hour of the morning the street was still largely deserted. It was still quiet, a few cars passed in the morning light. Several neighbors were just beginning to get moving. The bathroom lights of several houses were on. A television flickered through the kitchen windows of the neighbors across the way. One could almost hear the clock radios going off in the cold, still air, the Mr. Coffee machines bubbling on Formica counters. But the Kossers' house was still dark.

Alberta and Michael Kosser had lived near the Piersons for as long as anyone could remember. Like so many other couples in this part of Long Island, they were in many ways closer to each other than they were to their families: helping to raise each other's children, setting each other's standards. Jim Pierson and Mike Kosser never had much to say to one another. As people, they could not have been more different. Pierson was a loudmouth. The neighborhood showoff. Kosser was more serious and quiet. A private man, who kept to himself. But their wives were best friends, and from the moment their husbands left in the morning until

the moment they came home, the two women delighted in each other's company, trading laundry de-
tergents and wives' tales, gossip and family recipes.
Alberta came from an Italian family and taught Cathy
how to prepare a perfect lasagna. She in turn taught
Alberta her secret recipe for French toast—the kind
with crisp edges and just a hint of cinnamon and pow-
dered sugar. They had had two children each—a boy
and a girl—and a shared respect for the Catholic
church. Petite, dark, outgoing, warm, they even looked
alike, and people often confused them for sisters.

Alberta was shocked when Cathy became pregnant
for the third time at the age of thirty. Cheryl was already eight years old. Jimmy was eleven. James Pierson, always accident prone, was in a leg cast up to his
thigh. But no one was more surprised by the pregnancy than Cathy herself. She confided to Alberta she
didn't want another baby. Since Cathy was a Catholic,
abortion was not an option. But three months after
JoAnn was born, she went into the hospital and had
her tubes tied so such a mistake would not happen
again. After she came down with the kidney problems
she wondered whether God was punishing her, getting
even with her for her rebellion.

"My father," Cheryl screamed in the Kossers'
darkened house.

Mike Kosser arrived in the kitchen first. A tall, lanky
man with thinning grey hair and strong, muscular
arms, he was clad in grey sweatclothes. His chunky
twenty-year-old son, Mike Jr., was next, his eyes
bloodshot with sleep. His daughter, Anne-Marie,
eighteen, followed, shaking at the idea that something
was wrong. The only one missing from the Kossser
household that morning was Alberta, who was in the
hospital recuperating from minor surgery. Mike Kosser had taken the day off from his job as an auto mechanic so he could bring his wife home that afternoon.
From his kitchen window Kosser could make out the
silhouette of Pierson's body lying face down in the

snow. He and his son ran out of their house and over to the Piersons'. They knelt on the icy ground beside the stricken man.

"He's slipped and fallen on the ice," Kosser told police when he dialed the emergency number. An operator told him they would send an ambulance. He then returned to Pierson's side with a dishtowel to see if he could stop the bleeding himself. Kneeling there in the freezing darkness, he was convinced he still felt a pulse. With the towel, he tried to contain the bleeding but was unsuccessful. The wait for an ambulance seemed endless.

Concerned that the commotion would awaken her sister, Cheryl rushed back into the house.

"You're not going to school today," JoAnn, eight years old, would recall Cheryl telling her. "Daddy slipped and fell on the ice."

"Is he hurt?" JoAnn asked.

"Don't worry," Cheryl assured her. "Everything is going to be okay." Cheryl turned on the television and waited in JoAnn's room until the little girl was dressed.

At exactly 6:46 A.M. Roy Baillard, a young, heavyset police officer, dressed in a dark blue woolen Suffolk County uniform, pulled in front of the driveway at 293 Magnolia Drive. With him was a recent graduate of the Police Academy, a young woman who was just learning what it was like to be on the job. The two were finishing a midnight-to-8 A.M. shift and feeling that exhaustion that comes when the biological clock is turned upside down. Baillard rushed up the driveway to Kosser's side to see what could be done. Phil and Ginette Rogers, two volunteers with the Selden volunteer fire department, arrived immediately thereafter.

The body was face down, the legs crossed at the ankles, just steps from the stairs. Blood oozed from the victim's nose and chest. There was so much blood it was hard to see exactly where it was coming from. Ginette Rogers, a registered nurse, turned the victim onto his back. He was a large man, and her husband helped lift him. He had stopped breathing, and as they were about to administer mouth-to-mouth resuscitation Ginette Rogers determined there was no pulse.

"We're too late," she pronounced sadly. Almost as she did, a white and gold Selden volunteer fire department ambulance pulled up in front of the victim's home. So did another squad car—"reserves" as they call the extra hands summoned to scenes of accidents to help control the curious. Neighbors were just beginning now to notice the commotion. Baillard glanced up at the victim's house and saw that Cheryl and her sister were looking out the kitchen window. He would later say how pained he was to see the youngsters standing there, how sweet and vulnerable they looked, how he dreaded having to go inside to break the news.

"Girls, I've got some bad news for you," Baillard said, standing with Michael Kosser in the hall.

"Is he going to be okay?" JoAnn cried out. She was seated at the dining room table while Cheryl stood at the kitchen counter.

"Your father is dead," Baillard declared somberly.

JoAnn let out a horrendous high-pitched scream like that of a small animal and went running into her bedroom. Roy Baillard and Mike Kosser ran after her and found the little girl in her room, shaking under the covers that just a short time before her father had tucked over her. She was shivering as if left too long in the cold.

"It'll be all right, honey," Kosser said, lifting the child into his arms. "You know Bertie and I love you. We'll take care of you. Everything will be just all right."

It was only after he got outside that Roy Baillard heard the word *murder*. One of the other officers, a sergeant, had spotted four expended casings near the body in the snow.

* * *

Word spread fast that there was trouble at 293 Magnolia Drive. By 7:20 A.M. the crowded yellow and black school bus that was to have picked up Cheryl arrived precisely on schedule. The youngsters pressed their noses against the glass and watched in horror as the police kneeled beside the large human form. A pair of dark boots eerily peeked out from beneath the yellow rubber blanket.

MaryAnn Sargeant, Cheryl's best friend, who lived just up the hill on Magnolia Drive, was among those on the bus. She ran up to the bus driver and pleaded with him to stop so she could find out what was wrong. But as is Brookhaven Public School policy, the driver refused and sped on to his next location. The other youngsters on the bus were abuzz with intrigue.

"Think it's a murder?" someone asked.

"Gotta be. All those cops."

But MaryAnn was frantic. She called her mother the moment the school bus pulled into the Newfield High School parking lot.

"Mom, someone's dead at Cheryl's house," MaryAnn said, weeping at the pay phone beside the school gymnasium.

"Oh honey, I'm sure you're mistaken," Mrs. Sargeant said, trying to reassure the girl.

"Mom, honest, I saw the ambulance and everything. It looked like a man. I don't know." Mrs. Sargeant, a hardy, heavyset woman, put on her heavy winter coat and trundled down Magnolia Drive in the snow to investigate what was wrong.

The police continued to arrive in droves, their unmarked cars making an almost festive appearance in the street as if they were all parked at some early-morning party. By now it was clear this was not just another accident. Walkie-talkie bleeped in the cold morning air as hefty men made their way through the scene looking for clues. Yellow tape encircled the driveway.

"He was on the concrete," Cheryl told one reporter. "He never made it to the car. I just looked at him and ran to my neighbor's house."

A crowd meanwhile had gathered on the sidewalk. A news crew arrived. One officer told a reporter it looked to him like a "hit."

James Pierson's body was still in the driveway when Lieutenant Frank Dunn knocked on the front door of the Kosser residence and asked if he could use the telephone. He was the chief of Suffolk County's homicide squad, a tall, good-looking investigator with piercing blue eyes and the self-confident posture of a man in command. He had the usual list in mind to call: the Medical Examiner's office, the District Attorney, a ballistics crew, the police photographers. It was all standard practice, and with twenty-six years on the force he had probably done it five hundred times.

A group of people sat at the Kosser's kitchen table, although at this point he had no idea who they were. They whispered among themselves and drank out of coffee cups the way friends and family often do at the scene of a crime, as if an invisible wall separates the bereaved from investigators; one not wanting to interfere with the other, the intensity of grief in self-imposed isolation from the sterile clarity of inquiry. Dunn broke the silence with a simple introduction. Everyone nodded. He was accustomed to such nods— the unquestioning gestures of those in shock. He had made some observations already. The couple, who he would later learn were the Kossers, were hardworking folk with a good deal less money than their neighbor, Jim Pierson.

As he was about to hang up, something strange happened. A teenage girl at the table turned and asked him a question.

"What kind of cologne are you wearing?" she asked with what was almost a flirtatious smile.

"I don't know," Lieutenant Dunn replied, taken

aback. It seemed such an inappropriate thing to say given the circumstances.

"I think it's Ralph Lauren," she continued. "Yeah. Pretty sure. Lauren."

"I don't really know," he said, explaining that it belonged to his son and that he just splashed it on before leaving the house.

Dunn went out onto the driveway and walked up to the detective newly assigned to the case, K. James McCready. Dunn asked McCready who the girl at the table was. When McCready told him it was the victim's daughter, the one who had discovered her father in the driveway, Dunn looked McCready straight in the eye and said, "She did it. She stood at the door and pulled the trigger."

McCready smiled. McCready had worked dozens of homicide cases with Dunn. A wry investigator with Nick Nolte good looks and an uncanny sense about people, McCready would later say he was accustomed to Dunn's hypotheses and the conviction with which he tested them out. McCready did not dismiss it out of hand, it was as good as anything else they had, but at that point it looked to him like a mob hit.

"Look. Why don't you talk to her? Tell me what you think," Dunn said with conviction. It was Dunn's great gift as an investigator to focus with relentless energy on one theory and pursue it until its end. Theirs was a symbiotic partnership: Dunn focused on the specific, McCready always kept his eyes opened to everything else. They were a great team, McCready and Dunn. Both intelligent, articulate men. Both sons of cops. Both at their best when faced with an unsolved murder.

McCready sidled up to the Kossers' front door and introduced himself. He announced to the group that he would be the detective in charge of the case and needed to ask Cheryl as well as everyone else a few questions. It was simply luck of the draw that McCready was assigned this case. It is the way things worked in homicide. By rotation. When the murder took place, it was his turn at bat.

For the sake of privacy, Cheryl accompanied Mc-Cready, a five-year veteran of the homicide squad, to the Kossers' living room couch.

"Well, I got up," she said, her voice even. Mc-Cready decided she was understandably upset but not devastated by her father's death.

"It was six-fifteen and my dog wanted to go out. So I was getting up to let her out. And we got to the door and all of a sudden I saw him lying there in the driveway so I ran out to see if he was okay."

"And then what happened?" McCready asked, watching her eyes. So far everything she said sounded right. It "flowed" as McCready likes to refer to the patina of normalcy.

"Well, I wasn't wearing anything except my nightgown so I ran back and put on some sweatclothes and like when he didn't talk or nothin' I ran next door and screamed for help."

"And who came to help you?" McCready asked, noticing how she was twisting her hair through her fingers.

"Big Mike," Cheryl said, referring to Mr. Kosser. "He ran out there and told me he must have slipped and fallen on the ice. And he called for help." She hesitated for a moment, looked out the window, and returned her gaze to McCready. Then she said something that gave McCready pause, something in fact that would haunt him for months.

"Is my father going to be okay?" she asked. McCready hesitated. He had thought for certain that Roy Baillard had told the girls their father was dead. He was convinced of it. But then McCready stopped himself. Maybe he had misunderstood. It was after all early in the morning.

"I thought the officer told you your father is dead," he said gently, again watching her closely.

"Dead?" she said with total shock as if hearing it for the first time. "My father's dead?"

"Yes, I'm sorry," McCready said as the girl burst into tears and began to sob uncontrollably.

It was an odd exchange. But at that point McCready thought Cheryl was simply in shock.

James Pierson had been clutching a pile of envelopes in one hand, his car keys in the other. Police had placed four drinking glasses upside-down on the icy concrete to preserve the location of four shells immediately to the right of the victim's body. A fifth shell, also under a glass, lay way off to the side near a tree. Had one of the detectives inadvertently kicked it? Had there been two gunmen? Had the gunman shifted aim?

"Looks as though he was shot coming out the door," Baillard told McCready as he led him to the victim's house.

"Goddammit let me in here!" a woman's voice suddenly shrieked. McCready looked up and spotted a small, slender woman standing in the driveway, trying to force her way past the yellow tape. McCready decided to investigate the commotion.

"I'm Detective Jim McCready," he told the woman, his voice official.

"I don't give a damn who you are," Marilyn Adams shouted. "It's my brother and you have no right to—" She now tore into the yellow tape and was about to burst into the driveway when McCready grabbed her arm and forcibly led the woman past the crowd of onlookers and into his car. There he broke the news about her brother, all the while gauging her response.

"You're going to let me see him!" Marilyn Adams screamed. McCready made a snap judgment. She was the kind of sister who would know what her brother was up to; the kind who would ask too many questions and always want to be involved. Even then, McCready decided, if James Pierson had any reason to suspect he was going to be killed, Marilyn Adams would know about it.

James Pierson's home was like so many in Selden—cluttered with furniture selected less for style than durability and comfort. It had modern conveniences: a microwave oven and dishwasher, a big-screen TV and VCR. The artwork was without theme. A lithograph of a young girl with long blond hair clad in a diaphanous blue veil hung over the bed in the master bedroom. A grandfather clock sat on an angle in the hall. There were reproductions here and there of the paintings of Norman Rockwell—wistful scenes of American family life, the kind of life to which, many would say, the Piersons had aspired.

But as he walked through the rooms, James McCready was not particularly interested in the flower print on the couch or the whimsical rooster lamp on the living room end table or the fact that Cheryl's room with its cache of stuffed animals and sound system, its color-coordinated sheets and VCR, could have been a showroom for everything a teenage girl would want.

The thing that immediately struck McCready were the guns. Not that owning a gun is unusual in a place like Selden. Just about everyone owns a gun to hunt ducks or deer or simply for show, but Pierson's collection bordered on something else. A .357 Magnum sat in the bedtable next to his bed. Under the bed was a rifle. In the closet in the living room there was an Uzi submachine gun and four others. Was this simply for a hobby or was it actually for protection?

As he walked through the rooms, which were so neat and tidy Pierson might have been getting ready for company, it was clear to McCready that the deceased was much wealthier than his job as a foreman at a Huntington electronics firm could possibly provide. In a special subterranean garage he had had built that spanned the length of the house, he kept tens of thousands of dollars' worth of tools, three valuable antique automobiles, five motorcycles, and a Datsun 280Z. Was he involved in some illegal business? Had he fired some employee? McCready had heard Pierson always had large supplies of cash on hand and would lend money to anyone who asked. Had he been killed by someone who owed him money? He was his firm's representative to the union. Had he been involved in some battle for kickbacks? Pierson seemed an immaculate record keeper. In fact everything about his home was well organized and in place. The kitchen did not have one unwashed dish in the sink or crumb on its counter. The laundry room did not have one unfolded towel. Even the victim's desk—piled high in early preparation for tax season—seemed well organized and tidy. Pierson clearly was a man who liked order in his life, things in their place. If he had a problem, McCready was convinced it would be reflected somewhere in either his calendar or book of addresses.

The first hint of trouble in the family, however, came when a former New York City policeman arrived on the scene, who identified himself as the father of Cheryl's boyfriend, Rob. Cheryl had called Rob earlier that morning to tell him of her father's "accident." Rob, in turn, had summoned his father.

"Well, what do you know about the guy?" Steve Cleary, a detective standing not far from the body, asked.

"A widower. Real nice guy. Just had him and his daughters over for Christmas," Cuccio replied. "Real family man. Doing a tough job on his own. Wife died just last year. But I gotta tell you, he's been having big problems with his son."

It was information the detectives were eager to know.

Young Jim Pierson did not arrive home the day of the murder until nightfall. It was the first time he had returned home since his father officially asked him to leave for good. Young Pierson and his father had battled for years, and in recent months things had only become worse. James Pierson had already taken his son's name off a number of bank accounts, and the week before he died was in the process of eliminating his son's name as a beneficiary and as the executor of his will.

It was roughly 6 P.M., and the house was crowded with friends and relatives when the youth walked in the door. Young Pierson was, as always, outrageous in appearance. His orange-dyed hair went down his back in uneven lengths. Several earrings hung from each ear. His complexion was a pasty white. With his tight-fitting leather jacket, he had a kind of studied rage like so many punks his age. His sister Cheryl had tried to reach him during the day, but the landlady at the rooming house where he now lived said he was at work. Cheryl and the rest of his family had no idea what Jim was doing from one day to the next. His great ambition was to become a rock star and although he played his drums at night, all night, every night, his movements during the day were a mystery to the family. Apparently this week he had found work at a factory in Lake Ronkonkoma, about a twenty-minute drive from Selden. He would later say he had gone to work that day. His girlfriend had driven him. It was not until after work that his landlady, who picked him up at his job, broke the news to him about his father.

"How ya doin', Grandma?" Jim asked as he swaggered into the house. Totally inappropriate, but totally Jim.

Pierson's mother, Virginia, sat on the living room couch. Still in shock, the sixty-four-year-old woman alternated between tears and silence. Her right hand was trembling. Her daughter, Marilyn, had sent one of Pierson's friends to get her at the factory in which she worked but did not break the news until she got home. Even seated there that first night in her son's living room, Virginia Pierson would later say, she wondered whether her grandson was involved. As much as she hated the thought, she was mesmerized by how removed he seemed, how totally unaffected by the fact that his father had just been murdered. He did not cry. He did not rail with anger. He just ignored almost everyone else and helped himself to dinner.

"Hey, you want a jelly donut?" he shouted, spotting Lenny Rosen coming in the door. Rosen was one of his father's closest friends and had rushed back from Florida when he heard the news. Later, Rosen would say, he thought young Pierson's behavior odd.

It was a surreal scene as family scenes often are after a death. It was an eerie coincidence: James Pierson and his father died on the same date, exactly four years apart. A similar scene had taken place then. But now the grief was clouded by so many other emotions: fear, anger, suspicion. Who could have possibly wanted to murder this man, this good man, who had been through so much? Detective James McCready was there. He spoke with everyone who walked in the door.

"Okay, everybody, time to go," young Pierson announced as if organizing a volleyball game. Friends, embarrassed by the outburst, started putting on their coats to leave.

"What are you doing?" Marilyn asked.

"I'm in charge now," he replied. Marilyn would later say she figured the youth was just expressing his anger in this way, and she attempted to calm him down. But he would near nothing of it.

"We're staying," Virginia Pierson declared, standing for the first time.

"We don't want you here," Jim said.

"I'm staying," Mrs. Pierson said.

"I'm in charge now."

"You don't live here any more."

Young Jim Pierson did a check of the house and discovered Jim McCready down in the basement speaking privately to Lenny Rosen.

"You guys have no business snooping around here," he declared. Rosen and McCready quietly returned upstairs and got into their cars.

There was more shouting. Obscenities flew. Doors slammed. There were threats of physical violence.

"We don't want you here," Jim announced.

"Well then, I'm going to call the police," Mrs. Pierson declared. "There is a minor in this house, and as long as we don't know who killed her father I am staying."

Cheryl, who up until now had sat sadly with her boyfriend, finally interceded to make peace. Cheryl was always the peacemaker in the family. Sweet, funny, with an ironic twist to her words, she had always been the family's negotiator. She told her grandmother it was all right for her to stay. She hugged her brother, Jimmy, then retired to her room. Her boyfriend went home. It was a fitful night for everyone. Mrs. Pierson, who slept on the couch in the living room, kept repeating the same question over and over. "Who could have done such a thing?" Young Jim Pierson went into the study to watch television. The sound of MTV would punctuate the silence of the night.

With morning came practical details. A funeral to plan. Fetching relatives at the airport. Cheryl's boyfriend, Rob Cuccio, came over to drive Cheryl to school to get some clothing she said she had left the night before in her locker. Virginia Pierson's brother, John Lehning, flew up from Florida. His daughter, Marion, flew in from California as did all his sons, from the disparate places they now lived. Even his ex-wife, whom he had left for another woman, came down from Connecticut to lend her support. A frenzy took over the Pierson household as frenzies do at times of grieving. There was too much food and nervous laughter and borrowing clothes and sharing cars. Friends arrived. Friends left. The telephone rang constantly and always the sound of the television in the kitchen, which ran from early morning into the night.

So much tragedy had befallen the Piersons in the past four years that the scene in the living room—

sleeping cots on the floor, lines for the shower—was
now almost familiar. First it was Pierson's father,
Monroe. Then it was Cathleen's father, John Fleckenstein—Fleck as he was called—in 1982. Then it was
Cathleen's mother, Helen, six months later. Then tragically it was Cathleen herself almost exactly the year
before at the age of thirty-eight after fighting for years
the ravages of a rare and fatal kidney disease.

Now, with Pierson's death, the family was numb. A
wake was arranged at Arthur Giove's funeral home on
Middle Country Road, a strange-looking structure with
Colonial-style pillars and a white neon sign out front
with its name etched, appropriately enough, in black
script. Pierson had had a lot of friends, and the family
asked for a large room. Giove himself had been a
friend of James Pierson and he flew back especially
from Florida to oversee the proceedings. Friends and
relatives from miles around came to pay their respects
as the family hovered beside the open casket. Just the
year before the same people had gathered in that same
flower-strewn room for the funeral of Pierson's wife.
They all remembered Pierson that day—how hypno-
tized he was by grief, how ill prepared he had been
for the death, how devastated he and everyone else was
for the children. Now Cheryl, clad in a dark blouse,
sat quietly with her brother or wept in the arms of her
boyfriend, Rob Cuccio.

As she was returning from the ladies' room at the
funeral home, Cathy Zimlinghaus, the wife of Pierson's partner, noticed Cheryl seated alone on the sofa.
The two had always had a good relationship and Mrs.
Zimlinghaus would later say she welcomed the chance
to talk to Cheryl alone.

"Hi honey," Mrs. Zimlinghaus said, taking a seat
next to her.

"I'm so upset," Cheryl said.

"I know, dear." Cheryl was sobbing.

"I don't want to go live with my Aunt Marilyn,"
Cheryl said, wiping the tears from her face.

"Oh honey, then you won't have to," Cathy Zimlinghaus replied, wrapping her arms around the girl. Cheryl and her father had always been so close and of all the children, Cathy Zimlinghaus would later say, she imagined the loss would be hardest on Cheryl.

Mrs. Zimlinghaus told Cheryl she would help her any way she could and that if it came to that, she and her sister could come live with her family.

"But don't worry about your aunt," Cathy Zimlinghaus said. "It will all work out okay. You'll see."

"The problem's not my aunt," Cheryl said, sobbing.

"Well, what is it then?" Cathy Zimlinghaus asked.

"It's the kids at school. They're saying that I did it, that I killed Daddy."

"Oh, that's terrible," Cathy Zimlinghaus said, running her hands through the girl's hair, thinking how cruel youngsters these days could be. "They're just being mean."

Cheryl woke up screaming the morning before the funeral and awakened the entire house. She had been sharing a bed with her sister, JoAnn, and twenty-five-year-old cousin, Marion, and was convinced she had seen her father's face. Just his face. Magnified before her eyes. He was staring at her. He was laughing. Marilyn, who had slept on the living room couch, rushed in and massaged her niece's neck.

"I'm so scared," Cheryl said. "I'm scared. I'm scared." Her fear was contagious. JoAnn insisted that someone guard the door to the bathroom in case "the bad man" came to strike again. There was an uneasiness everywhere that someone was watching, would come back. Marion meanwhile tried to comfort her cousins. She listened as Cheryl told her about cheerleading, her new boyfriend, about the wonderful Sweet Sixteen her father had thrown for her the previous May.

The plan was for Marion to stay with JoAnn during the funeral. Cheryl had thought a funeral would be too much for the little girl. Instead Cheryl brought her sister to Giove's the day before to say goodbye to her father in private.

"It's okay, JoAnn," JoAnn would recall Cheryl said as she approached the coffin. Cheryl had JoAnn bring along a small pin she had given her father the previous Father's Day. It said: The World's Number One Dad. The little girl fastened it to her father's lapel.

Both of them wept.

James Pierson's funeral was held on a snowy Saturday. Some two hundred fifty men and women crowded the main chapel of Giove's funeral home, where a priest stood in front of the casket and spoke about James Pierson, the provider, the family man, the widower whose life had always revolved around his family. Then he took out a torn piece of looseleaf paper. He said he was going to read something that had been written by James Pierson's daughter, Cheryl.

It was entitled: "Our Dad."

"It is a great loss knowing someone died that was so dearly loved by everyone," the words began. "He treated some people like a brother or sister and some people like a daughter or son. Our dad believed in telling things how they were. He was strong willed but softhearted. He cared for a lot of people as they cared for him. He'll always be in our thoughts in everything we do. We truly believe he is lying with my mother now and is resting in peace away from all pain. He did a great job as a mother and father this last past year and we all knew he tried his hardest to comfort us through everything. He was our best friend as well as our dad. We will miss him dearly but now we have to take one day at a time and hope he will be proud. We believe that one day we will see him again."

The words were brief, but their simple veracity caused everyone in the room to weep. They were true words, real words, the words everyone would remember, particularly with everything that was to come.

# 2

Homeroom 226 at Newfield High School is an unlikely place to plot a murder. It has a large green blackboard and posters on the walls. It has neat rows of Formica desk all pockmarked with proclamations of love. It has a public address system, into which the school principal makes daily announcements, and an American flag. On the floor in one corner is the top of a ballpoint pen chewed beyond recognition. In another is a now discarded sheet of looseleaf paper in the shape of a plane. Chalk dust covers the dark linoleum floor. Bubblegum sticks to the bottom of several chairs.

What students talk about most in Homeroom 226 are things like who is going out with whom and whether it is "cool" to wear sneakers with untied shoelaces to class. Sometimes the talk is of basketball games. Sometimes it is of parties like the senior prom. Always there is talk of rock and roll, problems with parents, surprise quizzes, and how to cut gym. But it was here in this homeroom—within earshot of everyone else—that Cheryl Pierson first made plans to kill her father.

The day was November 7, 1985, a Thursday, the day the newspapers ran a story about a Long Island woman arrested for hiring two men to kill her husband. The woman's name was Beverly Wallace, and she was a forty-year-old waitress from Mastic Beach who said she had hired the men because her husband had physically and sexually abused her. It was the kind of case that attracted a lot of people's attention on Long Island that day. It had been featured on the evening news and repeated all day on the radio. Beverly Wallace was an attractive woman with shoulder-length dark hair. She did not look like a strange person. If anything, there was something commonplace about her. She could have been anyone's next door neighbor.

Cheryl Pierson could not be certain when she first heard the name *Beverly Wallace*. Cheryl almost never read the newspaper and only rarely listened to the news. She was one of those teenagers whose world was not usually affected by current events. Her interests ran more to the humanly dramatic television shows like "Divorce Court" and "General Hospital"—dilemmas and situations about illness and romance with which she could identify. She knew who the president of the United States was but not the vice president. The only New York governor's name she ever heard was Nelson Rockefeller.

But when she arrived at school that morning, she would recall a group of students were talking about some case in the newspaper.

"Did you hear about the lady who tried to kill her husband?" Cheryl would recall a boy in her homeroom class asked.

"Wow, that's crazy someone wanted to kill someone," Cheryl said.

"Well, if the money's right, I guess anybody would do it," the boy replied.

"Oh yeah? How much money would you do it for if someone asked you?" Cheryl asked, her voice turning into a dare.

"A thousand bucks," he replied with confidence, as if it were the price of a car.

Cheryl would later say she hardly knew this boy. Sean Pica was his name. He sat next to her in homeroom because their last names both began with *P*. Short, skinny, with braces on his teeth, he would never have been Cheryl's type. Basketball hero types with tall, muscular good looks was what Cheryl went for;

the kind who could protect and take care of her, who
would make her feel safe. Cheryl had no idea what
Sean Pica was studying at Newfield nor did she particularly care. They had different friends and totally different interests. He was not someone she would talk
to. He was not someone she would care about. About
the only thing that interested Cheryl Pierson about
Sean Pica was what he had had to say about this woman
named Beverly Wallace.

"We left it at that," Cheryl would recall of that first
conversation.

With her red and white kick skirt and matching saddle
shoes, Cheryl Pierson could have been a poster girl
for the all-American high school cheerleader. Attractive, popular, with an easy sense of humor, she was
the kind of girl everyone at Newfield seemed to know,
the kind that could have been Homecoming Queen if
she set her mind to it; a teenager who seemed destined
to have everything she wanted. The boys all wanted to
go out with her. The girls envied her clothing, appearance, and seemingly effortless charm.

She had been co-captain for five months of Newfield's junior varsity cheerleading team and took great
pride in having rewritten many of the school's cheers.
She was a stickler for timing and was probably most
proud of the cheer entitled "Move it up. Sock it to
'em," when the girls all kicked with the fine-tuned
precision of pistons. They would lock hands behind
their backs and swivel to the beat: "Move it up. Sock
it to 'em. We can beat 'em. Let's do it. We got the
power. We got the might. We got the team. That's here
to fight. So come on. And get uptight. Because the
Wolverines are here to fight."

Cheryl was an average student. She never did much
better than B. She had little interest in reading, math-
ematics, or current affairs. She studied hairdressing at
Newfield because she thought it would allow her "to
meet people." Cheryl was not an easy girl to get to

know. Her friends would say she was a far better listener than volunteer of information. But she had her share of friends—good friends, mostly girls at school and around her block to whom she talked for hours about songs she liked on the radio, boys she had crushes on at school, dreams she had about the kind of house she would like to live in one day, the kind of wedding. All the bridesmaids would have flouncy pink dresses. Her dress would have a floor-length veil. There would be a mammoth party that would last all night long. At the end of the party, a white stretch limousine would appear—so long it took up half the block, complete with television and stocked bar—and it would whisk her and her new husband off into the night like some magical white bird.

Cheryl was one of those teenagers who from a very young age are in love with the idea of love. Even as a youngster, she would spend unparalleled amounts of time dreaming, scheming, planning to bump into Joey, Glenn, Steven, someone. She would write them letters. She would write her girlfriends letters about them. Wherever she went, Cheryl studied young couples to decide whether they were truly "meant to be." She could tell by their tone of voice, how tightly they wrapped their arms around one another, how openly affectionate they were with their kisses whether they were "in love." To Cheryl, "true love" was the ultimate.

If anything, Cheryl Pierson was an old-fashioned girl; somewhat naive for her age; more gigglish and childlike than hardened and sophisticated in the ways of the world. *Sweet* was one word people often used to describe Cheryl Pierson. *Thoughtful* and *sensible* were others. She was not a wild teenager, not someone who used drugs. She did not drink or smoke or parade around in strange or revealing clothes. She had never been in trouble or shown even the most remote signs of delinquency. Cheryl Pierson still slept with a teddy bear at night. She had never been to a discotheque. She believed in God. She still was unclear how babies were born. She had never tried marijuana. The most important thing in her life was her family, what little of it there was left: her father, her sister, her brother.

Cheryl had been the second child of James and Cathleen Pierson. Her mother was twenty-two when Cheryl was born. Her father was twenty-six. Like so many of their friends, Pierson and his wife were young parents with a three-year-old son already at home. But they seemed to know what they wanted, and what Cathleen Pierson always said she wanted was a daughter. She had gone into a serious postpartum depression after the birth of her son. But not with Cheryl, and right from the start she doted on the child and wanted to show her off to the world. A little girl she could dress up in fancy dresses and big bows and get close to the way she had always wanted to be with her mother was what Cathleen Pierson said was the greatest gift God could give. And so it was right from the start. Cheryl was "Mommy's little girl" and her brother, James Jr., became "Daddy's little boy."

Cheryl and her mother would stroll the malls and shop for clothes and pick out special things for "the men" at home. They gossiped with the neighbors and folded the wash and played together for hours.

Cheryl was eight years old when her sister, JoAnn, was born and although completely unplanned, it was a pregnancy that her mother and father seemed most to enjoy. For the first time James Pierson took a real interest in his infant daughter and proudly held her in his arms and cuddled her in ways he had never done with his other children. Cathleen, too, was smitten with her new "little doll." Cheryl, the middle child, often felt left out.

To help Cheryl feel special, Cathleen Pierson taught her daughter to diaper her new sister and give her a bath. The three of them would go shopping together and prepare supper. Cheryl would sometimes have the chance to babysit, which she enjoyed because it made her feel grown up. Still it was inevitable. After JoAnn was born, Cheryl—like so many middle children—often felt unloved.

"She's your child too," neighbors would recall that Cheryl's mother complained to her husband. "Just give her a little time. You don't even know her."

"I don't know what to say to a girl," Pierson would reply, not ashamed to admit he did not know what to do or say to a daughter. He spent his time with his son, coaching the boy's Little League team at the local church, taking the boy to hockey games and Yankee Stadium. A daughter, he said, was his wife's responsibility.

It all came as such a shock. Cathleen Pierson was looking and feeling better than she had in years. With her childbearing years now behind her, she had decided to go on a diet and under a doctor's care had lost fourteen pounds. At five feet two, she was down from 130 pounds to 116 and, at her husband's insistence, had just gone out and bought herself a new wardrobe. Then one weekend without warning her weight suddenly shot up to 156.

It was horrifying. Her legs swelled up at the ankles. Her face became distorted. Her arms puffed out like a blow-up doll. When she went to see the doctor, he wanted to admit her immediately to a hospital, but the next day—March 20, 1979—was JoAnn's second birthday, and she wanted to be able to bake her little girl a cake, be at the party. Birthdays had always been so important to Cathleen Pierson. To all the Piersons. It was as if that day were a summary of all the others. So the Piersons had their party that year, and it was not until the last guest had left that Cathleen Pierson checked into St. Charles Hospital in Port Jefferson for observation.

The doctors gave her drugs and tests but with each day the young woman only got worse. What was to have been a week's hospitalization turned into another week and yet another, leaving James Pierson alone with little JoAnn, Cheryl, and his son.

"Patient crying and upset about prolonged hospital stay. Spirits improved after it was explained to her how important it was for her to be here. Later in the day in fairly good spirits"—nurse notes March 23, 1979.

"Patient seems depressed today because the doctor told her she would be staying for at least another two weeks"—nurse notes March 24, 1979.

"Patient is resting comfortably. The patient was seen by Dr. Pastori and Dr. Fox today. She is aware that they want to do the open biopsy for her kidney and that her stay will probably be lengthened. She says her husband is more upset than she is. She seems to benefit by being able to verbalize about her situation." —nurse notes March 25, 1979.

Initially Cheryl and her siblings moved in with their mother's parents, who lived across the street from the Piersons on Magnolia Drive. Visiting their mother's parents was always a treat for the children. They could stay up as late as they wanted, eat whatever they liked, and do the kinds of things that grandchildren get to do with grandparents when their parents are having a hard time.

No one knew just then how serious Cathleen's illness would be or how physically debilitated she would become or that it would take many months to finally figure out what was really wrong, and as each hospital day elapsed, James Pierson became increasingly distraught. He wanted test results and they never came. He wanted to know where to turn and no one could tell him. His frustration and rage were building.

"I was totally disgusted," James Pierson would later say at a deposition in a lawsuit stemming from this initial treatment.

When his wife was finally discharged on May 13,

1979, this once perfectly healthy woman was so weak she could not walk. Pierson literally had to carry his wife from one room to the other. She was incapable of going to the toilet without his assistance. She was incapable of taking a bath or cooking a meal. She remained in bed as Pierson frantically pursued other medical options. Eventually he got the name of Dr. Eli Friedman, an expert in chronic kidney disease at Downstate Medical Center in Brooklyn.

Friedman would become Cathleen Pierson's personal physician and for the next six years would assist the Piersons through many hospitalizations, two kidney transplants, and a wicked roller coaster of prognoses. He did not know it at the time, nor would he have thought to ask, but that very first day he met James and Cathleen Pierson—May 14, 1979—the couple's daughter Cheryl was alone at home with her baby sister. It was a particularly sad day for Cheryl. Not only because she was worried about her mother and feeling sorry for her father.

It was her tenth birthday.

Cathleen Pierson was never particularly close to her brother, John, so it seemed a bizarre twist that he ended up marrying her husband's younger sister. It was just one of those strange coincidences that at first did not seem to matter since from the start the two couples went their separate ways. They lived only a mile apart, but each was busy with their own concerns: getting the mortgage paid, caring for young children. There were the birthdays and anniversaries, the Valentine's Day parties and Easter dinners. But beyond that contact was limited.

It was really not until Cathleen's illness that the two couples were forced to confront themselves and each other in a decision that went way beyond who would supply the Christmas turkey. John Adams, a telephone repairman, who was one year older than his sister, would remember the first time his brother-in-law broached the subject.

"When Jimmy asked me to go out to dinner I knew something was up," John Adams would recall. "I couldn't believe he was asking me out to dinner. He would never invite us out. Never. So we were sitting there and I said: 'What's the game plan, guys? Why are we here?' And Jimmy says: 'We've got a little problem. Cathy needs a kidney.' I thought: Oh God, they're going to ask me. He said: 'Would you think about going for the test and thinking about donating a kidney?' Me? What are you crazy? I said: 'Me? I'm a coward. I can't stand blood. I can't stand needles. I'll do anything. I'll jump out of airplanes. I can't stand a needle. Yeah, I'll do it.' "

So John went for the test, and not only was he a good match, the match was perfect. Dr. Khalid Butt, director of transplant surgery at Downstate Medical Center, where Cathleen was being treated, predicted that Cathleen Pierson's chances for recovery were excellent.

"On Saturday, May 24," Dr. Butt wrote in a letter to Dr. Friedman, "I discussed a transplant with Cathleen Pierson, who was accompanied by her husband, her brother, and her sister-in-law, who happens to be the younger sister of her husband. It was rather a jovial group of two brothers and two sisters intermarried and trying to make light of a rather important decision. Inasmuch as Mr. John Adams, the donor, and Cathleen Pierson are completely matched on locus A, B, C, and DRW, I would expect the chances of success to be very nearly 100%."

As the date for the transplant approached, Pierson and his family became increasingly anxious. Cathleen in particular was showing signs of depression. Unlike some patients who seek to learn everything there is to know about their illness, Cathleen Pierson responded by making light of her situation or otherwise simply ignoring it.

"She presents a cheerful facade," one hospital social worker wrote on Cathleen Pierson's medical chart.
"But it is evident she is quite fearful and feels that no
one can truly understand what she is going through.
The past year has medically been difficult. For her 1)
No major past illnesses only to find self hospitalized
for 9 weeks and becoming worse. 2) Dependent on
husband and mother. 3) Not fulfilling role of wife and
mother. 4) Dying (?)"

"The less I know the better," Cathleen Pierson,
who at the time was thirty-two years old, told the
nurses.

Cathleen Pierson received her brother's kidney on
September 17, 1980. It was an extremely emotional
day. Pierson, who was always at his wife's side, waited
during the lengthy surgery in the hospital cafeteria.
Cheryl, who was then eleven years old, and Jimmy,
fourteen, were brought to the hospital to thank their
Uncle John for saving their mother's life. Pierson was
so moved by his brother-in-law's generosity he did not
know what to do. Always awkward at expressing his
feelings, Pierson often showed his affection through
material things and that week went out and bought his
brother-in-law a new car. It was a 1969 Corvette Sting-
ray convertible, for which he paid $8,000. It was
painted Daytona Orange.

On the morning of February 5, 1986, Sean Pica was
thinking about a new car too. He had skidded his Pinto
on a patch of ice, and it now sat sadly dented in front
of his house, the wheels all out of line.

Sean woke up that morning at about 5 A.M. He would
later say he took the fact that he awakened without an
alarm clock "as a sign." His mother was out, the way
she often was in the middle of the night. An intensive
care unit nurse by day, Joanne DelVecchio worked as
a private duty nurse in people's homes at night to earn
extra money. Money had always been a pressure in the
Pica household. Since the divorce, Sean's mother was

always complaining about how there was never enough money and how it was all Sean's father's fault. As angry as Sean sometimes felt at his mother's attitude, what he wanted most was to be able to help her.

Sean opened his bedroom door. He could hear the sounds of his thirteen-year-old brother, Vincent, breathing early that morning. They were deep, throaty sounds somewhere between a cough and a snore. When the two of them used to share a room upstairs, those sounds had driven him crazy. But now that his older brother, Joe, was in the Navy, Sean had his own room downstairs where he could come and go as he pleased. He missed Joe, but he also loved his new room.

The hall was dark, and all the lights upstairs were out. Butterscotch, the dog, heard Sean's steps and crept slowly to investigate what was going on. But Sean led him back inside the kitchen and closed the door. Sean reached for his black down jacket and stepped into the brisk morning air. It felt clean on his face. The sky was black. He shoved his hands into his jacket pockets and went for his car. The street at that hour was empty. A light was on only in the house at the bottom of the hill. No one, he decided, was watching. He opened the car door. There in the back seat—just where he left it—was the gun. A .22-caliber rifle. He had had it three weeks. Sean had always loved guns. With a gun in his hand, Sean would later say, he felt that he could do anything.

The ammunition was on the floor of the car in a paper bag. There in the darkness he loaded the gun one bullet at a time. He stopped at five, he would later say, because "if I didn't get him with five, I didn't deserve to get him at all." With the gun under his arm, he headed down the street and into the woods.

A year into the transplant, Cathleen Pierson was doing well. The Piersons and the Adamses had a party and had a cake especially made for the occasion. The shape naturally was that of a kidney, and Pierson took great delight in taking a piece and pushing it into his brother-in-law's face. Cathleen Pierson soon told her doctor her "libido" had returned. She had started bowling again. It appeared as though she was going to do well and the family could resume a normal life.

But the Piersons soon had other problems.

On February 5, 1982—exactly four years before his son—James Pierson's father, James Monroe, died. Pierson and his father had had their battles over the years, particularly when Pierson was a youth, but he was unprepared for his father's death and it affected him deeply. He reached out to his mother and sister in ways he had never done before.

The following December, totally unexpectedly, Cathleen Pierson lost her father too. John Fleckenstein passed away at the age of fifty-two, a victim of an unexpected asthma attack. He had gone into the hospital on something totally unrelated and his death was a complete shock to his entire family. "Fleck," as he was known, was Cathleen's stepfather, but as the adult male they had known longest, his loss left a huge void. Cathleen's mother, Helen, went into a serious depression, and her daughter did not know how to care for her.

It was just around this time that Pierson and his wife began making plans to move across the street into the Fleckenstein home at 293 Magnolia Drive. The plan was to build an extension onto the house and for the family to live with Cathleen's mother, Helen. Helen was never thrilled with the idea. But she had little choice. Destitute financially, she had turned to her daughter for financial support, and this was the plan they agreed upon. But just as a hole was being dug for that extension, Helen Fleckenstein's emphysema took a turn for the worse, and that July of 1983 she too died, leaving the Piersons with a much larger home than they ever needed and leaving Cathleen to contend alone with the responsibilities of her family. Cheryl's mother, who herself had been "Mommy's little girl," plunged into a serious depression. She became more withdrawn. She had lost her easygoing humor. Friends would say she had "given up on life." To add to the stress, she had a falling out with her brother because he had a vacation scheduled and decided to skip his mother's funeral.

"I didn't speak to her when she was alive," John Adams would recall he told Cathleen at the time. He and Marilyn took off for a Las Vegas vacation, and when they returned the Adamses and the Piersons stopped speaking. Cathleen Pierson would simply not forgive her brother, and he in turn would not forgive her obstinacy. It was just a few weeks after that, that James Pierson was putting electrical wire in the attic of the new extension when he stepped on a weak board and went crashing to the ground. He smashed all the bones in both lower legs and there was talk of whether he would ever be able to walk again.

It was a difficult time, and Cheryl increasingly was being asked to take over. Not only was she asked to be a mother to her little sister, but now she had to take care of her depressed mother and incapacitated father.

Cheryl was fourteen years old.

It was some time before Pierson's fortieth birthday that Cathleen Pierson took a serious turn for the worse. The swelling had returned. She was continuously vomiting and so weak she could hardly move. She had a second transplant on March 30, 1984, but it would do no good.

She began to suffer from hallucinations. Sitting at the dinner table with her family, Cathleen Pierson would suddenly see a giant rabbit. Later there were bugs, spiders, lizards wherever she turned.

"What is it now?" Pierson would ask with humor when all of a sudden his wife would gasp and point across the room. Jokes were how the family dealt with so many of their problems.

Cathleen Pierson threw her son a graduation party.

She and her husband grilled hamburgers by the swimming pool. But the snapshots that day told the real story. Her face was distorted, her body once again swollen. Even her expression was removed, as if she already knew.

The only irony was that in the end it was not Cathleen Pierson's kidneys that killed her, but her lungs. She was admitted to Downstate Medical Center in December of 1984 with pneumonia and would never leave. It was a sad and confusing time. After lying two weeks in a coma, she eventually died on February 13, 1985. She was thirty-eight.

"I remember we were sitting in the hospital," James Germana, one of Pierson's closest friends, would recall. "We were kidding around by the soda machines. He was teasing me that I didn't have enough change and all of a sudden he started to cry. 'What am I going to do? My wife's dying. What am I going to do without her?' "

Sean quietly closed the front door. It was around 7 A.M. and he could hear his brother Vincent just getting up. Sean took a shower and put on a clean pair of dungarees. He helped himself to a bowl of his favorite cereal, Fruity Pebbles. His thirteen-year-old brother, Vincent, came down the stairs and joined him at the breakfast table. He had promised his new girlfriend, Diana, that he would drive her to school that morning in his mother's car but stopped first to pick up his good friend Mary Freire, who lived across the street.

"How ya doing?" Diana Gabb would recall Sean asked her that morning.

"Good," she replied, standing barefoot in the doorway of her family's home. A petite, dark-haired girl, Diana gave Sean a peck on the lips, then invited him inside while she finished getting dressed. Sean followed Diana into her bedroom, took a seat on her bed and quietly watched as she stood at the mirror and applied the rest of her makeup. She laced three gold

chains around her neck and adjusted her pierced earrings. Diana always wore two pairs: tiny gold hearts
and diamond studs, then sprayed some cologne behind
her ears. Gloria Vanderbilt. Diana then took a seat
next to Sean on the bed as she slipped on her socks
and shoes. He kissed her again.

"He was calm as anything," Diana would recall
many months later.

Diana's brother, Lou, appeared and finally the three
of them joined Mary in the car and took off for the
bagel place at the Selden mall. Sean loved bagels, and
at the Selden mall you could get a bagel and eggs for
eighty cents. Except for Diana, who was not hungry,
they placed their orders. They sat on the bright yellow
benches, designed for lack of comfort so no one sits
too long. Sean, Diana would later say, seemed "perfectly fine" around 8 A.M. that morning. He was in
good spirits and, as always, plenty hungry. From the
bagel store they took off for school.

Diana and Sean had known each other from their
class in English. But it was not until the weekend before that they actually had their first date. It was Diana's birthday. "Our first date was February first,"
Diana, sixteen years old, would recall. "He showed
up at my house with roses. And we had a birthday
cake with my parents. They didn't say a word about
the party. But I kind of had a hint because we were
going to hang out at Eric's house. We were going to
celebrate my birthday. And I got there and all my
friends are there. And that's when it happened. Like
we hung out so much. He's telling me: 'I love you
too.' We'd be hanging out and he'd make me laugh
and like 'I love you so much.' "

It had been that night on the couch at Eric's house
that Sean kissed Diana for the first time. After that,
he and Diana were inseparable.

Sean kissed Diana goodbye that morning at her
locker, five days into their new relationship, and said
he would meet her later that day for lunch. He then

walked up the stairs to room 226. A lot of the youngsters had already arrived and were busy taking off their
coats. Someone mentioned the basketball game against
Smithtown the night before and how Newfield had been
clobbered 54 to 19.

Sean removed his coat and took his seat across from
the American flag. He noticed Cheryl wasn't there and
thought to himself that at that moment he was the only
one in the room who knew the reason.

Mrs. Hoban, the teacher, began taking attendance.
She called his name. "Yeah," he replied.

# 3

It was the Tuesday after James Pierson's funeral, and Virginia Pierson was now living at her son's home on Magnolia Drive, looking after his children.

The crowds of interested relatives had come and gone, and the immediate family was settling into as much of a normal routine as possible. The refrigerator was still packed tight with delicatessan platters neatly wrapped in plastic, bowls of potato salad, cartons of half-eaten pizza, stale donuts. The immaculate order in which the place had always been kept had given way to chairs moved in a circle to accommodate a crowd, pillows on the floor, and Mrs. Pierson's belongings here and there on hangers and tabletops.

The door to James Pierson's room was closed.

It was on that Tuesday afternoon that Mrs. Pierson, a tall, rugged woman accustomed to working all day on an assembly line, had decided she could no longer just sit on a couch. It was time to start doing something again. She decided to cook the family supper.

Marilyn's eighteen-year-old daughter, Kimmie, was there to help, and the two of them—grandmother and granddaughter—stood at the Formica counter and prepared deep-fried chicken cutlets first dipped in egg and flour. They peeled and washed potatoes and mashed them with butter and then prepared a salad with neatly sliced cucumbers. The activity was therapeutic. The oppressive silence of grief had given way to shouts of "Do you know where I can find the salt?" The stereo was on. Cheryl set the table.

But when it came time to actually sit down and eat, Mrs. Pierson could only stare at her plate and the empty dining room chair that only the week before had been occupied by her son. Virginia Pierson kept looking up at the window, expecting to hear a car pull into the driveway. How sad that chair was without him. The week before she had cooked her son's favorite dish. Risotto: rice cooked with bite-size chunks of chicken. He had been pleading with her for weeks to prepare it.

"Daddy, I'm coming!" he had declared to his mother when she had brought it over to him in a plastic box. He always joked that he would have to die and go to heaven before he ever got the chance to taste his favorite dish again.

It was now around 6 P.M., and Jim Jr. had already left for his new class at the Wilfred Beauty School in the Selden mall, where he had recently decided to learn how to become a hairdresser. JoAnn was watching television in the kitchen while Cheryl sat on her bed slipping a pair of white leather boots over turquoise stretchpants. Rob was picking her up. They were going to Newfield's annual talent show. When the doorbell rang, Cheryl flew to the door. Always the gentleman, Rob, clad in neat trousers and a leather jacket, greeted Mrs. Pierson and shook her hand. He said he would get her granddaughter home by around nine.

It was just as the youths were on their way out that Detective K. James McCready arrived at the house as he had periodically all week. He was a warm, outgoing man with a quick smile and an easygoing manner, and Mrs. Pierson would later say she was pleased to see him.

"So where's the gang off to tonight?" McCready asked cheerily as Mrs. Pierson invited him inside.

"A school show," Mrs. Pierson said.

"At Newfield?"

"Yes," she replied. McCready smiled. In that week

he had met the entire family and of them all liked
Virginia Pierson best. He admired her strength and
tenacity. She liked him too.

"Call me Mom," she had told him early on.

"She sure is dressed," McCready said, commenting on Cheryl's outfit. She was wearing a tight white
sweater and heavy eye makeup. He remembered hearing how strict Cheryl's father was about his daughter's
appearance and wondered if he would have been unhappy seeing her painted up that way.

"What'cha gonna do?" Mrs. Pierson replied.

"Kids," he said, shrugging his shoulders.

"Anything new, detective?" Virginia Pierson asked.
It was the question Virginia Pierson asked every time
she saw McCready, and he always responded the same
way.

"We're working on it," he said, winking in a sign
of reassurance.

"I know. I know," she continued, focusing her
steely blue eyes into those of the detective. "But I
want you to promise me one thing."

"What's that?" he said, smiling.

"That you won't give up. I don't care how long it
takes. But I want you to find who did this to my son."

"I will, Mrs. Pierson," Detective McCready replied, his tone solemn. "I promise. You've got my
word. And my word is always good. We won't stop
until we know." He put his arm around the woman
and watched the youngsters get into the car through
the living room window. It was a typical Selden scene:
three teenagers taking off in a car for the local high
school. Cheryl in a red and white Newfield jacket, an
ankle bracelet with Rob's name on it under her socks.
Rob cheerily at the wheel, putting his arm around his
girlfriend. Kimmie in the backseat. Lots of laughs and
smiles. Nothing out of the ordinary. If anything it was
rather commonplace, almost dull, a scene played out
on suburban streets all around the country.

But what McCready did not tell Virginia Pierson at that moment was that the police already knew.

James McCready had been a homicide detective since 1980, or as he will always remember it: almost five years to the day he shot and killed a thirty-two-year-old fugitive named Billy Costanzo. The year was 1975. He was still a police officer then, and it was the only time in his career McCready shot a man; the only time he ever had to test those raw reflexes of survival. But there he was on that grey June afternoon on a crowded stretch of highway and it had come down to this: Either Billy Costanzo or Jim McCready was going to live, and in that multiple choice McCready had no trouble making up his mind.

McCready had been working another case the afternoon Costanzo robbed the Chemical Bank in Elmwood. An all-points bulletin came across his car radio. There was a holdup of an armored car. When news next came across that one of his good friends had been shot, McCready leapt into action. He sped to the scene. A chase ensued. McCready joined it. His siren blaring, his gun poised, McCready finally caught up with the armed man. Undeterred, McCready pursued and finally found himself face to face with Costanzo in a driveway. Costanzo's shotgun was pointed straight at McCready's face. McCready fired first.

It was a bittersweet day. Everyone was so proud of him. But the idea that he had had to kill someone so repulsed him he did not know where to put all the pride. He called his wife that day at the elementary school where she taught. They were newly married.

"Judy," he said with tears in his voice, "I had to kill someone today."

But in many ways, that day had made McCready's career. To McCready and his family, being a cop was more than a job. It was a way of life, a chance to bring one's principles of right and wrong to a world built on chaos. It was an idealistic vision, but one the Mc-

Creadys had always followed. It was practically genetic. McCready's father was a cop. All three of McCready's brothers became police officers. His sister married a cop too, the Police Commissioner's son.

"To me what can you do with your life that is more interesting than investigating a murder?" McCready often said. "It's for real. It's not read a good book. Watch a good movie. This is the real thing where you can really make a difference. I learned it from my father. It's the best thing you can do. It's the best thing I know how to do. A cop is the only thing I've ever wanted to be."

James McCready was now heading toward the Coram Pond diner where he, Dunn, and two other detectives were supposed to review what they knew so far. The way McCready looked at it, time was always on his side in a murder case: Let those who are guilty think they have gotten away with it. Let them get sloppy. No matter how many years he had been a detective, it never ceased to amaze him how often criminals sabotage themselves if only given time. Patience was one of his great virtues as a detective. Careful methodology was another. A compulsive researcher, he was the kind of stickler for detail who always said he would rather be late and right than first and made a fool.

"If I have six nails in a coffin it might stay closed," McCready liked to say. "But if I have forty . . ."

The trouble was, after five days McCready did not even have a hammer. No weapon had been found, and there were still no firm leads or clear motive. Despite all his boasts of patience, it was getting to him. He would have so loved to have arrived at that diner with an ace in the hole. He did not even have a theory. They had set up a roadblock, interviewed the neighbors, canvassed Pierson's employers, queried his closest friends, and all they had come up with were more suspicions about his son. The union connection was a dead end. There was no evidence that anybody owed

Pierson money. If there was a spurned lover or an angry husband, they had not even heard about it.

It was Kenny Zimlinghaus, Pierson's business partner, who gave a little better insight into the man's character and helped suggest it might have been a random thing. He told McCready about how Pierson loved to flirt with danger; how walking the fine line of just getting away with something seemed to give him a thrill. There was the time, for example, Zimlinghaus told him, when Pierson and Zimlinghaus were in Las Vegas with their wives and, unprovoked, Pierson started shouting racist remarks at a group of black men minding their own business.

"Smell those niggers?" Pierson had shouted for no reason as he walked down the street. The men ignored him. Then there was the time Pierson got so mad at a neighbor upstate where he owned some property that one day, when no one was around, Pierson took out his Uzi submachine gun and shot up the man's car. When he was questioned by state police about the shooting, he took particular delight in the fact they had seized the wrong gun.

It was Lenny Rosen, Pierson's confidant and legal adviser, who kept coming back to Pierson's son.

"The son. The son. People kept telling us about the son," McCready would recall. But no one knew anything more than the fact that Pierson had planned to cut James Jr. out of his will. Still, Rosen told McCready one other fact that stuck in the detective's mind, something he would think about for a long time. Rosen told him that in the weeks before he died, James Pierson was distracted, definitely preoccupied with something. "I could tell when he was troubled," Rosen would say. "He called me in Florida. When am I coming back? He was lurching with something to tell me." McCready decided that before he was done, he would have to find out what that was.

* * *

It had been the house that had given Lieutenant Robert
Dunn pause; not specifically anything that was in it,
but rather what was not. It was an impression: once
again a gut response, an intangible sense that the
pieces in that house just didn't fit, that there was something missing. It wasn't the plethora of guns that Pierson owned, although the guns were clearly a part of
it. They seemed to fit with the rest of the impression
he had of the man—a lusty, boisterous, authoritarian
who used foul language and had a macho sensibility.
It was the lack of sexuality. The ''sterility,'' as Dunn
would put it, of his bedroom. Not one *Playboy* magazine. Not one matchbook with a woman's telephone
number. It was McCready's investigation. He was the
one responsible for gathering evidence, hunting down
leads. But Dunn's job was to keep asking questions.

It was the day of the crime, not long after Cheryl
had made her remark about the cologne. McCready
and Dunn were standing in the victim's bedroom beneath an oil painting of a young girl with long blond
hair clad in a diaphanous blue veil. To their right was
a somber portrait of Jesus Christ, positioned so that
the eyes focused directly on the bed. Dunn took in the
scene and made some wisecrack.

''Bobby went down the hall the next day and talks
to people in Sex Crimes,'' McCready would recall.
''And they say: It's a classic. Mama's dead. She's been
ill for a long time. The daughter takes on the mother's
role, and that goes from doing the cooking and cleaning to right on into the bedroom. And Dunn's saying:
'It's the daughter. It's the daughter. She shot him from
the door.' And I kept saying: No! The daughter doesn't
shoot him from the door. She wouldn't shoot him in
the back. She would take the gun and go 'Bam I've had
enough Daddy,' and shoot him right between the eyes.''

Young Pierson—''little Jimmy'' as he was called—had
started the hairdressing class in January in an unan-
nounced peace overture to his father. Pierson had been

after his son to learn a trade, to make something of himself. The youth had just left his job at Stony Brook Hospital, and, ironically, cutting hair was the only job he could think of that would permit him to keep his own hair long. Hair was one of the many sore points he had had with his father. The earrings in both ears were another.

"My father always wanted me to be responsible," Pierson would later say of their relationship. "I just wanted to have a good time."

James Pierson Jr. had just finished class at Wilfred's Beauty School that evening and was walking to his car when a familiar voice said, "How ya doing." He looked up and recognized McCready. "We've been getting more information on the case, and we'd like to go over it with you." McCready's tone was matter-of-fact. There was not the hint of threat in his voice. "This is not the greatest place to talk. Would you mind going with us to headquarters?"

"No problem." Jim Pierson said, his long hair blowing in the wind. "Come up with anything yet?"

"Yeah," McCready replied. "I think I know who one of the murderers was."

"Who?" young Pierson asked.

"You. I think you're up to your neck in it."

"Not me," he said adamantly.

"We've got some pretty good sources telling us it's you."

"It's not."

"Well, if it's not you, then who?"

"My sister," Pierson asserted as they were still driving together in the car.

"Whoa!" McCready said, feigning total surprise. "Your sister? It's hard for me to believe that."

"Yeah. Christmas Day she came to me and said she wanted me to kill our father."

"Why would she want to do a thing like that?"

"Beats me. I thought she was kidding."

Once at Police Headquarters, the questioning continued.

"Look, Jim, I know you're behind it," McCready said, suddenly becoming confrontational. They were now in an office with the door closed.

"You're crazy," Pierson said, seemingly unperturbed by the accusation.

"Who benefits by your father's death? You do. You and your sisters. Now I don't think JoAnn killed your father."

"I had nothing to do with it."

"You're lying to me," McCready said, raising his voice. "Just like you lied to me before."

"What are you talking about?"

"Remember down in the basement?"

"No, what?"

"Remember how you wanted me to leave? How you didn't want us cops snooping around anymore. You damn well knew then who killed your father."

"Nah. Not really."

"Wait a minute. You're telling me your sister came to you on Christmas Day and asked you to kill your father. Your father ends up dead in the driveway and you don't know who did it?"

"Well I asked her and she said 'no.' "

"You're a real dirtbag, you know that?" McCready said, showing his disgust as he slammed a chair against the desk. "You knew what was going down all the time."

"No way," Pierson shouted. "She came to me. She came to me and asked me to help her. But I didn't . . . I didn't think she was serious."

"When was this?"

"Christmas Day. We were at our aunt's house."

"Which aunt?"

"Marilyn. She and my father were having a fight in the kitchen. And Cheryl and I were just sitting in the living room, and she just told me she wanted me to find someone to kill Daddy."

"Did she tell you why?"

"She said he wouldn't let her out on New Year's Eve."

McCready stared at him.

"Because she couldn't go out on New Year's Eve," McCready said, his voice heavy with sarcasm.

"Yeah. He was really strict and stuff. And she had this new boyfriend. And. Anyway, I just thought she was kidding."

"I think your father was fucking her," McCready said, dropping the bombshell, waiting for the youth's response. Had that been Cheryl Pierson's motive? Or was it money?

"I don't think so," young Pierson said matter-of-factly. "Not that I know of. I kind of doubt it."

The lack of emotion surprised McCready. Had someone suggested that about his father and sister he would have been outraged.

"So she told you it was because she wanted to go out on New Year's Eve." McCready continued, his voice skeptical.

"Yeah. That's what she said."

"So what did you tell her when she said that?"

"Well, I asked her if she was serious, and she said 'yeah' she was. And I told her I'd help her. I didn't mean it. I just said it. That's all."

"Was that the only time she asked you?"

"No," Pierson replied. "She called me too. She called me a couple of times."

"When?"

"Before New Year's. And once afterward. She wanted to know if I found someone yet."

"And what did you tell her?"

"I lied. I told her yeah, but that the cops were watching the guy and so he couldn't do it yet."

"And then what happened?"

"Well, her boyfriend asked me too."

"Oh yeah?" McCready asked. Suddenly Cheryl's murder charge had expanded into a charge of conspir-

acy against her boyfriend, Rob Cuccio. McCready
wanted to get up and pull Cuccio in for questioning.
But it was the wrong moment. He glanced around the
sparsely furnished room with its green metal desk and
frayed green vinyl chairs. He waited for Cheryl's
brother to reply.

"Yeah. He came over and asked if I had found anyone yet to kill my father, and I told him the same thing
I told Cheryl. That I had but he couldn't do it yet."

"Who else did Cheryl ask to kill your father?"

"I don't know."

"Well then, who did it, Jimmy?"

"I don't know."

"You did. Didn't you, Jimmy?"

"No way! I told you I thought she was kidding."

In fact, McCready had already established that Jim
Pierson could not have shot his father. He might have
in some other way been involved, but his alibi for that
morning was tight. He was at work. He clocked in.
McCready inspected the time card and spoke with the
youth's boss.

Robert and Tina Cuccio knew something was wrong.
It was midnight, and their son was not home. He had
a ten o'clock curfew on weekday nights and was never
late without calling. The talent show was usually over
by 8 P.M. They called Virginia Pierson at around 11:30
P.M. and asked about their son. She told them he had
left more than an hour before. They paced the floor.
Either he was in an accident or had otherwise gotten
in some kind of trouble.

The Cuccios lived with their two sons and daughter
in the heart of Selden. For more than twenty years
Robert Cuccio Sr. made the long drive all the way to
the 43rd precinct in the Bronx where he was first a
police officer and eventually made a detective. Religious people, who believed that "God had been good
to us," they had recently opened their home to an
orphaned youth, Brian, who had become friends with

their son Robert at Newfield High School. The Cuccios were like that. They were community-minded people. Their children taught catechism at the local church. Cuccio was the coach at his church's Little League. Now that he was retired, he earned a living operating a coffee truck on one of the main arteries off the Long Island Expressway. His wife worked as a clerk in a local bank. They were decent, hardworking people who had struggled long and hard to provide a good life for their children. They were proud of their daughter, who was already in college. Robert too. He was studying accounting at Dowling University. So far it had been a good semester.

"I thought maybe he was arrested for drunk driving," Robert Cuccio would recall many months later.

In all his twenty years as a policeman in the Bronx, Robert Cuccio Sr. saw many ugly things. Murders. Suicides. Family violence of all kinds. He was a cynical man, a man who was difficult to shock. But nothing could have prepared him for what was to follow.

It was after midnight when Jim McCready returned to 293 Magnolia Drive. Robert Cuccio was already under arrest. Through the lit window McCready could make out the form of Virginia Pierson, clad in a housecoat, ambling toward the door.

"Hello, detective," she said solemnly, as if from the hour alone she knew it was something important. She invited him in out of the cold.

"Remember how I promised I would find who killed your son?" McCready asked, standing in the doorway. Mrs. Pierson nodded. A wave of tears crossed her face as she invited him in.

"I have," he said, now moving to the living room. He led her to a couch because he wanted her to be seated. "But you're not going to like what I've got to tell you."

Her entire body trembled.

"Jimmy?" she asked, her voice cracking. He knew

that is what she would think. It is what she had thought all along, but out of loyalty to her grandson had been unable to say it out loud. Protect your own. Protect your own. That was the Pierson family's first commandment, as basic a tenet as life itself.

"No," McCready replied solemnly. "No, it's not your grandson. But it's Cheryl."

Initially she just stared at McCready in horror as if hoping she had heard wrong. He nodded.

"Cheryl!" she said, standing. "No. But why?"

"I don't know," he said quickly. "That's why I need to talk to her. That's why I'd like to take her down to headquarters right now and try to find out. But first I have to place her under arrest. Where is she?"

"Sleeping."

"Would you mind going in to wake her up?" There was a part of him that wondered if Mrs. Pierson would request an attorney. At this point he had no warrant for the girl's arrest.

"Cheryl!" McCready, still standing in the living room, could hear Mrs. Pierson cry out. It was not a particularly urgent call. It was as if Cheryl had just received a special delivery letter or a telephone call from school. "Will you come in here please? There's someone here who would like to talk to you."

Clad in blue sweatpants and a sweatshirt, Cheryl stumbled bleary-eyed into the living room. Her face was clean, and sleep had made her pale. Standing there, rubbing her eyes, she looked like a disoriented child who had just been awakened at the end of a long car trip.

"I think you've got something to say to your grandmother," McCready told her solemnly.

"What?" she asked, her eyes wide with surprise. She shrugged her shoulders.

"You have something to tell her about who killed your father."

"I don't know what you're talking about," Cheryl insisted with conviction.

"I think you do," McCready said, motioning through the window. The door opened and in walked Detective Steven Cleary and Cheryl's boyfriend, Rob. Cheryl studied Rob and the detective.

"Rob, tell her," McCready said.

"Cheryl, I told them. They know everything," Rob said solemnly, looking down at the floor. Mrs. Pierson stood speechless, her eyes following them as if at a tennis match.

McCready asked Mrs. Pierson to go into the bedroom with Cheryl and watch her get dressed. As if on automatic pilot, Mrs. Pierson complied. She stood in the doorway while Cheryl opened the top drawer of her dresser.

"Hurry up, Cheryl," Mrs. Pierson recalled saying as Cheryl stood there rummaging through the drawer for what seemed like a long time. At last she reached for a pair of socks.

Meanwhile McCready tried to reach Marilyn. She had no telephone because, in the throes of a bitter divorce, her husband had cancelled her service, and McCready first had to call a neighbor. He knew Mrs. Pierson had a bad heart and did not want to leave the elderly woman alone. Cheryl and Rob waited in the police car with another detective while McCready waited inside the house for Marilyn.

"That bitch," Marilyn shouted at the top of her lungs when she finally arrived and was told the news. "I'll kill her. Let me at her. I'll kill her."

JoAnn Pierson remained asleep.

Only nine months earlier, Pierson and his daughter Cheryl had danced at her Sweet Sixteen.

The Sweet Sixteen occupies a special place in the lives of little girls. It is a magical time, a delicate coming of age, a proclamation to the world—but perhaps most important to the girls themselves—that young ladies of sixteen are no longer just children. First kisses in the moonlight. First tubes of lipstick.

Darkened dance floors. Dreams of going steady. That is what Sweet Sixteen parties are about. Part fantasy, part celebration, they are an initiation rite into the world of romance.

Cheryl Pierson had waited a long time for her Sweet Sixteen. Like a wide-eyed child staring up the chimney at Christmas, Cheryl imagined the myriad possibilities: all the presents, dancing with a lot of boys, maybe even falling in love. Cheryl was good at that. As a child who contended with parental illness, she learned at an early age that fantasy was often a more comfortable place than daily life. Not that her dreams were that unusual or indeed all that different from those of other girls, but she had an extraordinary capacity even at sixteen to retreat into her own imagination; more perhaps the way young children do.

Cheryl and her parents had been planning her Sweet Sixteen for years. Even at the hospital, Cheryl and her mother talked endlessly about place cards, invitations, what she would use as a centerpiece, the kind of cake, whom she would invite. They would see a dress in a magazine and think yes, that was something Cheryl could wear. It was Cathleen Pierson who decided to hold Cheryl's Sweet Sixteen at the Island Squire. It was one of the most expensive catering places in town and carried along with it the most prestige. Clearly for the Piersons the party was an important symbol as well. They said they wanted to "do it right," to show their friends that they had arrived.

When Cathleen Pierson died, just three months before the party, there was talk of cancelling Cheryl's Sweet Sixteen. But a guest list had already been compiled, the catering hall hired, even the disc jockey had been reserved. At first it was hard to know what to do.

"She would have wanted it," Pierson would eventually say, turning the Sweet Sixteen into a posthumous tribute to his wife. "And we're going to do it."

And so they did. More than one hundred twenty were invited. The room at the Island Squire was ablaze with pink balloons. Round tables were all set out with pink and white flowers. There was a big buffet with lasagna and orange-glazed chicken and a long table in the rear piled so high with presents that they had to be moved to the floor. Cheryl wore a white silk jumpsuit off one shoulder that tightly hugged her waist. Her hair was all done up in "banana curls" and she beamed as she ran from table to table getting hugs and kisses as if she had just won some important prize. All the boys Cheryl ever liked were at that party, and she danced with them all. Her brother, James, all dressed up in a suit, danced with little JoAnn. Pierson worked the room like a politician, ebullient with his hospitality. He seemed so proud of his daughter, so proud of himself.

"Can I have a Sweet Sixteen party someday too?" JoAnn asked, tugging on her sister's waist. Cheryl promised the little girl that she could.

Everyone danced to the rock music and, in special deference to her father, the Twist. Many would remark that Cheryl was as happy that night as anyone had ever seen her.

Cheryl blew out the candles and cut into her cake. It was all pink and white and gooey with frosting, and as everyone applauded James Pierson gave his daughter a hug. The disc jockey selected the song "Sixteen Candles," and Cheryl walked out onto the darkened dance floor with her father.

> Sixteen candles makes a lovely light.
> But not as bright
> As your eyes tonight.
>
> Blow out the candles.
> Make a wish come true.
> For I'll be wishing
> That you love me too.

You're only sixteen.
But you're my teenage queen.
You're the prettiest, loveliest girl
I've ever seen.

Sixteen candles
In my heart will glow.
Forever and ever
For I love you so.

It was a moving moment, the kind that didn't require a photograph to become etched in people's memories. As Pierson cradled his daughter in his arms, there were few in the room who didn't think back to how helpful Cheryl had been all those many months going back and forth to the hospital, how attentive Cheryl always was to her father, how he continually bragged to friends that although everything else in his life was going wrong, Cheryl was his life's one source of joy.

---

*Until my mother got sick, my father never bothered with me. He always did stuff with my brother. Little League and stuff, and I always stayed with my mother. When my mother got sick, my mother wasn't around and I felt no one was paying attention to me. And my father started paying attention to me. At first I was really happy that he did it because before then he didn't even know that I existed. Then it got out of hand, I guess.*

---

"I know the whole story," McCready said. He, Cheryl, and another detective were seated in the lieutenant's office at Police Headquarters. The door was closed.

"I may not know all the details," he said. "But I know that you did it and why you did it. I've heard about it from Jimmy. And I've heard about it from Rob. But I'd like to hear about it now from you. I'd like you to tell me in your own words. I'd like to know exactly what really happened.''

Cheryl was seated in a grey metal armchair across from an American flag that was so old and dusty it looked as though it might only have forty-eight stars. The room, with its old file cabinet and beat-up coat rack, made her look small. It was usually occupied by beefy men with holsters around their ankles or seasoned criminals who had been in and out of the jails all their lives. With her makeup off, her eyes were like that of a small, frightened animal. A doe frozen with fear in the spotlights of a car. With her shoulders hunched to her neck, she held on to her elbows. Her teeth were clenched. She looked down at the floor.

"I know what was going on between you and your father," McCready ventured. Initially Cheryl did not speak. She was sobbing as he read her her rights.

"Is it true?" She did not reply. She was shaking. Gary Leonard, the other detective in the room, handed her some water.

"Is it true?" McCready asked again gently. Cheryl Pierson looked at him. Her eyes seemed to speak, but she did not. It was hard to know whether, if only given time, words would follow.

"Listen," he said. "You don't have to be embarrassed. We've been around. We know about these things. So just tell us and don't worry about it. Okay?"

Cheryl's tears were now a hiccup. She nodded.

"When did it start, Cheryl?" he asked. She looked off to the side.

"When I was eleven," she finally said, choking on the words. Her voice that of a little girl.

"How did it start?"

"Wrestling. We would just like be wrestling and stuff.''

"What do you mean?"

"Well, we would wrestle and . . ." Then she began to cry again.

"What would happen?"

"He . . . he would . . . grab me?"

"Where? Where did he grab you?"

Now she didn't speak. She pointed to her crotch. Then pointed in slow motion to her breasts. Was it the ugliness of the gesture that caused her to weep anew?

"Like I knew it was wrong . . . But it was my father. And like well since it was my father . . ." she volunteered.

"When else did your father touch you?" McCready asked.

Again there was silence.

"When we watched TV," Cheryl said at last. "He had a blanket and stuff and like it started like that. My mother was sick and she'd be in the living room on the couch. And like we'd be watching TV in the bedroom. And no one could see."

"Were you wearing clothes?"

"Yeah at first we did. But then we . . . didn't." Her voice trailed off.

"Where was your mother during this time?"

"Well like she was sick," Cheryl told him again. "She used to sleep on the couch. And like I'd go in there with him and watch TV."

"What exactly did you do?"

Again no response. She was weeping.

"I know it's hard," he said gently. "But we know about these kinds of things and you shouldn't be ashamed."

Still she could not reply. McCready changed his question.

"When did he do this to you?"

"At night," Cheryl said, at last bursting into tears. The tears were soon a hiccup, her words a mixture of nods and shouts.

"What time of night?"

"Late." She was now rocking in her chair.

"Where was your sister?"

"Asleep."

"Where?"

"In her bedroom."

"And your brother?"

"Working."

"Was he always working?"

"No, sometimes he was asleep too."

"Did you ever have intercourse with your father?"
It was the question McCready had to ask. The one to
which he was almost sure he knew the answer.

Once again she did not speak. She nodded and
looked down at the floor.

"How old were you?"

"Thirteen."

It was this silence. This hesitation that McCready
found most convincing. McCready and Leonard questioned Cheryl for forty-five minutes, and McCready
would later say that what she said and how she said it
"flowed." If it was not for her sister, she told him,
she could have "lived with it." But that now that she
had a new boyfriend and was spending more time outside the house, she was convinced her father was about
to start abusing JoAnn. She told him about her conversation with Sean Pica, about the article in the newspaper, and how he had said for the right price he could
kill someone. She told McCready of a first attempt:
how this classmate, Sean Pica was his name, threw a
brick through the window of a house across the street
and how afraid she was that her father would find out.

"Why didn't you tell anyone?" McCready asked.

"I didn't think anyone would believe me," Cheryl
Pierson said.

But K. James McCready believed her. Right from
the start.

It was sometime around 3 A.M. when Jim McCready
returned for a third time that night to 293 Magnolia
Drive. He already knew how he would break the news.
Shortly, swiftly, and to the point, as if he were telling
someone of a suicide. His eyes were bloodshot from
fatigue. He had been running straight since 6 A.M.

He approached the driveway and knocked on the door, the door through which James Pierson had walked seconds before being shot.

"We need to talk," he said after being invited indoors. To his dismay, Virginia Pierson and Marilyn Adams had summoned Pierson's good friend, Lenny Rosen. It was not that McCready thought that Rosen was in any way connected to the crime. His concern was that the more people who were informed of the arrests, the greater the likelihood that "the shooter" could get tipped off.

"This is truly a tragic situation," McCready said solemnly. "Jimmy was having intercourse with Cheryl."

No one even gasped. Neither Virginia Pierson nor Marilyn Adams said anything. They just sat there and listened.

"It started when Cheryl's mother took ill," McCready continued, his voice rhythmic and soothing, not unlike the sounds of a priest giving the sacrament. "She told me all about it and I believe her. She needs your help. There is nothing left you can do for your son. So you may as well help her. She needs your help. She's still young. She's got her whole life ahead of her. You're the only thing she has."

And Marilyn and Virginia agreed. Help. Protecting one's own. That was what families were about. That was what James Pierson always said. Loyalty to his family was the most important principle he knew. "Family is family," he had always said.

"She's going to need all the support we can give," Marilyn said vehemently as Virginia Pierson nodded. They talked about calling a lawyer. At this point, they would later say, all they could think about was that this was James Pierson's daughter, the daughter he loved.

# 4

"I'm real sorry about your mother," the boy had said, putting his arm around Cheryl's shoulder. They were standing at her locker. It was late February of 1985, the week following her mother's funeral, and Cheryl had just returned to school after a brief absence.

"Oh thanks," Cheryl said shyly, looking down at the floor. Cheryl and this boy hardly knew each other. They had only met a few weeks before at a schoolwide lesson in square dancing, which Cheryl had thought silly until she switched partners and found herself facing a tall senior with dark good looks and a strong, self-confident manner. He said his name was Rob.

Cheryl and Rob saw each other from time to time after that, but it was not until he learned that her mother died that he asked if they could get together some time after school. Cheryl explained that these days she really had to get home. Without her mother, she now had to look after her little sister, cook the family dinner, do the wash. The boy said he understood. Then one day Cheryl invited this new boy to a party. It was her Sweet Sixteen, and she could not wait to see him there.

The evening flew by, most of it a blur. But there was one moment, Cheryl would later say, she would never forget. It was the last dance of the evening. The disc jockey played "Sixteen Candles" for one last time and this new boy, Rob Cuccio, asked Cheryl to dance. It was a private moment filled with all those wonderful heady feelings of excitement, challenge, and longing, the kind of moment Cheryl had always dreamed about. Rob looked into her eyes, just as she had always hoped someone would, and on that very special night asked her to go steady.

It was not long after that night that Cheryl told Rob she wished her father were dead.

---

*I would be watching TV in his bedroom and my father had a blanket there so if he heard something, you couldn't see nothing because the blanket was there. With the touching stuff, I don't think I realized it. Then like it was to the point where it wasn't with our clothes on anymore. That's when I think I realized it. I said something to him to the effect of: Why are you doing this or something like that. And he said he wasn't doing anything wrong.*

---

It was an old-fashioned notion, but after Cheryl's Sweet Sixteen, Rob Cuccio began to call on Cheryl in her father's home. He would arrive, be invited in, shake her father's hand, and take a seat on the couch by the television in the living room. Out of the corner of his eye he would study Cheryl, her sister, and her father. It was an awkward situation. He did not know what to say. Rob was accustomed to going out with girls, being able to get to the movies, out to dinner. Not sit there and be judged. But since he liked Cheryl, he was willing to see her on any terms. He imagined that with time her father would soften. Once the four of them went bowling. Another time, Pierson took them all out to dinner. Then Rob asked Cheryl to accompany him to his senior prom.

"You're only a sophomore," Pierson had told his daughter. "They call them senior proms for a reason. They're for seniors."

Cheryl was devastated. Rob went with someone else. With the summer, as Rob was getting ready to go to college, the romance cooled, and Cheryl heard through friends he had begun to see someone else. She felt her father was to blame and was convinced she would never meet another boy. She was convinced she would always be stuck in that house and never be able to leave. It was the first summer since the death of her mother, and Cheryl would say the worst of her life. Without school as an outlet, her days revolved around getting her sister off to day camp, preparing the family's meals, doing the wash, making the beds, scrubbing the bathtubs. She never saw her friends.

"I felt sorry for the girl," recalled Jack Wern, one of Pierson's friends from work, who was a frequent visitor at the Pierson home.

Ellen Somar, Pierson's banker and also a good friend, suggested that Pierson hire a housekeeper.

"He told me Cheryl did not want any strangers in the house," Ellen Somar would recall. "He was ready to do it. She didn't want one."

With the fall Cheryl and JoAnn returned to school, and Cheryl once again went out for cheerleading. To her disappointment, she was not accepted by the senior varsity team and was so disappointed and made such a fuss that the school appointed two captains that year for the Newfield High School junior varsity cheerleading squad. Cheryl was one of them. Suddenly her afternoons were booked with "practice" and games out of town. Dinners now were increasingly McDonald's and other fast foods. James Pierson taught himself to cook and would surprise his daughters with pork chops and steaks.

One day in October, totally by surprise, Rob Cuccio, Cheryl's love from the spring, appeared one day at Newfield hoping to rekindle things, and Cheryl and Rob began seeing each other again. Just like "love in the movies," Cheryl told her friends this was "true love." He gave her a little silk pillow, which she hung from her rearview mirror, inscribed with the message "Our Love Is Here To Stay." Rob became a frequent visitor at the Pierson home and a part of the family's daily life. But still Pierson would not permit his daughter out alone.

"You're only sixteen," Pierson would continually tell her.

"I wish Daddy were dead already," JoAnn would recall her sister, Cheryl, said. She said it often. It was just about this time that Cheryl Pierson made plans with Sean Pica, the boy she sat next to in homeroom, to kill her father.

Mary Freire was on her way to school. Sometimes her pal Sean Pica would give her a lift and sometimes they would take the bus. They had lived across the street from each other all their lives, and getting to school and Sean were always synonymous. Since he had not said anything, she assumed that that particular day they were taking the bus.

It was a Thursday morning about 7:20 A.M. and Mary as usual was putting her coat on to go to school. Mary's mother was cleaning the breakfast dishes and noticed her daughter had forgotten her $1.50 lunch money on the kitchen table. Mrs. Freire, who had lived on Windover Drive twelve years, grabbed the money and went for the door.

"Mary!" she cried out, but her daughter did not hear. Through the window, she could spot Mary running in her winter coat down the block. Sean was walking down the street too. They usually went to school together. But then a strange image caught her eye. A grey car. It stopped in front of Sean. A large man got out and shoved Sean into the back seat. Stunned and in a panic, Mrs. Freire ran upstairs to the bathroom where her nineteen-year-old daughter Terry was in the shower. She opened the door.

"Terry! Terry! Someone just kidnapped Sean," Mrs. Freire yelled.

"What?" Terry Freire asked with the water still running.

"A car. A man. They took him away," Mrs. Freire said breathlessly.

"I don't think so, Mom," Terry said with authority.

"But there were these guys pushing him into a car," Mrs. Freire insisted.

"Maybe they were the police," Terry said calmly, turning off the faucets.

"The police? What would the police want with Sean?"

"I think he may have been involved in the murder of that guy Pierson."

Mrs. Freire let out a scream. Terry grabbed a towel.

"No. No. Terry. No. Please tell me, no. What are you talking about?"

"Mary told me. The kids were talking about it at school."

Mrs. Freire was in a panic. Was her Mary involved? Her older daughter tried to calm her down. Mrs. Freire did not know what to do. She called Sean's mother.

"She's not home yet," Sean's younger brother, Vincent, replied.

Joanne DelVecchio was just coming back from the home of a bedridden patient as a private duty nurse. Sometimes she would work all night and go straight to her job in the intensive care unit at the hospital. But on this particular night she was heading home.

She pulled into the driveway and walked up the stairs. Vincent had left a note on the kitchen table.

"Call Mary," it said, and so she did.

"Joanne," Mary said, "I . . . Sean . . . I saw Sean being abducted today. Two big men in a grey car. I'm worried. Maybe we should call . . ."

"Oh, it's probably nothing," Joanne said, the sensible mother of sons. Experience had taught her the best posture was never to panic.

"But I saw them . . . they were . . ."

"It's probably some joke or something. I'll call the school and let you know." Joanne has a cheery way of talking at times of crisis that drives some people mad.

Joanne dialed Newfield High School, but no one was there yet. She glanced at her watch. It was 8:20 A.M. She had promised to drive her good friend Claire Gould from across the street to the garage to get her car fixed. Whatever was going on with Sean could wait. It took a lot more to get Joanne going than simply a frantic call from Mary, and a promise was a promise. Nothing made Joanne more crazy than someone saying they would do something and then not doing it. It was a lesson she had taught her friends. It was a lesson she had taught her sons. It was the subject about which she was probably most adamant: "A commitment is a commitment. If you say you're going to do something you better well do it."

Every Thursday since 1975 a group of four women on Joanne's block would get together for lunch at each other's homes. This Thursday was Claire's turn.

After Joanne dropped Claire off at about 9:15 A.M., Claire went for the vacuum cleaner in her broom closet only to discover she was out of Electrolux bags. So she put on her boots and headed straight over to Joanne's house. When she arrived, Joanne was on the telephone with Leonard Lupetin, the school's assistant principal.

"He never showed up," Joanne whispered to Claire as she came in the door. For the first time all morning JoAnn looked concerned. Claire took a seat at the kitchen counter. It was a familiar spot; she had spent hours there. Joanne was always complaining about the counter, how she wanted to have it modernized and redone. Grey was the color she wanted.

Claire waited while Joanne called the 6th precinct, then tried to reach one of Sean's friends. No one seemed to know where Sean was.

Then the telephone rang. It was Mr. Lupetin to say that he had *Newsday* on the telephone and that they had some questions to ask about Sean.

"What would *Newsday* want with Sean?"

It was then that Joanne decided to take off for school.

"Want me to come?" Claire asked.

"No," Joanne said, still dismissing the incident as some mistake. "I'll go. You cook."

Newfield High School was like so many high schools across the United States. It had a football field and large gymnasium and hallways decorated with student artwork and announcements of upcoming special events. Mr. Lupetin's office was like the assistant principal's office in any modern suburban high school. It had a large desk with his name prominently displayed in the front. It had a comfortable wooden armchair. A dedicated school official, he had been with the school system thirty years and was proud of it. There had been difficult students over the years. But Sean Pica was not one of them. He had never even heard his name before.

As he waited for Joanne to arrive, Lupetin had pulled the young man's file. He was an average student. Nothing special. Absolutely no record of problems. He noted that Sean was getting ready to represent the school in a statewide carpentry contest.

Now that Joanne was in his office, Mr. Lupetin tried the police again. He must have tried three separate times.

"Look, I've got a mother in here with me and she is frantic," Mr. Lupetin said in his quiet but firm tone. "Please can you simply check and see if any of you guys are talking to him."

This time he got through to someone who could give him news about Sean's whereabouts. He listened intently, thinking about how he was going to communicate what he was hearing to the woman sitting across from him.

"Look, I'm going to tell you right now it's serious," Mr. Lupetin said. "Sean's been arrested for murder. For the murder of James Pierson."

"Murder? Sean?" Joanne said, imagining some mistake. She began shaking and asked Mr. Lupetin to call Claire to help accompany her home. But Claire was in the shower getting ready for her guests and didn't hear the phone. It was Mary Freire who eventually drove to school to escort Joanne home. Once there, Joanne stepped out of the car and fell to the ground. Her voice echoed the length of the block.

A single solitary scream.

Room 100 in Suffolk Criminal Court is a long, windowless courtroom with imitation wood paneling, harsh overhanging neon lights, and ceiling fans that produce an incessant buzz. The bare floors make every footstep echo, the result to the uninitiated seems to be intimidation by design. But most of the people called to appear here are not intimidated, they have been here before. A court appearance is just an annoyance. A day missed at work. A confrontation with a lawyer over money they would much prefer to spend someplace else.

On this Thursday, February 13, 1986, however, there were three young people who did not look as though they belonged. None of them had ever been arrested before. Still clad in the outfits they had worn the previous day to school, they looked more like children playing hooky from class than criminals. The girl wore her red Newfield High School jacket emblazoned with the name of the basketball team: Wolverines. With dark circles under her eyes, she looked fragile, a Siamese cat left out in the rain. One of the two boys was so young he still wore braces. The third was a handsome youth with a neatly kept mustache.

It was an emotional scene. From the rear of the courtroom three families watched, total strangers suddenly pulled together in the most stressful situation of their lives. A time that would forever be known as "the week it happened." They sat in discrete units. Marilyn Adams, a slender woman in a tight-fitting light suit, sat off to one side scanning the scene like a hawk. Her mother was beside her. So was her brother's close friend, Lenny Rosen. At that moment, Marilyn Adams would later say, what she wanted most was for her niece to come home. She did not want to believe that Cheryl really contracted for her father's murder. And she did not want to believe the reasons Cheryl gave as to why.

On the other side of the room sat Sebastian Pica, Sean's big, burly father. A former New York City policeman, he had spent his working life in and out of courtrooms, making arrests, learning the routine. For years he had watched the mothers and fathers of murderers walk into courtrooms in slow motion, their eyes cast downward to the ground.

Now the accused was his son.

Until his son's arrest, Sebastian Pica had never heard the name *Cheryl Pierson.* He had not read about the murder. The whole story seemed so absurd. Why couldn't this girl have asked for help? Why was his son involved? The Sean who had kissed him goodbye at the train station just the day before was not capable of murder.

Robert Cuccio Sr. was in still another part of the courtroom. Also a former New York City police officer, he had last been stationed as a detective in the Bronx. He too had seen plenty in his day as a cop. He knew about sex and family violence. But knowing the Piersons as he did, it simply made no sense. He had liked Cheryl's father. Sure, he had seemed strict. But Cuccio had liked that. He respected Cheryl's father. This was a man who took care of his children. It made no sense to him either. If there was a problem, why didn't his son simply tell him? He had always thought they were close.

"How could they have done such a thing?" Robert Cuccio said to Marilyn, reaching out to her at one point.

"Maybe they didn't," she said. "Maybe they're covering for someone else. Maybe this is just a bad dream."

Paul Gianelli is one of the best-known attorneys in

Suffolk County, a busy lawyer who is constantly racing
from one crisis to the next. The last time he had attracted national attention was when he represented the
parents of a seriously handicapped newborn who had
refused to allow doctors to perform the one operation
that would save the child's life. He had represented
sexual abusers over the years and murderers of all
kinds. But this was his first case of patricide. It had
been Lenny Rosen who knew of Gianelli's reputation
and had recommended him to Cheryl's aunt.

Gianelli entered the rear courtroom door and began
to walk down the middle aisle, his heels making click-
ing noises on the floor, when all of a sudden he spotted a familiar face. Joanne DelVecchio's friend and
neighbor, Claire Gould. She stood and rushed in his
direction. Unbeknownst to him, Claire had been trying to reach him all morning. She and Gianelli's wife
had been pregnant at the same time, and they were all
at the same Lamaze group. Their families got together
socially after that. She knew he was the best lawyer in
Suffolk County and that he was the man to represent
Sean.

"Paul, I need your help. My friend's son has been
accused of the Pierson murder. Can you help them,
please. They really need you."

"Oh Claire, I wish I could," Gianelli said sympa-
thetically. "But I'm here to represent the girl."

"You are?"

It was one of those small-town occurrences that would
mark the entire Cheryl Pierson case—coincidences that
would entwine the lives of all these families in one way
or another, in ways at this point they could not even
imagine.

It was late before the defendants were finally brought
into the courtroom. they were the last on the calendar.
Rob was the first to be called. He pleaded not guilty
to the charge of conspiracy. Bail was set at $5,000,
which his parents met on the spot. Then Cheryl was
brought in. She wept as she stood handcuffed in a red

Newfield High School jacket and sweatpants. Then Sean. This was the first time Sean's parents heard the words *contract killing*, the first time they heard that his motive was money.

"Cheryl is more a victim here than a defendant," Gianelli told the judge. "She has been a virtual prisoner in her home for the last five years. Her father was six foot two and she was five foot two. She did all the work around the house. Many students have often seen her with black and blue marks from brutal beatings that she got. There was intercourse and one of the concerns was that this was beginning to happen to her eight-year-old sister."

Cheryl's bail was set at $50,000. Sean's bail was set at $100,000. The lawyers met with the press outside the courtroom and answered questions. But there was one horrifying detail the lawyers kept to themselves.

"We've got to get her out of jail," Gianelli told Cheryl's aunt, whispering outside the courtroom as they stood against the wall.

"Where are we going to get that kind of money?" she asked frantically.

"They're going to have to lower it. And we're going to have to get her out."

"How? Why would they do it?" she asked. She had never been in this situation before. She felt as though she were asking a surgeon for advice.

"She's pregnant with her father's baby."

# 5

Shock. Stunned. No warnings. Disbelief. These were the words being used everywhere in and around Selden in the days following the arrests.

How could this have happened? How could this have happened here? Why didn't Cheryl Pierson tell anyone? How come no one noticed? The same questions were being asked over and over as if not to find an answer was to somehow invite repetition.

Selden is not the kind of place that normally attracts public attention. Its terrain is flat and unremarkable: one long stretch of neon signs touting bagel stores, auto repair shops, gas stations, water bed stores, discount druggists, beauty shops. Situated fifty miles east of New York, Selden is smack in the center of Long Island near towns appropriately named Middle Island and Centereach. Nowhere near the ocean, it is bordered by the Caldors shopping center to the east and the Smithaven Mall to the west. Just like countless towns across the United States where men and women work hard to provide a better life for their children; its residents carpenters, auto mechanics, beauticians, school bus drivers, security guards, nurses, secretaries, carpenters, policemen. Few who live in Selden ever dream about running for president or becoming a doctor or changing the world. Most content themselves with the joys of a simple life. Going to church, raising children, finally paying off a mortgage. They keep signs like "Bless Our Mortgaged Home" thumbtacked to the kitchen wall. They drive around with bumper stickers like "Wife in Trunk." They seek out restaurants emblazoned with the offer "All You Can Eat."

The Piersons were just that kind of family. James Pierson coached his son's Little League. He and his wife bowled Sunday nights at the local lanes in Centerreach. His children rode dirtbikes around the neighborhood. He and his wife vacationed with friends in Las Vegas. He took his family hunting upstate in the fall and on expeditions to amusement parks in the spring. Throughout the illness in their family, the Piersons stuck together, and they were for many in the community an inspiration.

Just about everyone who had ever met Cheryl Pierson and her father pushed their memories for clues. If what Cheryl claimed was true, then everything they had ever thought about James Pierson was a lie, and if it wasn't, then the lie was everything they had ever thought about Cheryl. It was like any deception: It begged the veracity of everything else, a blurred photograph that only now was coming into focus. What else lurked beneath the surface? What really happened to James Pierson on that snowy Wednesday morning? Cheryl's reasons were in many ways more frightening to the townspeople of Selden than a random act of violence. Parents looked at children. Children looked at parents. Husbands and wives looked at each other.

Pierson's friends kept thinking back to his fortieth birthday party, to Cheryl's Sweet Sixteen, to all those public events, to dinners around his table, to his son's graduation party, to his wife's funeral. They played back those scenes over and over like a scratchy old 16mm home movie as if the answer would lie in a gesture, a comment, a pause. Something that if they saw again might tip them off, might make them look more closely.

James Germana had known James Pierson ever since the eighth grade. He was the best man at Pierson's wedding. He was with Pierson when his children were

born and when his wife was about to die. He knew
what kind of man James Pierson was, how much he
loved his family, how protective he was of his children, how old-fashioned he was in his values. William
Praetorius, who handled Pierson's insurance, knew
how strict James Pierson was as a father, how firm his
principles, how clear his ideas about child rearing, how
important family dignity was to him. Arthur Giove,
who owned the funeral home where Pierson was eu-
logized, knew how dedicated he had been to his wife,
how not a day would go by when he would not be at
her bedside, how devastated he was when she died.
Kenny Zimlinghaus knew of his many travails with
work and health and that the only joy left in his life
was Cheryl.

''It was the kind of relationship I would have wanted
with my daughter,'' Kenny Zimlinghaus would say
sadly.

It was impossible to understand.


Christmas 1985 had been a particularly sad day for the
Piersons. James Pierson had been dreading it for
weeks. It was to be the first Christmas since his wife
died. His wife was always so good at fussing with
presents and decorations and candles and special
cards. All year long Cathleen Pierson combed the
stores. Even in July her closet would be filled with
surprises she planned to give the children the following Christmas. It would have been their twenty-first
Christmas together. Half his lifetime.

He was to spend it that year at the home of his sister,
Marilyn, who shared a house with their mother. The
Christmas tree was up. The wood stove was hot. The
windows were frosted with snowflakes. The oblong
table in the kitchen was decked out with wreaths and
candles and a bouquet of mistletoe. The air was rich
with the aroma of turkey. Everyone was trying so hard
to be cheerful.

Marilyn decided to invite over her nephew, Jimmy.

He and his father were not speaking but made a special exception for Christmas. Christmas was the one day of the year when the slate of family animosities was wiped clean. The youth arrived early and helped his aunt set the table. He had come with a blue dress shirt for his father he and his aunt had picked out together in the Smithaven Mall. When Pierson and the girls finally arrived, their arms too were laden. Virginia Pierson was in the kitchen finishing off the preparations for dinner.

"Hey Mom, I want to show you something," Pierson said, stepping into the kitchen before he had even taken off his coat.

"Yeah what?" his mother replied. She was standing over the stove, laying the sweet rolls out on a baking tray.

"Come on Ma, I need you here. I need you here right now."

"Okay. Okay," she said. "Do you want to eat tonight or not?"

"I want to show you something."

"What's the rush?"

"I want to show you my new car." She looked through the window.

"I can see it from here."

"No, I want you to see it up close. So come out here." She put on her overcoat and followed him outside.

"You like it?" he asked, standing there.

"It's very nice," she said, looking out at a royal blue 1980 Chrysler Cordoba with a plush royal blue interior and a shiny white top.

"Really?" he asked.

"Yeah. Really."

"I mean do you really like it?"

"Yeah. I really like it. I really like the color."

"Good," he said, handing her the keys. "Because it's yours."

The rest of the family laughed and applauded. It was

vintage Pierson. He was often loud and brash with his family, but it was hard to find anyone more generous. "He'd tell you to go to hell and give you the money to get there" was how many described James Pierson and how his bravado was just a cover for his far more vulnerable interior. His mother threw her arms around her son and wept. In many ways he was still her little boy.

Marilyn had made eggnog, and the family ate cheddar cheese balls as they watched the yule log on the television set. Cheryl had been planning for weeks to give her father a leafblower. It cost $600, which Cheryl asked her father to take out of a bank account he kept in her name. Pierson initially refused, complaining it was too much money. Cheryl insisted but refused to tell him what it was for because she wanted to keep "the surprise." Finally Marilyn persuaded her brother to give Cheryl the money after all and accompanied her niece to the local Sears to pick the item out. Pierson gave Cheryl her mother's diamond watch and a heavy gold bracelet. JoAnn received a bicycle and a Cabbage Patch doll her mother had stashed away for her during that year before she died. Pierson gave his son a card with $300. Pierson and his son were cordial that day, but nothing more.

All in all, it was a bittersweet day: joys and surprises punctuated by sadness and irritation. At one point Pierson and his sister got into an argument over the way she had prepared the potatoes and then again over the fact that she still had one of his cars. The children gathered around to listen.

In an adjoining room, seated on the living room sofa, Cheryl asked her brother to find someone to kill their father.

---

*On the ride to see my mother in the hospital he'd tell me how guys would try to use my body and stuff. He'd be like: I'm not using your body. I really love you. And all this kind of*

*stuff. All guys are the same. You shouldn't do
it until you get married. If I catch you, I'll kill
you. But then he'd say if I was ever in trouble
I should come to him.*

---

"Where's Cheryl?" JoAnn Pierson, eight years old,
wanted to know. It was early Thursday morning, February 13, 1986, exactly a year to the day that her
mother died. The girl had awakened to find her grandmother and aunt alone in the den.

"She's at cheerleading practice," Marilyn replied
cheerfully, not knowing what to say. Marilyn knew she
had to be in court later that afternoon to try to post
bail for Cheryl. She was afraid to send JoAnn to school
that day out of fear that the other children might already know. Frantically Marilyn asked the advice of
friends about what to do. It was Bruce Bandes, Pierson's attorney and friend, who suggested a child psychologist. A professional, he said, would be best.

"I know someone good," Bruce Bandes had said.

It was now Thursday night. Cheryl was already in
jail as Dr. Gary Cox-Steiner drove up the Pierson
driveway on Magnolia Drive. Dr. Cox-Steiner took a
seat at the oblong wooden table in the dining room,
the same table where JoAnn had shared so many meals
with her sister and father. Marilyn Adams was already
seated.

"I'm the kind of doctor who talks about feelings,"
Dr. Cox-Steiner told JoAnn. "There is something we
have to say. It is very difficult, but it has to be said."

JoAnn sat intently at the table and watched the man.
She was a pretty girl with curly reddish brown hair
and wide, intelligent eyes. She held a doll in her arms
that she stroked with her hands.

"It's been discovered that Cheryl was involved in
having your father killed," Dr. Cox-Steiner said.
JoAnn began to cry, clutching the doll to her body.
She looked at her aunt. Marilyn nodded solemnly.

He waited a moment to continue.

"One of the reasons she says she did it is because she says your father did something to her that fathers are not supposed to do with their daughters. Sexual things."

"You know how Mommy and Daddy said to tell them if someone touches you down there," Marilyn then said, pointing to her crotch.

At this point JoAnn jumped from the table and began to scream. "No. No. It's not true. It can't be true. Cheryl didn't murder Daddy. My daddy wouldn't do that. My daddy never . . . My daddy loved us."

The child was sobbing.

Marilyn reached over to hug the little girl. Dr. Cox-Steiner tried to comfort the child as well. There was a long period of silence. It was a tense, terrible moment.

Then JoAnn abruptly grabbed her doll and ran from the table.

"Shall I go after her?" Marilyn asked, standing. "Shall I go see if she is all right? Should you go?" She was weeping too.

"No," Dr. Cox-Steiner replied. "Give her a moment. Let her have a little time."

JoAnn reappeared. She had stopped crying. She seemed calmer. Instead of a doll she was now carrying something else in her arms. It was a bulletin board covered with photographs, all of her family. Her mother. Her father. Her brother. Her sister. One was of her brother's graduation. Another of Cheryl's Sweet Sixteen. Another was just of her parents, standing arm in arm.

With great pride, JoAnn Pierson explained who everyone in the pictures was. Dr. Cox-Steiner listened.

In every photograph, everyone was smiling.

Leonard Rosen and Bruce Bandes, two of Pierson's friends, cosigned a cash note for $25,000 and bailed Cheryl out of jail. It was an awkward moment. They would later say they knew James Pierson too well to believe he could do that to his daughter. But they also knew how much he loved Cheryl and would have done anything to keep her out of jail.

So Cheryl was released from jail ten days after her arrest and went to live in the home of her father's sister, her new guardian, Marilyn Adams; the same home in which she had shared Christmas dinner with her father just two months before; the same house where in the middle of the dinner she wandered into the living room to ask her brother to help her find someone to kill their father.

Now arriving at her aunt's house with two shopping bags filled with clothes, Cheryl felt strange. It was the home she had come to as a child for family dinners. Birthdays. Thanksgivings. Valentine's Day dinners. She felt awkward, ashamed. She did not know what to say.

Marilyn Adams lived in a modest home with three small bedrooms. She and her husband, John, were divorced the previous November, and she now lived there alone with their two grown children. Her mother lived there, too, in an apartment over the garage. It was a cramped place with none of the amenities to which Cheryl was accustomed. Since there was no extra bedroom, Cheryl now had to share a single bed with her eighteen-year-old cousin, Kimmie. JoAnn had to share a bed with Marilyn. All of them had to share a kitchen and an ocean of incomprehension.

Marilyn had promised herself she would not talk about the murder. She knew it would serve no good. But it was impossible to avoid. Sitting there in the kitchen, the subject hung over them like a shroud. Once little JoAnn and Virginia Pierson had excused themselves for bed, Marilyn could no longer contain herself.

"How could I have told you?" Cheryl said, sitting at the kitchen table, the same table where she had had

Christmas dinner with her father. "You would never have believed me. He was your brother."

"You're right," Marilyn replied. "I wouldn't have. But then I would have thought about it. And you know I would have done something. You know I would have tried to find out more."

"Yeah. But then you would have told him," Cheryl said. "And then what?"

"It would be better than this. Anything would be better than this."

The radio was on. Sixties rock. No one spoke for what seemed like a long time. Then Marilyn turned to Cheryl and raised the awful subject of the pregnancy for the first time.

"We'll schedule an abortion," Marilyn said sadly. "Please don't mention it to JoAnn."

Cheryl nodded.

Again there was the awkward silence.

"But the thing I still don't understand, Cheryl," Marilyn said, shaking her head, "is if it was so bad, if it was as horrible as you say, how come you didn't kill him yourself?"

"How could I have done a thing like that?" Cheryl replied. "I loved my father."

---

*I think right after my mother died I started thinking about it more. 'Cause he was doing it to me more and more and I kept thinking about it all the time. Because that's what made me think too. Because I was out more then. I was at cheerleading practice and I went to the movies with Rob a couple times. And when I used to go out with his parents, my sister was home all the time with my father now. And I'd come home and I'd see her sleeping in his bed. Now I don't know if she wanted to sleep there because no one else was in the house or watch TV with him. But I knew that was how it started with me. And he used to wrestle around*

*with her and stuff just like he started with me*
*and I seen that it was going to start and I*
*didn't want it to. And I think he felt that I was*
*going to move out soon and that she was going*
*to be the only one there.*

Tall, with short-cropped dark hair, ramrod-straight
posture and a penchant for crisply pressed blue pin-
striped suits, Edward Jablonski was a thirty-eight-year-
old trial lawyer who exuded the word *prosecutor*. Never
rumpled, never at a loss for words, and with penetrat-
ing dark eyes that seemed to notice everything, he
could play himself in the movies. Jablonski was chief
of the Suffolk County District Attorney's Major Offense Bureau and as such had prosecuted some of the
most notorious criminals in the county. Devil wor-
shippers. Multiple stranglers. Thugs who beat a taxi-
driver to death and set his cab on fire.

The case of Cheryl Pierson was not one that Ed
Jablonski initially found all that compelling. There was
no great community fear involved. From a legal stand-
point, so far as he was concerned, there was no particular challenge. The detectives had secured
confessions in the case. Cheryl's motive seemed
straightforward. Whether or not she was under emotional distress would be up to a jury. Sean was a hired
hit man, and Jablonski was convinced he would get
him convicted of murder. He could not understand all
the attention the media was giving the case. What was
even more problematic for him was the outpouring of
public sympathy for Cheryl.

"All she had to do was go to the police," Jablonski
would say. "That's what they are there for. That's why
we have a Family Crime unit. Not to hire someone to
murder the person. If you accept her behavior, then
anyone who gets fired from their job or has their house
burglarized could hire a local kid to get even. That's
anarchy. That's Dodge City."

He would later say it was Cheryl's premeditation that bothered him most; the notion that a girl who felt incapable of telling anyone of her father's sexual advances was nevertheless sophisticated enough to hire someone to have him killed. It struck Jablonski as callous and amazingly resourceful, certainly resourceful enough to have been able to pick up the telephone and call an operator for assistance. The toll-free number for the New York State Child Abuse Hotline is on page one of the Suffolk County telephone book. Newfield High School has a large staff of guidance counselors. It even has a special room set aside for youngsters with problems. There was talk of not seeking a murder indictment against Cheryl Pierson; that with all she suffered she had emotional cause and it might be more suitable to charge the girl with manslaughter. A grand jury convened. Cheryl's brother was its main witness, which meant that he could not be prosecuted if later on it was discovered he played a role in planning the murder. But, at last, the prosecutor would have inside information about Cheryl, about Cuccio, about Cheryl's relationship with her father.

"I got the impression he was trying to defend his father," Jablonski recalled of young Pierson's appearance before the grand jury. When asked specifically whether he was aware of a sexual relationship between his father and Cheryl, James Pierson Jr. said he was not. Asked if the two ever watched television together in his father's bedroom, he replied they did but "it was normal," the kind of affection one expected between a father and a daughter. Both were dressed. Neither was under the covers. The bedroom door was open.

Young Pierson's observations had surprised Ed Jablonski. He thought for certain he would have heard more of Pierson's alleged sexual relationship with his daughter. Out of allegiance to his sister, young Pierson could even have manufactured some impressions.

But he did not. He seemed not to know anything about it.

The grand jury returned indictments for murder against both Cheryl and Sean. Jablonski had already decided to hold off charging Cuccio until he could get him to agree to testify against the others. If convicted, Cheryl and Sean faced a minimum of fifteen years in jail, because even though they were only sixteen years old at the time of the crime, a sixteen-year-old convicted of murder in New York State is automatically treated as an adult.

"She started talking about it," Sean would recall. "But it was more or less just talking about it. 'Well, how much would you charge if something like that ever happened?' I said, 'I don't know.' I guess one thousand dollars or something like that. You know. And she said, 'One hundred thousand dollars!' And I said, 'No. Just one thousand dollars.' It wasn't like anything was happening. We were just talking. And then the next thing I know she's all serious about something. She asked me if it was all right if her boyfriend came in to talk to me. And I said, 'For what?' She says, 'He wants to make sure you're serious about doing it.' And I'm just . . . 'What?' "

From the start, Sean Pica's involvement in the murder was as big a mystery as Cheryl's. Sean was a popular student, no less so than Cheryl. He had his own crowd. He was about to represent the school in a state-wide carpentry competition. He was working on getting his Eagle badge at the Boy Scouts. He was the kind of person people would call on in a pinch to baby-sit for their kids; the kind just about anyone who knew him could trust. He was a short, dark-haired youth. Not unattractive. Sean wore braces on his teeth and had only fuzz for a beard and looked far younger than his years. Outgoing, with a quick sense of humor, he was well known around the neighborhood.

*Gentle* was one word friends used to describe Sean

Pica. *Sensitive* was another. He was the kind of boy who was not ashamed to wrap his arms around his mother in pubic and declare he loved her, the kind of boy who enjoyed taking the time to talk to the only elderly man on the block, the kind who took special interest in helping those who needed assistance.

Sean lived with his mother in a two-story Roxbury Colonial which his parents had bought two years before he was born for $21,500. The development in which they lived had many other young families. Those initial deposits did not only buy a house. They bought each other's company. Their children would be each other's best friends.

It was in 1975 that Sebastian Pica left home for the first time and took an apartment in New York City. His sons were nine, seven, and four. Shortly after his move, Sean's older brother, Joe, came down with a fever. Unperturbed, Joanne figured it would go away. But when it didn't, she took him to the doctor, who diagnosed leukemia; Joe had less than five years to live. It was a devastating period. Sebastian Pica returned home, and in time Joe miraculously recovered. Ben and Joanne went for counseling, but the marriage was long over. They were officially divorced on Valentine's Day, 1979. The following June Ben married his second wife, KarenAnn, a police officer who had worked at the 111th precinct with him in Queens. Not long after Ben's marriage, Joanne met an X-ray technician on a blind date named Jim DelVecchio, whom she married three months later.

''Jim is your real father,'' Joanne would tell the children. ''Ben is only your biological father.''

Even after the divorce, Joanne and Ben bickered constantly over money, discipline, and many other matters pertaining to the boys. The children were asked to choose sides, and then made to feel that their father had let them down when he walked away. The family was dealt an even harsher blow three years later when Jim DelVecchio took off one day for a softball game and never returned. Again for Sean there had been a father, a father he loved, a father who left him.

Jim's leaving left Joanne mortified and feeling like a failure yet again. Money was even tighter, and it was more difficult to discipline the boys. Joanne found it hard to contain her anger.

"I don't hate men," Joanne would say. "I'm just realistic."

Joanne and her boys made up a game. Anytime they went anyplace and saw what was clearly a nuclear family, they would put their hands over their ears and in mock unison cry out "Happy Family." It was the one thing, of course, that Joanne DelVecchio had so desperately wanted.

Clearly these divorces took their toll on Sean.

"Sean always felt it was his fault," John Rosalia, Sean's old friend, would recall.

John and Sean grew up directly across the street from one another in exactly the same style house. Both were juniors at Newfield, and they often rode dirtbikes together. They froze snowballs in the winter and threw them at each other on the Fourth of July. They built a tree house together in the yard of the neighbors' house next door.

"Just the week before this happened I held Sean up as an example to my son," John's mother, Carmen Rosalia, said. Carmen was part of Joanne's Thursday lunch group; her husband drove a yellow cab in Manhattan. "This is the worst tragedy of our lives. How could this happen? Why did this happen? Sean was one of the most pleasant kids on the block. I look at this and I feel unnerved. Why was I spared? We're all a family here. When one of us had a baby, we all got together and made a week's worth of dinners. When we moved out here, we were all alone. It was our chance to make our own little world. And that's what we did. We were fifties people. Never touched by the sixties. We had our families. We had each other. A terrible thing has happened to all of us."

* * *

Five days after his arrest, Sean spent his seventeenth birthday—February 18, 1986—at the Suffolk County jail.

A lonely, drafty place surrounded by barbed wire, the Suffolk County jail sits on a tract of land in what many refer to as the armpit of Long Island—smack in the center of where the two forks go off into their far more affluent directions: the North Fork and the Hamptons. It is about a forty-minute drive from Selden. To visit a prisoner there, one must sign up on a sheet early in the morning and wait one's turn. Prisoners are entitled to exactly one hour a day. No more. A maximum of two visitors at a time, which means that if ten people show up, they often spend more time with each other in the uncomfortable waiting room with its small aqua plastic bucket seats than with the person they came to visit.

Friends and relatives arrive convinced that the police have made some mistake. They come to show their support, to share their sorrow. Naturally in those first days, Sean's mother and father went to see him, as did grandparents and neighbors from up and down the street. But at first Sean wanted to see no one.

"He was too ashamed," recalled Sebastian Pica, Sean's father.

As family and friends sat there in the jailhouse, it was hard not to play back the events of that "week it happened." Joanne would later say she knew something had been bothering Sean but had no idea what. He had been speaking about getting his own place. A house or something, where he could get a good deal. But she just assumed it was an adolescent scheme. She sat the youth down, drew up a budget, and showed him how unrealistic it was. They then spoke of other things. She ran over the details time and again. The Wednesday of the murder she had been at work. She worked that night too.

Diana Gabb, Sean's new girlfriend, was at the jailhouse too, waiting her turn. She remembered how Sean had driven her to school that Wednesday and how he drove her that Thursday too and how that night he was supposed to leave on a ski trip with his mother. Diana had pleaded with him to cancel the trip and stay with her, but Sean had to go. At lunch that day— perhaps to make amends—Sean took Diana to the Smithaven Mall and said he wanted to buy her an ankle bracelet. Diana told him she did not like ankle bracelets because they always broke. Sean had Diana try on a necklace. It was made of 14K gold and had her name written on it in script. The problem was it did not sit right and kept on flipping over. When Diana next admired two heavy gold bracelets, Sean bought them for her. They cost $1,100. He put down a deposit of $150 on layaway.

Joanne, too, remembered that first day, after "it happened," a Thursday, the same day Sean was supposedly paid $400 in carpentry class for James Pierson's murder. After school she and Sean took off with her youngest son, Vincent, for New Jersey. The plan was to spend the night at the home of her boyfriend, Larry. The boys were supposed to miss the next day of school so that they could all go skiing. A news report came over the car radio about James Pierson's murder.

"I asked Sean if he knew Cheryl," Joanne would recall of the car trip to New Jersey. "He told me he did. He said that she was in his homeroom."

There was nothing more said, Joanne recalled. When they awakened Friday morning, it was snowing so hard they questioned whether they should risk the drive. But, true to form, Joanne insisted. They had said they were going skiing, and it was going to take more than a little snow to stand in their way. An hour's drive took almost four, and when they finally arrived everyone was exhausted. Sean announced he did not feel well. He was running a fever. He spent the day lying down on a table in the ski center's cafeteria. They drove

home that Friday night, just the day before James Pierson's funeral, the day Sean was said to have called
Cheryl for the first time and to have asked that she
meet him at a local pizza place where he demanded
the six hundred dollar balance, two motorcycles and
permission to live in a vacant house Cheryl's father
had owned.

Ben Pica had not seen his son that week at all. But
the Monday after "it happened" Sean had a midwinter
recess at school and he went to visit his father and
stepmother in Valley Stream, about a forty-minute
drive west of Selden. They had a good time. Sean's
father drove Sean to the train station that Wednesday
afternoon. The Long Island Railroad was running late
because of the snow. They had one final chat, "a good
chat," Ben would recall, about an argument his son
had recently had with his mother about his new girlfriend. He kissed his son goodbye. The next time he
saw him, Sean was in handcuffs and under arrest for
murder.

"I think he should get his braces taken off," Ben
Pica said at one point at the jailhouse, just making
conversation.

"But they cost so much money," Joanne Del-
Vecchio's mother replied.

"Yes. But it could be dangerous in there if he got
into a fight."

"Well, he better not get into a fight in there," she
replied naively. Sebastian Pica winced and looked out
the window.

It was tense for everyone. They were still at the point
where Sean's involvement could be denied; when there
was speculation that he was taking the blame for
someone else, that the police had forced him to sign
a false confession.

There was another visitor at the jail that day. He
was someone whom Sean had not seen in a long time;
not since that day he announced he was taking off for
the softball game from which he never returned. Awk-

ward in the presence of the others, the man kept to himself. But as time went on, Jim DelVecchio would have a lot to say.

Meanwhile at Newfield High School, Mrs. Hoban, in whose homeroom the murder plot was first initiated, was devastated. She asked everyone she knew whether there was something she could have done; something, anything she could have noticed. Could it have been prevented? She was not alone; these questions preoccupied almost everyone at the school.

Dr. Arthur Dermer, the school's principal, got on the public address system and reminded students of the existence of the Time Out Room, a comfortable room on the ground floor. It is furnished with couches and is staffed around the schoolday clock with a teacher for students who need to talk.

"If anyone has a problem. Please step forward. Tell us. Ask us to help you. That's why we're here."

After Leonard Lupetin, the school's assistant principal, broke the news to Sean's mother, he went home and told his wife he felt like a failure. He always thought of himself, after thirty years in the school system, as the kind of teacher and administrator youngsters could approach, could turn to when they were in trouble.

"All they have to do is walk in the door," he said, at a loss for answers. "Did we miss something? There is something not in line here. I'm hurt that they didn't feel they could tell me."

Many years before, Leonard Lupetin had had Cheryl's father as a student. He remembered him as an average student. A boy's boy, "full of the devil," with a big mouth. In recent years he had seen James Pierson in the bleachers watching his daughter cheer. It was an image that had always moved him that Pierson turned out to be such an attentive father who was not afraid to be proud of his daughter.

Students were confronted by journalists as they entered and left the school building. Many girls on the cheerleading squad quit; they couldn't stand the pressure, the questions, the constant scrutiny. The ones who stayed tried to pretend they had never met Cheryl. But something strange was happening at the high school, something that couldn't be explained away by the tension of the last week. Graffiti appeared on the lavatory walls: "Free Sean!" Sean Pica was emerging as a hero at Newfield. A hometown Arnold Schwarzenegger. A modern-day Robin Hood.

"It's scary," said Debra Handel, a psychologist at Newfield High School. "That kids look at Sean as the way to go instead of the system. Years ago a policeman was your friend. So were teachers. The heroes today are not public servants. They're driving in Porsches with thick gold chains. The Mr. Ts. They're not poor social workers in the Peace Corps. Do it quick. Do it easy. Get what you can. I suppose if we all weren't so disillusioned with the police, politicians, and all the other public figures it would be different. But why trust the system? In these kids' minds, quick is better. Sean circumvented all the nonsense of the system, and if you believe Cheryl, then in these kids' minds, what he did was truly heroic. My big fear is, if he gets off, kids will begin to think they can get away with murder."

# 6

No jail. That was Cheryl's lawyer's position and one he kept. "She's been punished enough," Paul Gianelli would say at every turn.

He was hoping that the District Attorney's office would finally acquiesce, particularly once some corroboration of the sexual abuse emerged, and Gianelli was confident it would. The results of a paternity test following Cheryl's scheduled abortion would be important, as would any other physical corroboration. Cheryl had told Gianelli that she and her father had had sexual intercourse in his bed the night before the murder, and the prosecutor's office had sent her father's sheets to be tested for semen stains and pubic hairs. An analysis was also done on Cheryl's nightclothes and her father's bathroom towels.

Strategically, he knew that Cheryl's case could turn into bad publicity for the District Attorney's office. If there was an outpouring of public sympathy for Cheryl, then the District Attorney would have to back down from their current hard-line stand. Paul Gianelli at one time worked in the District Attorney's office. In fact he ran for District Attorney and lost. He knew the politics of justice. Public scrutiny, he decided early on, could be his most powerful tool. But for this to happen, it would be important to separate Cheryl's case from that of Sean, so that the attention would be on the abuse Cheryl suffered and not on the intricacies of the murder plot. But he knew, too, that the District

Attorney would fight hard to keep the cases, for that very reason, together.

---

*Two weeks before my father died, I wasn't talking to him and he kept asking me what was wrong and he knew when I was supposed to get my period. And he's like "did you get it? did you get it" for like a week straight. And I kept yelling at him: "No! Thanks to you!" And stuff like that and he's like "You're not!" I'm telling him: "But I never missed it before" and all this other stuff. And he started to get worried and started looking through the phone book for clinics and stuff so nobody would find out. Then . . . and then . . . so that's why I thought I was. Yeah. I was really upset. I was really upset that this is what he was putting me through. Because I love little kids and for me to have to go through all this stuff because of him. I was really annoyed. I knew he was hurt and upset about it and he wasn't going to come after me or yell at me or scream at me if I yelled at him 'cause it was his fault. I don't know if he called. He said . . . I forgot which one he said but he said he found a good one and stuff.*

---

Dr. Sanroman in Port Jefferson shares an office with the gynecologist who just sixteen years before helped deliver Cheryl. The office is just down the street from Mather Hospital where Cheryl was born.

It was two weeks after the murder. Marilyn sat with Cheryl in the waiting room. Cheryl was nervous. She had never been to a gynecologist's office before. She had no idea what was involved in an examination. Marilyn tried to explain what had never been explained to her before. She asked the secretary for a piece of paper and drew a diagram. Marilyn stayed with her as she took off her clothing and put on a gown for the sonogram. Cheryl watched the screen overhead as the nurse pointed out the tiny dot on her uterine wall that was the embryo. Until that afternoon, Cheryl had never heard the word *uterus* or *ovary*. She had no idea exactly how one gets pregnant, let alone what was involved in an abortion.

The doctor explained that it was too early in the pregnancy to perform a surgical abortion, that earlier could cause damage to the lining of the uterus. But that if they waited about three more weeks it would be fine, and he scheduled to do it in the hospital on March 20, by coincidence her sister's ninth birthday. He advised Cheryl that it was not a painful procedure and she should not worry; that she would be admitted one day and be able to go home the next.

Marilyn Adams got the name of a psychiatrist for Cheryl to see. She also contacted the local school authorities and arranged for Cheryl to be tutored at home. Gianelli had told Marilyn he would have a better idea how things would proceed once the results of the paternity test were in hand.

Meanwhile, tension was mounting at home between Cheryl and Marilyn Adams. Cheryl wanted to see her boyfriend, Rob, but given the circumstances, Marilyn was against it.

"You're out on bail for murder, Cheryl. Remember?" she would say. "It doesn't look good."

"My bosses are dead," Cheryl would respond.

"As long as you're living here you're going to listen to me," Marilyn Adams would say.

Still Cheryl went her own way. She would tell Marilyn that she was going to see her girlfriend and then be seen driving around the neighborhood with Rob. Not a day would pass without a blowup. An accusation about Rob. Criticism about how she behaved with JoAnn. Remarks about who took up too much of the single bed she shared with Kimmie. If not that, it was endless questioning at every turn of what was really at issue.

"We're such bad people?" Pierson's mother would say to her granddaughter. "If you were in trouble you could have come to us. I was there every Saturday morning. Ironing. Why couldn't you come to us? Why couldn't you say something?"

"Why didn't you stay away from him?" Marilyn would ask. "Why did you like to be with him all the time? There was a lot of help out there, Cheryl."

Cheryl didn't answer.

"You could have gone to somebody. My brother does not deserve to be in the ground! He could have gone for help. I would have taken him to get it. Who do you think you are, God?"

Cheryl would run into the bedroom she shared with Kimmie and lock the door.

It was on March 9, 1986, that *Newsday* published a lengthy article on the front page of its Sunday editions entitled "Homeroom 226: A Lesson in Murder." It was as controversial as its sensationalist headline. It touched off a slew of questions that no one seemed to have thought about before, in terms of both the intricacies of the murder plot itself and what appeared to be going on in each of these young people's minds.

Incest is an uncomfortable subject, and it is rarely discussed by the general public. The statistics alone are explosive. Four in every hundred women are approached sexually before the age of eighteen by someone they know, usually their father or stepfather. The intricate psychology is fascinating: that incest is often a secret kept by an entire family, that, in fact, secrecy is its most powerful fuel, that it is often passed down from generation to generation.

*Newsday* located a number of neighbors who had suspected the abuse, although none were certain it was sexual. Diana Erbentraut, a student, recalled how Cheryl came to school once with a black and blue mark on her face after her father had discovered a Valentine's Day card in her purse. Others noticed how obsessed Pierson was with his daughter; how they went everywhere together on his motorcycle, how he lavished her with showy gifts.

Both Cheryl and Sean were interviewed for the first time at length, and it was learned that Cheryl had never told Sean why she wanted her father killed. She said she never believed that he would really do it; that her comments to him in homeroom were all just talk.

"She never stopped asking me," Sean countered.

There was an outpouring of sympathy for both youngsters. Letters poured into the District Attorney's office against prosecuting Cheryl. Sean received mail. One woman offered his family $15,000 for bail. The camera crews began to show up in the schoolyard, and the youngsters were interviewed about what they knew and what they thought about the crime.

James McCready and his wife, Judy, voraciously pored over the article at home that Sunday. McCready was quoted in it only once in describing his interview with Sean and how the only time Sean broke down in his office after confessing to the murder was when McCready asked him his father's profession.

"A police officer," Sean had said.

But what occupied the discussion between McCready and his wife was what should become of Cheryl. Judy McCready, who taught third grade at the local elementary school, felt strongly that Cheryl should be excused with probation. Jimmy McCready felt strongly that she should go to jail.

"She's never going to hurt anyone," she said.

"But she took a life," McCready said.

"Yeah. But she thought that was her only way out," his wife said.

"She's not a stupid girl. She could have called the police."

"She's only a kid."

"She took a life and she should be punished for it. I'm not saying fifteen years or anything. But something. Otherwise, another kid is going to go out and do the same thing.''

It was the kind of debate that went on in homes all over Long Island.

The District Attorney's office knew that the weakest part of its case had nothing to do with Cheryl. The trouble was Sean.

The day of his arrest, Sean confessed. He told detectives of Cheryl's offer, his acceptance, and a first, unsuccessful attempt the previous December in which Pica threw a brick through the window of Pierson's other house on Magnolia Drive. The plan was to stab Pierson when he came to check what was wrong. But the alarm never went off, and Pica went home. In January, Pica said, he finally got a gun, and the day he confessed he led police to the spot overlooking Long Island Sound where he said he threw the weapon.

Photographs were taken of Sean standing on a jetty pointing to where the gun was, but police divers spent an entire day looking and came up with nothing. According to their calculations, Sean had disposed of the weapon at high tide and, since metal doesn't float out to sea, by low tide it should have been easily visible. But it was not. Indeed nothing that Sean told detectives about the murder weapon rang true. He bought it, he said, in Queens at a cemetery near 48th Street where people came to sell hot merchandise. But first he bought the ammunition at a gunshop in Coram.

''No one buys ammunition first,'' McCready would later say, wondering aloud why someone would confess to a murder but lie about a gun.

By now McCready had canvassed enough of Newfield High School to hear the rumor that the gun had been stolen and, if it was, the odds were pretty good it involved a neighborhood chum of Sean's, Michael Kerwick. Kerwick was legendary among the troublemakers. Kerwick was Sean's oldest friend and the one his mother constantly pleaded with Sean to avoid. Everyone around the block knew that Michael robbed houses and sold off the hot merchandise. Everyone knew Michael used drugs. Everyone said that had Kerwick been arrested for Pierson's murder, no one would have been surprised.

On a hunch, McCready decided to check all the robberies that had been committed in Selden and Coram over the last three months to see if someone had reported losing a .22-caliber pump rifle, and his "good old-fashioned detective work" paid off. Someone had, on January 10, 1986—three weeks before the murder.

Convinced that this was the murder weapon and that Michael Kerwick had stolen it, McCready was eager to play out his hunch. He called Kerwick's father.

"Your son has been implicated in the Pierson murder," McCready said. "We'd like to bring him down here for questioning."

The family of Michael Kerwick retained a lawyer, and the two of them met with McCready in District Attorney Edward Jablonski's office, an immaculate room on the eighth floor of a modern structure that does not look as though it belongs on Long Island. There is not a paperclip out of order; not a file folder visible. The room is so clean it looks unoccupied. The only ornament is a black mug embossed in gold with the following message: "Thou Shalt Not Kill," a memento from the homicide squad.

The date was March 11. Michael Kerwick, a tall, curly-haired youth with an easygoing charm, arrived on schedule. He was deceptively clean cut in appearance. He took a seat directly across from Jablonski and McCready. The deal cut was that anything he discussed honestly and truthfully in that office would not be subject to prosecution.

McCready began.

"I know the gun was taken during a burglary," he said. "And I know you took it. We found the gun. Your prints are on it."

Kerwick, with his dark, curly hair and wide, angelic eyes, played dumb.

"I don't know what you're talking about," he said.

"I also know where you got the gun," McCready said, continuing his bluff. "No one's protecting you up there in the grand jury, Michael, so you may as well come clean. We know where you got the gun. It was right over the fireplace. I can tell you when you were there too. I can tell you what else you took. You better tell us everything, Michael, or you're going to find yourself indicted for murder."

At this point Kerwick, who had been kneading a pen in his right hand, suddenly threw it clear across the room, just missing Jablonski's left cheek. Then he jumped up from his chair, ran over to the door, and punched it so hard his knuckles were bloody. McCready and Jablonski looked at each other. No one else moved. It was the moment they had been waiting for.

Kerwick sat down.

"Okay, I stole the gun," he said, pounding his fist on Ed Jablonski's desk. "But I didn't kill him."

"I think you better tell us exactly what happened, Michael."

"Okay, I stole it. I didn't want to keep it in my father's house."

"But you gave it to Sean."

"Yeah."

"Did he ever tell you he was planning to murder someone?"

"He mentioned it once."

"What did he say?"

"He said that Cheryl wanted to give him a thousand dollars to blow away her dad. I told him that he just better forget about it, that it was crazy. I thought he had."

"So when did you give him the gun?"

"Well first I had it for a while."

"What did you do with it?"

"I just had it. Then a couple of times Sean and I

went and shot it off." McCready's stomach grew taut as he envisioned new evidence.

"Oh yeah?" he said, not wanting to appear too eager.

"Yeah. We went to the survival course in Coram and took aim at a tree."

Michael told the detectives many things that day. He told them about how he and Sean had committed dozens of burglaries over the past two years. He told them how the two of them used drugs. He told them that the day of the murder he went over to Sean's house and confronted him in his bedroom.

"I punched him out," Kerwick said.

Kerwick swore to the detectives that he had no idea where Sean hid the gun. All he knew was that it had been "broken into pieces." Then Michael Kerwick did something almost as good as lead them to the gun. He led McCready to the spot where he and Sean had shot off the rifle in target practice, the same rifle that had killed James Pierson.

The "survival course," American Air Gun Games of Coram, is a place where on the weekend men and women dress up in Army fatigues and chase each other in the woods with toy guns filled with paint in a day-long game of war. Kerwick led McCready to the exact tree where Sean took target practice. There McCready knelt on the wet ground for hours and dug through the leaves. Eventually he found the shells covered with dirt like buried treasure. He sent them off to the ballistics lab with the following question. "Do these striations match the ones on the shells that killed Pierson?"

The answer: They did. The prosecution no longer needed the gun.

Dr. Kathleen Oitzinger met Cheryl Pierson for the first time on March 5, 1986, in her small office in Setauket, about a twenty-minute drive from Selden. A tall woman with shoulder-length light brown hair, Dr. Oitzinger is a psychotherapist who specializes in dysfunctional families.

Cheryl arrived that first day with her aunt Marilyn, who waited in an adjoining room as the teenager talked about her situation. Pregnant and under indictment for murder, speaking about her father's sexual abuse with a professional for the first time, Cheryl was surprisingly forthcoming, Dr. Oitzinger would later say. There was a naivete to Cheryl that was also disarming.

"She was one of the few kids who's never puffed a joint," Dr. Oitzinger would recall. "She had never been allowed to go to a movie alone. Never been able to go to the city. What she really wanted to do was go to the zoo. The Bronx Zoo. She wanted to go to a disco. She wanted to go to Adventureland. She had a fantasy of a real vacation. Of Florida. Of being on the beach. Of her senior prom, of creating her own beauty salon someday with a section for children. With a merry-go-round horse, a rocket ship."

But there was a chilling coldness to how Cheryl spoke as she recounted in detail why she had been driven to take her father's life.

"One of the differentiations I had to make right in the very beginning was whether this was someone who was psychotic," Dr. Oitzinger would later say. "She was detached from any kinds of feelings, from any kind of remorse. This is the way it happened. This is what it was as if there were no other alternatives."

Cheryl did not have any apparent psychosis, but her capacity to disassociate herself from reality was pronounced. So was her capacity for denial.

"This becomes a defensive style," Dr. Oitzinger said. "A way of life. That whenever there is stress, what you do is just detach. Even though she spoke to Sean the night before. Even though they had been planning the murder for months, when she found her father's body in the driveway she actually believed he had fallen on the ice. And I believed her." Dr. Oitzinger determined that in Cheryl's troubled psyche, what other people did not know was simply not true.

The bleeding began sometime in the morning. Cheryl was supposed to go on a trip into Manhattan. She was now enrolled in special classes—away from Newfield High School—and her beauty class was supposed to take the Long Island Railroad together and visit some fancy high-style salon. She had been looking forward to the trip; anything to get her out of town, away from the legal headaches and the difficult business of the abortion. But when Marilyn Adams called the doctor, he instructed her to keep Cheryl home.

Marilyn was scheduled to go to the Department of Social Services that morning. There were all kinds of papers that needed to be filed so that Cheryl and JoAnn could collect the benefits they were entitled to from the government. Their father's estate was now estimated to be worth about a million dollars, but it was not clear when the estate would be settled or how much—if anything—would go to Cheryl. Marilyn, who was already in a financial squeeze after the divorce, needed money to help pay for the girls' food and clothing so she was loath to reschedule her appointment. Marilyn told Cheryl she would be back later that afternoon. But by the time she returned, Cheryl had already been taken to the hospital by Marilyn's next door neighbor, Yvonne.

Marilyn raced to St. Charles Hospital, a large brick structure that sits on a hill overlooking Port Jefferson Harbor. Marilyn had many memories of St. Charles Hospital. It was where JoAnn was born. It was the hospital where she gave birth to her son and where Cathleen had stayed all those weeks when she first took ill. There had always been a privacy to these visits. Friends knew to call first before showing up. The Piersons were like that. The good times were the times to share, but not the bad. They were the kind of people to keep tragedy, and most importantly anything that might result in disgrace, to themselves.

But now as Marilyn walked in the front door of the hospital, James McCready was there to share in the family's drama. He had already been on the telephone with Ed Jablonski and Jablonski, in turn, had summoned the Medical Examiner. Under an agreement that Cheryl's attorney had initiated with the District Attorney's office, the remains of the fetus were to be sent to a high-technology laboratory to determine the paternity. It was in everyone's interest, they had all decided, to know.

The dilation and curettage was performed at the hospital that afternoon, the same procedure that would have been done had Cheryl not spontaneously miscarried. Marilyn saw Cheryl before surgery, then went home, prepared dinner for her family, tucked JoAnn into bed, packed a night bag, and returned to the hospital to spend the night with Cheryl because she did not want the teenager to be alone. As she lay on the other single bed in Cheryl's room, listening to the muffled footsteps of the nurses in the hall, so many things ran through her mind. She thought of her dead brother; the questions she would ask him, the things she would say. None of it made any sense. She lay there, trying to envision the worst that could have happened between Cheryl and her father. She knew how difficult her brother could be. She knew how often he abused his physical strength. She knew how he liked to think he could get away with anything. As uncomfortable a thought as it was, she could even envision him fondling his daughter as part of a crude joke or a desperate, lonely act of tenderness. Perhaps Cheryl had tried to seduce her father. But intercourse was beyond Marilyn's comprehension. She could not imagine he would risk the indignity of getting his daughter pregnant. Her brother simply would not do that to his daughter.

"I cried myself to sleep," Marilyn Adams would recall.

* * *

Boy Scout troop 454 meets most Monday nights at the Boyle Avenue Elementary School. About two dozen boys, aged seven to seventeen, gather in the school gymnasium, divide off into patrols, and review scouting skills. It was Sean Pica's troop, and it was here that Sean was elected to the Order of the Arrow.

Being a Boy Scout was an unusual pastime for someone like Sean. Many youngsters his age look down on Scouts as being "uncool." But not Sean. Sean was proud of his being a Boy Scout. He worked on leadership skills and accumulating enough badges to receive the Scouts' highest honor of being named an Eagle. It was with the Scouts that he went on his first hike and fired his first rifle. Sean delighted in planning campouts for the other scouts. He enjoyed teaching such skills as building a fire, installing a tent, and making knots to the younger recruits.

Sean loved the Boy Scouts. He loved it for many reasons, not the least of them Bruce Kirschner, his scoutmaster. At a time when Sean was hungry for a father figure, Bruce, thirty-nine, gladly filled those shoes. Married, but with no children of his own, he tragically had recently lost his own teenage brother. Sean called Bruce Dad, and they developed a special friendship that went beyond Scouts. Bruce regaled Sean with stories of Vietnam, of comradeship and bravery and the chaos of war. Sean did carpentry work for Kirschner and his wife at their home.

When Bruce Kirschner learned of Sean's arrest, he felt in part to blame.

"I sensed Sean had a drug problem," Kirschner would later say. "He told me. But I don't think you can say 'no' to the boys. I think different from others about this. I never condoned it in the troop. I know boys in the troop who do drugs. Whether they can handle it or not, it's up to them. Everybody experiments. Sean used to talk to me. He would ask me about certain things. He used to drink a lot also. He was concerned it was addicting and habit-forming. It was more like peer pressure than anything else. I know he did have a problem and I told him: If your mother asks, I'd tell her but I wouldn't volunteer it. When I spoke to JoAnn a few times, she never asked.''

After the murder Bruce Kirschner resigned from the Boy Scouts. He said he believed his own behavior had been "erratic" and that he might not have listened to Sean as carefully as he should.

"I'm a Vietnam Vet," he explained. "I have flashbacks. He knew I was a Vietnam Vet. He knew I spent two years there. I was in Danang. I was a medic. I went to Camp Eagle in Pleiku. When I have flashbacks I don't talk to anybody or get angry and I take it out on my wife. Luckily she understands, she went to a group. She became a volunteer. She knows. Sean never said he was out of control. He just said he was doing some nice drugs. Drinking this and that. Experiences. I don't preach it's not okay. That's the way I am. Nothing's bad. You have to decide for yourself what you're going to do. I don't think I was a great Scout leader.''

Kirschner said that prior to the murder Sean had told him that he was brought in for questioning by the police about some stolen property.

"I didn't say anything," Kirschner recalled. "Sometimes I was a good ear. Sometimes I didn't want to be bothered. I'd say: Talk to me later. I felt usually if the boys had a bad enough problem, I sent them to talk to the priest. It was up to the boys to do that. If I didn't want to be bothered, I'd say talk to the church and if you don't want your folks to know, go to the church.''

Church is where Joanne DelVecchio took her sons almost every Sunday. It was a ritual in their house just as saying grace was a ritual. They all knew the prayer by heart, and they took turns reciting it.

Joanne DelVecchio had been raised a Catholic, the daughter of a carpenter and his wife, the eldest of three children. The principles of the church were important to her, and she liked the unity that going to church as a family represented. She taught catechism. Every week ten neighborhood children would come to her living room, and she would speak about the role of religion in their lives. They discussed topics like how not to cave into peer pressure and how to be honest. She was a good teacher, and as with most things she did, she embraced this instruction with dedication and energy.

Doing things the right way had always been important to Joanne DelVecchio. Even though she worked two jobs and at one point went back to college to get her degree, Joanne always made time for her children. She was her sons' den mother at the Cub Scouts. She was her sons' class mother at school. She was one of those mothers who never missed a parent-teacher conference and volunteered her living room to raise money for the school. When money was tight at home, she would prepare pancakes for dinner in the shape of the letters in her sons' names. She would be the first to admit that she had long been hard on herself and those she loved.

Joanne was aware that Sean had problems: She knew he had tried drugs. She worried about what he might be doing with his friends. There had been a package missing from underneath the Christmas tree that year, a watch Joanne's boyfriend, Larry, was planning to give her. One of Sean's friends had taken it. She had a good idea who. She worried about bad influences on her son and that he was getting difficult to control. Joanne tried from time to time to talk to Sean's father about it. But when she approached him, he would reply, "Sean never has problems with me." There was even a fleeting moment when she heard about a program for wayward youth called PINS, Persons In Need of Supervision, that was run by the courts. But, as always, it was the shame of reaching out that stopped her, a reluctance to admit failure, a sense that in the end no one really could help.

"What could I have done, turn him in?" Joanne would ask months later. "What could they or anyone else have done? They would have given him a slap on the wrist and told him to do what I was saying all along: Sean, don't do that.''

"She was like: What happened?" Sean would recall. " 'Cause I kept on telling her I'll do it tonight. Then I'd come to school. 'Something happened. Couldn't get out of the house.' Or something. You know. She'd ask me every day. And like . . . I didn't want to tell her I couldn't do it. I didn't want to do it. But I didn't want to let her down, kind of I guess . . . you know. Because I said I would do it from the beginning. Like I got myself involved in something and didn't really even realize what I was really doing . . . you know. It was more like a plea: Like Sean! When are you going to do it, Sean? Things are getting worse and worse. She never ever said, 'How come you're not doing it? What are you scared?' Nothing like that. It was just like uh . . . It was just like. 'Sean things are kind of getting kind of worse.' You know. 'I don't like it. Are you going to do it? Can you do it? Like can ya . . . can ya do it tonight, Sean please . . .' And you felt like she was at your whim, you know? And I felt like I was the only one that could help. It sounds strange, I guess. Huh? The way she talked. She told me that her father put her in the hospital and threw her out of the car once when it was moving. She said that he beat on her. Believe me: I never thought like maybe she's lying to me. I guess it never even entered my mind.''

The Lifecodes Corporation is a high-tech genetics diagnostic laboratory situated in Westchester that is capable of doing some of the most advanced genetic screening and analysis available in the nation. It was founded in 1982 by a team of scientists who, using the most up-to-date tools, perfected a technique that permits the isolation of DNA, the body's molecular blueprint. DNA can be extracted from blood, semen, or tissue. Because DNA varies from individual to individual, it can serve as a highly specific identity profile. Scientists at Lifecodes claim that the likelihood of finding two individuals with the same genetic blueprint to be one in eighty million.

It is the most powerful tool to establish paternity. Investigators claim they can determine it with 99.9 percent certainty.

Until the development of this test, which came into use only in 1985, it was virtually impossible for a laboratory to ascertain the paternity of a fetus of less than three months' gestation. The only test available prior to that time was a blood test that could only be used on a fetus of more than six months' gestation, because it is not before this stage that a fetus develops actual blood.

The paternity of Cheryl Pierson's fetus was the first legal application of this highly advanced test. Cheryl's miscarriage was sent in test tubes and containers. Charles Hirsch, the Suffolk County Medical Examiner, had also sent the laboratory blood and brain tissue samples from the autopsy of Cheryl's father. Although it was supposed to have remained a secret, news of Cheryl's miscarriage hit the papers. The public eagerly awaited the test results. Meanwhile the debate over Cheryl's guilt or innocence continued to rage.

If there was a turning point in the case of Cheryl Pierson, it came in the form of a sterile one-page letter from Elmsford, New York, to the Suffolk County Medical Examiner. It had lots of words like *accession number, case number, fetal tissue, enzyme, DNA, probe.*

"Using the DNA probe, genetic markers were found in the fetal tissue that were not present in the mother or alleged father," the letter said.

It boiled down to the following explosive conclusion: James Pierson was not the father of his daughter's baby.

"Talk about being fooled!" Detective Steven Cleary declared, referring to a case from about a year before: the murder of a forty-two-year-old Mastic, Long Island, man, a charter bus operator. His wife had discovered the body in the driveway of their suburban home. He had been shot eight times, five times in the head. He died on the way to the hospital.

Detective Steven Cleary had interviewed the woman. He had comforted her at the funeral. Frequently she called him at work to check on the investigation's progress. Cleary worked on that case around the clock for weeks and turned up nothing until one day, nine months later, he received an informant's tip: The murder was planned by the wife.

This deception had an important impact on Steven Cleary as well as other members of the homicide squad. It was an intangible thing, a sense of being had. A sense in particular of being had by a manipulative woman. It was only coincidence that this woman happened to be Beverly Wallace, whose case had inspired Cheryl Pierson. Detectives had had doubts about Cheryl's story right from the start, and the results of the pregnancy test only fanned them. The other laboratory tests performed on the sheets where Cheryl had said she and her father had had sex the night before came back with no evidence of sexual activity. Her nightgown similarly was tested with negative results.

"It's her word against a dead man," Jablonski declared, deciding to reevaluate the entire case against Cheryl Pierson. He was not alone in his skepticism.

Sue Lenz, a detective in the Suffolk County Sex Crimes unit, kept wondering whether the police—in their race "to get the shooter"—had not inadvertently given Cheryl and her boyfriend the perfect motive.

"The motive was comfortable," she would say. "Any half-smart juvenile would jump on it."

Even psychologists and social workers who would otherwise have been predisposed to someone like Cheryl found the case troubling.

Dr. Vincent J. Fontana, chairman of both the Suffolk County and New York City task forces on Child Abuse and Neglect, wanted to know why Cheryl did not simply take her younger sister and run away.

"You have to consider whether the father was acting out in a disciplinary way," Dr. Fontana said. "She was having sexual encounters. I feel in this situation the father is not around to defend himself. If she was going to the extreme of wanting to kill her father, she should not have hesitated to go to law enforcement. She can't say: I was afraid to. She did the worst thing. She was not living in a desert or on an island. She was surrounded by friends, neighbors. Someone would have believed her. Someone would have listened."

Meanwhile Marilyn Adams was on the telephone with Ed Jablonski every day. It was the vindication Pierson's sister had been waiting for:

"I told you he didn't sexually abuse his daughter," she told him. "She just wanted to run off with her boyfriend."

Only James McCready stuck fast to Cheryl's allegations.

"Ed, I talked to her," McCready would tell Jablonski. "Ed, I know what I'm talking about. This broad was not bullshitting me. I'm telling you she's not that good an actress. Everything she said flowed. Every way she said it. I'm telling you, this guy did everything to her. I don't care that she was also having sex with her boyfriend. I'm telling you. I believe her.''

Cheryl moved in with the Kossers, the neighbors next door on Magnolia Drive. It was no longer possible to remain with her aunt and grandmother. Even before the pregnancy results came in, Marilyn had begun to doubt Cheryl's word. At every turn there was a confrontation, an accusation, shouts of ''liar,'' ''murderer.'' It had been late one night in her cousin Kimmie's bedroom that Cheryl had first raised the possibility that the baby was not that of her father. It was actually the night Cheryl was released from jail, the first night she was spending alone with her cousin in her single bed with the Mickey Mouse—print sheets. Kimmie had already turned out the light.

''Kim,'' Cheryl said.

''Yeah, what?'' Kim said. She was almost asleep.

Cheryl did not say anything at first.

''What's the matter?'' Kim insisted.

''You know the baby?'' Cheryl said.

''Yeah.''

''It's not my daddy's,'' Cheryl said. ''But please don't tell anyone. Okay?''

''What are you telling me that for?'' Kimmie asked.

''I had to tell someone. Please don't tell.''

But Kimmie told.

''Who are you, God?'' Marilyn would shout at her niece.

There was nothing Cheryl could say.

''I'd look at them and they'd look at me and I knew I had to get out of there,'' Cheryl recalled.

Cheryl waited until after March 20, her sister's ninth birthday. It was after the miscarriage but before the results of the paternity test were in. One morning Cheryl packed her bags, picked up her little dog, Noel, kissed JoAnn goodbye, and was gone.

Now Cheryl shared a bed with Ann-Marie Kosser, Alberta's twenty-one-year-old daughter, and she shared a bathroom that looked out onto the driveway where her father had been shot.

It was a cramped place. Money for the Kossers was never as easy as it was for the Piersons. So there were many less dinners out, fancy Christmas presents, catered parties for their children. But there was always plenty of food on the table and good times. The kitchen was the center of family life for the Kossers. Long after the dinner dishes were washed, the family sat around the table nibbling on pretzels and sweet peanuts, shooting the breeze, catching up on gossip; just the way Alberta and Cheryl's mother had for so many years.

Alberta and Mike Kosser had suspected for years that Cheryl had an unnatural relationship with her father. But it was impossible for them to imagine that it involved intercourse, as Cheryl now claimed. The idea of a parent engaging in sex with his child was so unfathomable they preferred not to think about it. Still, something gnawed at them; and there had been indications over the years that something was "just not right."

Alberta remembered the day not long before Cathleen died when she complained to her about her husband's relationship with his daughter.

"I don't like the relationship Jimmy has with Cheryl," Cathy told her. "I don't want to think that's a father."

Alberta thought at the time that she might have observed some inappropriate behavior. But she also thought that if she had, it was up to Cathleen to do something about it. After all, she was Cheryl's mother. Alberta never asked. It would have been wrong, Alberta had reasoned, for her as a friend and neighbor to pry.

After Cathleen died, Cheryl and JoAnn came over for dinner regularly. It was an arrangement Alberta had worked out for a time with James Pierson. He would give her money, and the girls would eat their meals at her house. The girls would bring a portion back to him. It was during one of these dinners, Alberta recalled, that JoAnn blurted out that "Cheryl slept with Daddy last night." They were standing in the kitchen. Cheryl gave her sister a dirty look.

Mike Kosser recalled the time John Fleckenstein, Cheryl's maternal stepgrandfather, came over all upset and announced that "he hoped he didn't really see what he thought he just saw." Apparently, according to Kosser, Fleckenstein had walked into the bedroom and discovered Cheryl lying on top of her father in a sexual way. Kosser listened. In his mind it was for Fleckenstein to do something or say something. He was the grandfather. Often Mike Kosser thought "I was the one with the evil mind."

Now they both felt to blame. It troubled them profoundly that Cheryl had never come to them, had seen no other way out. They wished James Pierson was still alive. They believed that he was a "sick" man and could have been helped. But their hearts went out to Cheryl, and now, wracked by the guilt of their own inaction, they welcomed Cheryl into their home.

The Kossers had their work cut out for them. Cheryl was a teenager in love, and she wanted to be with Rob all the time. She didn't seem to care that she was under indictment for murder. She didn't seem to care that she could be going to jail for a very long time. In the very first week Cheryl stayed with them, the Kossers came home and walked in on Cheryl and Rob having sex in the basement.

> *Rob used to come over. But he had to go home at ten o'clock or whatever. My father didn't like it every night because I had too many things to do. I had to do my sister's homework. I had to do my homework if I had any and I got home late from practice. I had to make dinner, clean up the dishes, and finish the wash. When my friends were over, I would be*

*folding wash in front of them and stuff. He didn't like it all the time because I had a lot of things to do and I had seen my friends during the day and I didn't need to see them at night.*

*He used to ask me about a housekeeper. But I felt with what he was doing to me, that's how I was making it up to my mother. She always liked a clean house and everything and I felt that if I got a housekeeper I would be just giving up and I wouldn't . . . because she used to be proud of me doing all that stuff and I figured after she died that I would just be giving up and letting someone else take over. Meanwhile that was her house and I wanted to do what she would do. So I figured that she would be proud of me.*

Ellen Somar, Pierson's banker, kept thinking back to Thanksgiving and the time she, her husband, and son had spent with the Piersons. Pierson and his daughters had just returned from a long weekend in Florida, all aglow with stories about Busch Gardens and Epcot Center. They were all in the kitchen at Marilyn Adams's house. The television in the kitchen was tuned to the football game. Ellen Somar and her family dug into plates of pumpkin pie.

"It was such a loving time," Ellen Somar would recall. "It was natural. It was normal. There was absolutely no indication that there was anything wrong."

Now, looking back on it, the idea that Cheryl had already hired someone to kill her father was totally inconceivable. Ellen Somar knew what a stressful time it was for the Piersons. James Pierson had repeatedly told her how hard it was being on his own. He had said things that surprised her, like how angry he was at his wife for having left him with the children; that a family had been her idea and now she was gone, how it had become too much. They had talked about hiring a housekeeper. But Cheryl, he said, did not want a "stranger" in her mother's house.

"You can't let a sixteen-year-old dictate to you," Ellen Somar had told him. But if what Cheryl said was true, then why wouldn't she have wanted someone there? She kept thinking back to Pierson sitting at the table in Marilyn's kitchen with JoAnn on his lap and how Cheryl massaged her father's neck. There was nothing secretive, strange, or self-conscious about the gesture. It was just an affectionate scene between a father and a daughter.

Robert and Tina Cuccio kept thinking back to Christmas Eve. It was the first and only time they had spent with James Pierson.

Their house was filled with flowers. The plastic-covered gold lamé couches in the living room sparkled in the candlelight. Tina Cuccio cooked up a storm the way she always did on Christmas Eve. No luxury spared. Little JoAnn was all dressed up in a black velvet dress and black patent leather shoes, her blond hair pulled back with ribbons. Right from the start, Pierson seemed at home.

"We hit it off," Robert Cuccio Sr. would recall of that meeting.

"My mother was so impressed with Cheryl," Tina Cuccio recalled. "She was so mature. She had her head screwed on. She was not like so many other girls her age."

They would remember it as a lovely evening.

Kim Adams, Marilyn Adams's twenty-year-old daughter, kept thinking back to the day she, JoAnn, Rob, and Cheryl had spent looking at the Christmas decorations in the city. The tree at Rockefeller Center and the shop windows on Fifth Avenue. They had had lunch in Chinatown and walked around the Lower East Side.

"She was talking about what she planned to get my Uncle Jimmy for his birthday," Kim recalled.

James Pierson's forty-second birthday was just one week later. Cheryl baked her father a cake. Pillsbury vanilla with Betty Crocker milk chocolate frosting. His favorite. She woke up early that morning and dialed WBLI, her father's favorite radio station, to ask that they broadcast her birthday message: "Happy Birthday, Jim Pierson, Love Cheryl." She was the "lucky caller," and her father won two free dinners to El Torrito's. That night her grandmother came over with a cake of her own. She and Pierson's two daughters sang "Happy Birthday." Cheryl gave her father a neatly wrapped package of razor blades and a bottle of cologne. Prince Matchabelli.

Gruff and restrained to the point where he often spoke to them in monosyllables, young Robert Cuccio was not happy to be talking to the police. But he had no choice.

His curly dark hair neatly combed to the side, Rob sat glumly in Ed Jablonski's office. His hands were in his lap, and were it not for his mustache, he would have looked more like a schoolboy about to be admonished by the principal than someone who had been arrested for conspiracy to commit murder. In fact, he had just come from court, where he pleaded guilty to criminal solicitation, a lesser charge, and the promise of no jail in exchange for his cooperation.

"When did you and Cheryl meet?" Ed Jablonski began as Rob's attorney sat beside him and listened.

Cuccio then told Jablonski how they had met in gym class at a square dance and how Cheryl had invited him to her Sweet Sixteen. Rob said he had wanted to go out with Cheryl but her father would not allow it and that he spent week after week at the Pierson home watching television with the entire family. Eventually, he said, he grew suspicious.

"Just the way he was with her," Cuccio said. "The way he touched her. The way he hit her. The way he'd get so upset whenever she'd pay any attention to me.

It wasn't the way a father should be with his daughter. It's not the way my father was with my sister.''

It was around Christmas, Rob Cuccio said, that he decided to confront Cheryl about her relationship with her father. He and Cheryl had become more intimate by then. During lunch he would take her back to his parents' house when no one was home.

''She'd just lie there,'' Cuccio recalled. ''Like she was dead. I'd ask her 'what's a matter. What's a matter?'' It was just weird. So I asked her. It was around Christmas. I told her I needed to talk to her. And her father drove her over, and I asked her straight out if there was something going on with her father, and at first she said no. But I just kept insisting and finally she told me. She said it started when her mother got sick when she was around twelve and went into full swing when she was about fifteen.''

''So when did you first learn about Sean?'' Jablonski asked.

''November,'' Cuccio replied.

''What happened?''

''I drove Sean to the house with Cheryl.''

''Was that the first time you met him?''

''Yes.''

''Had Cheryl said she wanted her father dead at this point?''

''Yes. The first time she told me she wanted her father dead was around the time of her Sweet Sixteen.''

''In May.''

''Right.''

''So you met Sean and knew about the plot even before Cheryl told you about her relationship with her father.''

''Yes, I did.''

Jablonski nodded. His doubts about Cheryl's story expanded.

''What happened when you got to the house?'' he

asked, thinking about the three youngsters inside the Pierson home.

"Well, it was during lunchtime at school. Sean wanted to use the Uzi, but I said no because it would get traced back to Cheryl. So he was going to strangle him or something."

"And then what happened?" Jablonski asked. He was taking notes on a yellow pad, notes he knew that he could refer to later at a trial.

"He made a first attempt. He was going to throw a brick. There was a house across the street that Cheryl's father owned, and he was going to throw a brick through the window, and when Cheryl's father came to see what was wrong, he was going to stab him. But he didn't throw the rock in far enough."

"When was this?"

"About two weeks after we went to the house."

"Now getting back to the actual murder, did he tell you when it was going to happen?"

"Yes."

"How was that?"

"He told Cheryl. She was at a game. He told her he was going to do it. She told me, and I told her not to worry about it. He's said it before."

"When did you pay him?"

"The next day."

"Where?"

"School. Me and Cheryl went to school."

"Where did you get the money?"

"From the safe." Cuccio was referring to the special combination safe built into James Pierson's living room closet.

"When was that?"

"The day it happened."

"What time?" Jablonski wanted to know. It was the first time he was hearing details about when Cheryl actually went to her father's safe to get money to pay her father's killer.

"Around three o'clock or so."

"How did that come about?"

"The lawyers were there, and Cheryl and I went to the safe while they were in another room." He explained that Cheryl stood on a chair and removed the combination from a light fixture in the ceiling while he stood guard at the door. Earlier Cheryl had told a reporter she had gone to the safe the morning after her father died, because until that time she had no idea Sean was involved. Her description had been elaborate, including details of how she had to tiptoe past her grandmother, who was still sleeping on the couch. Clearly, Cheryl's account to the reporter was a lie, because when the lawyers opened Pierson's safe the same afternoon of his murder, it was already devoid of all cash.

Cuccio's information confirmed Jablonski's impressions. Cheryl was trying to present herself as an innocent victim. But so far as he was concerned, she was a coldblooded killer. Confronted with her father's body, she was cogent enough to think about getting money out of his safe before his lawyers.

"So when exactly did Cheryl tell you she was having sex with her father?" Jablonski asked, still skeptical of the girl's story.

"Just before Christmas."

"So when Cheryl and her father came to your home Christmas Eve for dinner, you must have been pretty upset sitting there."

"Yes I was," Cuccio replied, demonstrating no emotion. Rob's attorney changed his position in his seat.

It had already been determined through a DNA test of his blood that Robert Cuccio Jr. was the father of Cheryl's baby.

---

*Rob used to say he could always tell if someone was a virgin. I told him I had never been with anyone else. The first time Rob and I were together I didn't know how to act. He would get mad if I just lay back. It was on the couch in his parents' basement. I was nervous. I wasn't with Rob for the first time until after my father died.*

Cheryl took a shower. It was 8 A.M., and she had taken the day off from a job she had cutting hair at a beauty salon called Great Expectations. It was a warm Saturday morning in September, about seven months after the murder, and Alberta waited in the kitchen for Cheryl to get dressed. An undertaker and his wife had put a deposit down on the Pierson house next door, and Cheryl had to sell all the furnishings from her family's home. The plan was to hold a yard sale at Alberta's place and divide up the profits three ways. Cheryl's brother, Jimmy, was supposed to help. But as usual he had been up all night the night before and was still fast asleep. Cheryl knocked on the door.

"Go on, Cheryl. It's okay," Alberta said, reassuring the girl as she turned the handle.

Young Pierson had invited a few friends over to spend the night, and they were sprawled on the living room floor. The place had taken on the air of a college fraternity house after a week-long party. Dirty clothing was scattered everywhere. Lightbulbs were out in the hall. The carpet was caked with matchbook covers and half-smoked cigarettes. A half-eaten pizza lay on the kitchen counter. The wall phone from the kitchen had been ripped from its stand and was now lying with the cord all tangled on the floor. The air was stagnant. All the windows were closed.

Cheryl turned on the kitchen light. She had a roll of masking tape in her left hand, a black felt-tipped pen in her right. Then methodically, efficiently, as if she had done this her entire life, Cheryl began reaching for appliances and attaching to each one a price. Toaster, $4. Kitchen clock, $6.50. Ceramic cannisters in the shape of mushrooms, $10 for the set of four.

By the morning's end, Alberta's backyard was crowded with appliances and paintings, stuffed animals and clothing, office furniture and power tools. Cheryl had taped a sign, YARD SALE, to a stop sign near the firehouse down the street. Strangers stopped their cars. With no apparent emotion, Cheryl took their money.

"You can't sell that, Cheryl," Alberta would repeatedly say, reaching for a ceramic dish, an old music box, a cameo brooch. "It meant so much to your mother. Keep it for when you're married."

"I don't want it," Cheryl would reply. "I don't want anything from that house. I don't want any of those memories."

By afternoon's end, she had collected $57.

---

*What am I going to do? Tell someone? Like you know sometimes Alberta asks me: Why didn't you come to me? Why didn't you tell me? Because if I would have come to her and told her I knew she would have believed me. It wasn't to the point where she wouldn't have believed me. But what's she going to do? She's going to confront my father or try to get help and he's going to find out and then we're both in trouble. Then he's going to try to take it out on me or on her and her family. I didn't want that. I didn't want anybody else to be hurt.*

---

The summer was over. A crisp fall breeze made its way across the potato fields. Soon winter sweaters would be coming out of closets, cotton T-shirts would be folded and packed for another year. Tryouts would be held for this year's cheerleaders. The class of 1987 would at last be seniors. Newfield High School was already in session, and the hallways were abuzz with tales of summer vacations and new romances and the upcoming plans for the senior prom. It was the year for which Cheryl Pierson and Sean Pica had so eagerly waited. But on that bleak September morning, neither one was anyplace near Newfield High School. They were sitting in a chilly second-story courtroom of State Supreme Court, the courtroom of Harvey W. Sherman, a white-haired, grandfatherly-looking man with a pleasant smile and an official but gentle manner. It was only a pretrial hearing, but the courtroom's three rows of wooden seats were completely filled.

In the second row Sean sat with his mother on one side, his father on the other. His mother's second husband, Jim DelVecchio, sat directly behind Sean. Larry, JoAnn DelVecchio's current boyfriend, was there as well. Cheryl, in the grey wool suit her father bought her the previous Christmas and the one she wore to his funeral, sat between Alberta and Mike Kosser. Cheryl's brother, uncle John Adams, and a cousin who will be called Susan sat close by. In the first row sat Virginia Pierson, Marilyn Adams, and Cathy Zimlinghaus. The battlelines were already drawn.

On this particular day the issue before Judge Sherman was the confessions and whether they should be entered into evidence. But what was said in that courtroom that day paled beside all the many things that were not.

During those first days of pretrial hearings, Cheryl's twenty-five-year-old cousin Susan, who had traveled to Riverhead from Vermont, accompanied Cheryl to court. She had not seen Cheryl in a long time, and Susan wanted Cheryl to know that she had her support. Well dressed, with long, curly blond hair and a delicate model's stature, she was a striking addition to the courtroom.

Susan and Cheryl were never particularly close growing up. It was more like extended family than anything else. They occasionally got together for Christmas and Easter and several weekends during the year. Susan was eight years older than Cheryl, and

Cheryl looked up to Susan as being more sophisticated. Susan's mother always had a special affection for Cheryl's father.

Susan had heard over the years that Cheryl's grandmother had been abused as a child. She knew that after Virginia Pierson's parents died, she had been sent to live with strangers who mistreated her. There were stories about being fed only cornmeal for months at a time. Being locked in the basement. It was a sad coincidence but Susan's father was also orphaned as a child and similarly mistreated. But with Cheryl's arrest, Susan discovered something else that she and Cheryl had in common; something she had only started to even remember herself, something that was beginning to come to the surface during therapy following her divorce, something that she also had told no one.

Susan had been sexually abused by her father also.

Court adjourned at around 4 P.M. The lawyers each said their piece to the news reporters and were already framing their opening remarks for trial.

"Whether she was abused or wasn't abused is not the point," Ed Jablonski, the prosecutor, said. "She should have gone to the police. That's what they're there for."

"She was a prisoner in her father's home," Paul Gianelli, Cheryl's lawyer, said. "She could see no other way out. I'm hoping that if a jury hears what Cheryl's life was like, they will understand her silence."

But the real drama in the courtroom was a silent one, played out in the looks and glances and all those things unsaid that criss-crossed all the various family members. Cheryl had not seen her grandmother and aunt in months. Not since they had been living in the same home. Now Virginia Pierson glared at her granddaughter with apparent hatred. The atmosphere had changed for Cheryl. Skepticism was in the air among the reporters. Gianelli was now being asked questions he had not been asked before, questions about corroboration, questions about proof. Questions time and again about the pregnancy.

At one point Cheryl had wanted to use the ladies' room during a courtroom break. She was feeling faint and needed some water. But when she opened the door, Cathy Zimlinghaus, her father's longtime friend, was standing there.

"I'm not going in there while she's there," Cheryl screamed.

The lines were drawn.

Kenny Zimlinghaus left the courthouse with his arm around Virginia Pierson. He vowed then he would come every day until the case was over. Jim Pierson was his closest friend. Cheryl was lying. He was willing, he said, to stake his life on it. Susan had not seen her Aunt Virginia in a long time, but now the old woman would not even look her way. Alberta Kosser and her husband Mike avoided the glances of Pierson's mother and sister as well. John Adams ignored the glares of his ex-wife. It was clear from where he sat in that courtroom whom he believed. Cheryl.

But the truth was, as John Adams left the courthouse that day prepared to testify on Cheryl's behalf, the more he thought about it, the more doubts he had as well. He would have never admitted this in open court. In fact, he said he would have lied to save his niece from going to jail. But so far as he was concerned, the pieces of the crime just did not fit. He believed Cheryl and her brother had other reasons to murder their father and that chief among them was money. With Pierson's various properties, life insurance policies, and bank accounts, his estate would eventually be valued at close to one million dollars. He felt his nephew was behind the murder and that Cheryl became involved only after she became pregnant with her boyfriend's child.

Susan left the courthouse that day with Cheryl. They went back to the Kossers' place, changed into dunga-

rees, and telephoned the local pizza place for a pie.
They drove over to pick it up. It was the same pizza
place where Cheryl had driven to talk to Sean Pica
after her father's funeral to discuss when he would receive his additional money.

"I just want you to know I'm here for you," Susan
told her cousin on the back trunk of the Monte Carlo
Cheryl's father had given her for her sixteenth birthday.

Susan invited Cheryl to come visit her in Vermont.
She asked about Rob and her plans for marriage. She
told her a bit about her own life and how difficult it
had been since the divorce.

But what she did not tell Cheryl was that when she
was thirteen her father began to make sexual advances
at her. The only daughter of six children, she was in
the shower when her father, who at the time was a
prison guard, would walk in.

"He would come and ask if I wanted him to soap
my back . . . wash my back, kind of," she would later
say. "In my own way he got the point . . . I would
become silent like . . . I couldn't tell him to get out?"

She said it was not a matter of her father just being
affectionate.

"It wasn't, and I knew it wasn't. My father thought
he had the right to see his daughter growing up physically. He believed his rights were different from other
fathers."

His advances were not limited to the shower.

"I came home from the beach really sunburned
once," Susan continued. "I was fried on my back and
legs. He came in: 'Oh, I'll put cream on your back
and your legs.' And he like did my legs . . . like between my thighs and that's when I like . . . froze. He
tried . . . I said, 'Dad, get out.' And he said, 'There
is nothing wrong with a father touching his daughter.'
I said, 'Dad. It's wrong.' He said, 'There's nothing
wrong. I'm not doing anything to you.' I said, 'It's my
privacy. Get out.' "

Susan would later say that what she wanted more than anything now was to be able to confront her father and tell him what she thought of his behavior. She never wanted to kill him. But she needed to talk to him. She even thought about what she would say and how:

"I could start off with Cheryl," she would say. "My story would be: How can you not believe her? How can you not believe Cheryl. When you . . . When your own beliefs . . . Of course you can only believe that what Jimmy did was right? Or you're saying that it never happened. Dad. Dad, it happened with me and you!"

But now seated with Cheryl on the back of the Monte Carlo, waiting for the pizza, Susan kept those thoughts to herself and listened. What Cheryl most wanted to talk about was Rob. How much she loved him. How they were getting married. How they would have a large wedding. Lots of children. A big white stretch limousine that would carry them off to their honeymoon.

"Do you have any regrets?" Susan asked her cousin that day in the sunshine.

"Only that I didn't do it myself," Cheryl replied.

# 8

Virginia Pierson—James Pierson's mother, Cheryl's grandmother—only barely knew her parents. About the only thing she would remember was that her father worked in a lumberyard; her mother made coats. They lived on Manhattan's Lower East Side, and by the time she was thirteen she was an orphan and sent to live in a foster home.

"Ah. What do you want to know about that for?" she would say as an adult, refusing to elaborate. "What's past is past."

It was as a teenager that Virginia saw a boy one day on a street corner and decided then and there she would marry him. He was a tall, rugged youth with dark, wavy hair and a mustache who exuded a sense of strength and self-confidence. James Monroe Pierson, "Monroe" as everyone called him, did not like to speak about his childhood either. After they were married, Monroe and Virginia settled in Brooklyn, where she got a job on the assembly line at the Good Humor Ice Cream plant and he drove a truck for a hospital supply company. They had two children, James, Cheryl's father, and three years later, Marilyn.

Monroe Pierson had strict ideas about children. He taught them to remain silent at the dinner table, to leave nothing uneaten at the end of the meal, and not to drink so much as a sip of water until their dinner plates were scraped clean. He regulated the manner in which they consumed their meals and would chastise them if they ate more of the meat at any one time on their plates than the vegetables. When adults visited the Pierson home, the children stayed in another room. Monroe Pierson was always to be addressed by his children as "sir."

"We learned parents were parents, and you respected them no matter what," Marilyn Adams would recall of her childhood.

*Gestapo* was the word James Pierson often used to describe his upbringing. Monroe Pierson would have been the first to admit that of his two children he was far more demanding of his son.

James as a child was an altar boy, a short, skinny youth with fire-engine red hair and a cherubic face sprayed with freckles. Shy and introspective, he was known around the neighborhood as a "sissy" because he excelled in school and was not ashamed to sing in the choir. Once when he came rushing home in tears because a boy had called him a name, Monroe ridiculed him and forced him to go outside to take on the other youth. He perpetually criticized James, calling him "a good for nothing."

"What do you want from him?" Virginia Pierson would complain when young James Pierson brought home perfect marks from school and instead of a compliment his father issued a warning: "You better get an A next time too."

"He's got to grow up, get married, and support a family someday," Monroe would reply. He said it often. What he wanted, he said, was for his son to be "a man."

Marilyn was a sickly child. When she was seven years old, she was hospitalized for two years with a rheumatic heart and not expected to survive. Her family only was allowed to visit once a month. It was a stressful period on everyone. Indeed an incident took place during this time that many years later friends would point to as an explanation for certain aspects of James Pierson's personality as an adult: why, for example, when he married he trailed his wife wherever she went, why he always needed to know what his wife was saying on the telephone and with whom, why he was so demanding about how she dressed, how she spoke, how others looked at her; why in the Pierson home no one except for Pierson himself was allowed down in the basement; why night and day the bedroom doors were always left open.

It was one event, the kind of childhood trauma one revisits as an adult not unlike the seconds preceding a serious car accident, an incident that once it had taken place would never be mentioned again except many years later by Pierson himself, who reportedly told his wife, who in turn told two of her closest friends, an incident Pierson's mother would vigorously deny.

It was that Virginia Pierson had begun to see another man, Cathleen Pierson had told her friends. Monroe found out about it and was so distraught that he grabbed his nine-year-old son, Jimmy, and went to confront his wife at the home of her lover. Little Jimmy was made to climb the stairs, walk up to the door of the strange apartment, and knock. When a man answered, he was to ask to see his mother.

He did.

At age nine, little Marilyn was finally released from the hospital on the condition that the family move to a place where she would not have to climb stairs. For six months Monroe Pierson carried his daughter up and down the three flights of their Brooklyn walkup. Then one day, acting on a tip from friends, the family drove out to what was then a dot on the map with a serene-sounding name that could have been a new brand of sleeping pill. It was a place called Selden. The Piersons paid $9,000 for their three-bedroom house. The year was 1958. James Pierson, Cheryl's father, was thirteen. His sister was ten. Selden was still a wide expanse of pastures and farmland. Cows grazed in the afternoon sun. The family planted a cherry tree in the backyard. It was a new beginning.

But the commute to Brooklyn proved to be too much for Virginia, who was making good money at Good Humor, so she decided to stay in the city during the week. Monroe initially got a job driving a truck out on Long Island but soon after was laid off and had trouble finding a job. Eventually he secured menial work at a local hospital but was plagued as a young man by ulcers, high blood pressure, and other illnesses. While Virginia emerged as the principal breadwinner, Monroe remained at home and looked after the children. Marilyn was recruited to cook the family's meals and clean. It was an unusual arrangement, which as they were growing up the children resented. The only time the entire family was together was on weekends.

As friends of James Pierson looked back on it, contradictory images of the family would emerge.

James Germana, one of James Pierson's oldest friends, would remember Pierson and his family as a boisterous, "happy" group always ready to crack open a beer, turn up the stereo, and invite friends over for a party. Pierson's parents were strict, Germana would recall, but they also knew how to have a good time. Virginia Pierson was in love with Elvis Presley. There was not a record of his she did not own; not a detail of his personal life she did not covet. Her son, James, was crazy about Chubby Checker and the Twist. The colonial-style house in which they lived was filled with music, people, laughter.

But Paul Vohlbehr, another of James Pierson's boyhood friends, had a somewhat different recollection.

"Something never seemed right there," Vohlbehr would recall. "They always drank, and there were times when they got tough with us. They were always loaded. They didn't get violent. But I remember his dad taking smacks at us: 'Don't get in trouble.' They would give us funny little hits. I always felt 'oh they're drunk.' They drank all the time. Mostly beer. They'd smack him across the face. I remember him getting it from both of them. It didn't seem like a normal family. We would always make an attempt to get him out of the house as soon as we could. I felt uncomfortable there.''

Marilyn Adams would recall that of her parents it was her mother who struck the children. Her father, she said, would verbally chastise his children when they did something wrong. He had a big booming voice and that was punishment enough. But it was her mother who sometimes lost control. There was once, she recalled, when her brother was impolite at the dinner table, and his mother hit him so hard she dislocated the boy's jaw. There was another time, when Marilyn was a teenager, that her mother became so infuriated with her that she shoved Marilyn's head in the toilet and kept her underwater until she almost drowned.

Shortly after he arrived in Selden, James Pierson met a group of boys who would remain his friends for life. They all attended Newfield High School and played baseball together. They whiled away the summers cruising around the local towns, stopping at nearby farms to fling vegetables at each other, taking long drives to upstate New York and camping out in the woods. It was the era of T-shirt sleeves rolled tight around packs of Lucky Strike, flashy large convertibles, and slicked-back hair. Pierson and his buddies wore tight black trousers with heavy belt buckles worn to the side, cigarettes behind their ears, white socks, black shoes, sunglasses. They all seemed to be competing with one another to look the most like James Dean.

As an adolescent, James Pierson walked around as if he wore a giant BEWARE sign across his forehead. No longer the shy, retiring choir boy, he was always trying to show how tough he could be. ''What's a matter, you can't take it?'' he would say, on a perpetual hunt for confrontation. He would slap friends too hard on the back. He would trap them in arm holds. Intimidation became his signature. So did driving fast; so fast that when he turned corners, the hubcaps popped off in different directions. Asked to slow down, he would just let out a laugh and drive faster.

"When you were in a car with him you were at his mercy," Paul Vohlbehr would recall.

James Pierson as a youth needed to be in control, and it was a trait he would keep. It was the flip side of his generosity, of his being the constant caretaker, of his always being ready to help a friend in need. What he demanded in return was deference, respect, attention, submission.

At seventeen James Pierson was in a serious automobile accident. A friend was driving, and Pierson was in the passenger seat with his right arm out the window. Another car jumped a stop sign and hit the car in which Pierson was riding. Seeing the accident in advance, he grabbed the head of the young man seated to his left, buried it in his lap, and saved the young man's life. But the car rolled over onto Pierson's arm, and it was not clear at the start whether the arm could be salvaged. It dashed all hopes of Pierson pursuing his beloved baseball.

"I think that's when he developed his temper," Marilyn Adams recalled. He became so frustrated at dinner one night after the accident by his inability to hold a fork that he threw his plate against the wall. A volatile temper would remain an important component of James Pierson's character. So would his rage at physical infirmity.

One of the worst times he lost his temper, Marilyn Adams would recall, was when their father discovered that Virginia Pierson was having an affair in the city. She and her brother were now teenagers. Monroe Pierson, who had been in poor health, confronted his wife, drove her back to Selden, and forced her to tell the children she was "in love with another man."

"You're my mother!" James Pierson shouted, turning over the table. "You're not supposed to do things like that."

Not long after that Monroe, at the age of forty-five, suffered a massive stroke. Confined to a wheelchair, he would never walk again. More and more James Pierson had to assume the role of man of the house. He as much as anyone was devastated to see his strong powerful father made powerless in this way. His greatest fear, friends would later say, was that some day the same thing would happen to him.

When James Pierson was twenty years old, Virginia Pierson introduced her son to a shy brunette named Cathleen Adams. She was the daughter of friends she knew from a local tavern.

"It was love from the start," John Adams, Cathleen's brother, would recall many years later. "I would say probably instant on both parts. I remember the first date. Because I made fun. He pulled up in a yellow convertible with dice. Two dates, and they were always together."

Cathleen Adams was the daughter of the former Helen Schweder and a man whose identity she would never learn. There were always stories, rumors, hushed whispers about who the man really was. But Cathleen Pierson would go to the grave without ever finding out.

There would be many things about her past Cathleen Adams would never learn. She would never know for example that her mother's father, John Schweder, was an alcoholic who stole his daughters' lunch money at knife point, sold the family's furniture for drink, and was ultimately committed to a psychiatric hospital, where he died. Helen Schweder was twenty-one years old when her first child, John, was born. She was twenty-two when she had Cathleen. But although they were told one thing or another over the years, Cathleen and her brother would never know for certain whether they were born out of wedlock or were even from the same father. Indeed it was not until they were adults and John was tested as a potential donor for Cathleen's kidney that the two concluded their genes were too close a match not to be from the same set of parents. Still, they would never know the identity of their father.

"You didn't ask too many questions in that household," recalled a friend from Cathleen's childhood and a bridesmaid at her wedding. Helen's early life in many ways would remain a mystery to her children. She could be violent and unstable, and they were sent to live in a foster home and from time to time with Helen's older sister, Anna. Helen married for what she said was the second time when her children were ten and eleven. They were adopted by her new husband and took his name, Adams.

Helen's brief marriage to Charles Adams was stormy.

"They were constantly fighting," John Adams would recall. "Once it was a ridiculous fight. I was eleven or twelve. We were just sitting there. We were going to go fishing for the weekend. And she told him, 'Well, you're not going.' And he says, 'Well, I am going.' She picked up the steak knife and threw it at him. It just missed him. He was gone about two or three days. But he came back Saturday and said, 'Wanna go fishing?' "

Two years later Charles Adams died following an automobile accident. Things at home got worse.

"I was always treated like a dirtbag," John Adams would recall of his childhood. "My mother was always telling me I was a real moron. I was a no good. Even in school. I went to therapists and psychiatrists. But I could never get to first base. I was always hiding. I was the kind of child who always had to prove myself. No matter what I did for my mother, I was never good enough. My mother hit me with pots. Big pots because I didn't cry. Sticks. Two by fours. I'd sit there and take it and smile. She broke my wrist. She dislocated my shoulder. I wouldn't tell anyone. I said

I fell or something. She was breaking my airplanes. My ceiling was full of model airplanes and cars and stuff and she would say 'get out' and she'd come into my room and destroy them and everything. Then she'd grab me and throw me down the stairs.''

John Adams frequently ran away from home but because he was ashamed never told anyone the reason. He was always hoping things would get better, that his family would be like other families. ''I was always waiting for the rainbow,'' he would say. But it never came. Not even after Helen married again—this time to John Fleckenstein. Friends would recall how little Cathleen, always eager for her mother's attention, resented the appearance of this new man. She was accustomed to sleeping in her mother's bed, now she had to sleep in her own room. But married or not, Helen's behavior remained unchanged and her wrath continued.

''She just sat and watched,'' John Adams would recall of how his sister, Cathleen, Cheryl's mother, responded to the beatings. ''What could she do? She was a little girl. All the neighbors knew. They never did anything.''

On June 26, 1965, James Pierson married Cathleen Adams. He was twenty-one years old and she was eighteen and out of the house at last. The ceremony was held at a white clapboard church in the small harborside town of Northport where Cathleen was raised. She wore a white floor-length gown that accentuated her tiny waist and a veil that cascaded onto the floor. She was a petite woman, only five feet two, and her groom towered over her at six feet, a skinny young man in a yellow jacket and blue bowtie, who looked far too young to be getting married. As they stood there on the church steps, posing for the photographers, there was an awkward innocence about the two of them—this eager young man and his small-town majorette who twirled batons better than anyone at

Northport High. The couple drove off in a blizzard of rice to a honeymoon in the Poconos, where by all calculations Cathy got pregnant with "little Jimmy" on their wedding night.

Even then James Pierson was a man with direction; a man with a vision of how things would be for himself, for his family.

"My wife will never work," he would announce, lifting his bride in his arms. He so liked holding her up like that, the woman he would spoil, protect, take care of, the way he always wished his father could have done for his mother. Even then James Pierson had a strong sense of obligation, of responsibility, of what it meant to be a husband. If he had to summarize his principal obligation in one word, it might well have been *provider,* a role at which in many ways he would excel. The Piersons bought a small house. Cathleen quit her job. They prepared for the birth of their son. Yet right from the start, there were those who were uncomfortable with the way James Pierson behaved at home.

"He had a strange way of showing his love," recalled James Germana, the best man at Pierson's wedding, of James's behavior toward Cathleen. "They would always be wrestling and screaming at each other."

"If he wanted to show her affection, he'd punch her in the arm," said Barbara Pallas, who knew Cathleen as a teenager.

"We stopped seeing them," recalled Frank O'Brien, one of Pierson's closest high school friends and an usher at his wedding. "When he first married her, he would drag her across the living room by her hair. He had to show his strength all the time. He always had to show his forcefulness. When he had kids, he saw society changing."

"Damn it," James Pierson would say. "They will do exactly as I say."

Contradictory images of James Pierson would

emerge for good reason. He was a man of extremes—
a man who punctuated his speech with four-letter
words but was on a perpetual quest for "class," a man
who often bullied his friends but then was the first to
bail them out of trouble, a man who worked sixteen-
hour days to provide for his family but then would
often intimidate and ridicule them into submission.

"Back then Jim was a younger version of himself,"
recalled Stu Helmig, Pierson's boss from 1968 to 1974.
"Gruff and tough. But with a gentle heart. Cathy was
a sweetheart. He was an extremely strict father. Too
much right from the beginning. I can remember when
his son Jimmy was a real young boy. Three years old.
They would come over to my house and visit. We
didn't have children at the time. All the boy had to do
was breathe the wrong way, and his dad made him sit
in a chair in the room for an hour. He didn't think
anything wrong to smack him. Jim was a very physical
guy. Jim was the type of guy who was constantly proving his manhood. He was always trying to be Mr.
Tough Guy. Grab you by the arm and twist it behind
your back. I wasn't thrilled with it. I never analyzed
it. Underneath all that was marshmallow. He didn't let
you see it. But it was there."

Jim Pierson, who at the age of twenty-five became
the father of a second child, Cheryl, began as an installer for a company called Broadway Maintenance,
which was under contract to install cable television in
people's homes throughout Long Island. Efficient, intelligent, and liked by the other employees, Pierson
did well and was eventually named foreman. He was
in charge of about two hundred men.

In 1974, however, when he was thirty, he was dismissed from the position when he lost his temper on
the job and began yelling obscenities at a superior. It
was just around this time that Pierson had a fling.
"Nothing serious," James Germana would recall. "He
was just trying to prove that he was still young." It
was also just around this time that Pierson acquired an

interest in guns. He got a license to carry a .357 Magnum revolver. He wore it in an ankle holster wherever he went. He would shoot squirrels out the kitchen window. When he got bored, he shot sparrows.

Pierson and his wife argued frequently during this period. Occasionally when Cathleen would spend an evening out alone "with the girls," Pierson would follow her there. He listened in to her telephone conversations. Cathleen rebelled and complained to friends he gave her "no space to breathe."

On one occasion Cathleen left her husband. It was only for a week. She ran to her mother, who had recently moved to a house across the street on Magnolia Drive. Ironically, Helen had moved to Selden because she, too, was having problems in her marriage. She and John Fleckenstein had decided to divorce and sold their house in Northport. When they reconciled, it was too late to stop the sale and they needed to find another place to live. When Cathleen told them about a vacant house across the street at 293 Magnolia Drive, they grabbed it. Now neighbors, Cathleen and her mother saw each other frequently. Helen encouraged her daughter to return to her family.

Thanks to Stu Helmig, James Pierson was eventually transferred to another division of Broadway Maintenance, a division that was under contract to fix traffic lights throughout eastern Long Island. It bothered Pierson that now he could no longer wear a coat and tie to work. But the job grew on him. He became active in the union. He earned about $30,000 a year and found he had extra time to do jobs on the side and off the books. He also supplemented his income by buying and selling used cars, eventually progressing to fancy sports cars and antique automobiles. He soon was earning more money after hours than he was from his daily job, which he invested in real estate and other ventures. His daughter JoAnn was born in 1977. He became involved with Cathleen's illness in 1979 but in 1982, when Cathleen seemed to be doing better, Pierson started a side business with Kenny Zimlinghaus that repaired broken cable television boxes. They called it Superior Cable and, for a time, did well. Whatever profits he made he always kept in cash, which he lent out to "friends." The loan operation, which was naturally done off the books, became another lucrative venture. It was one of the reasons Pierson always kept large quantities of cash on hand in his safe and meticulous records. The word *loanshark* made Pierson laugh.

"It's my money," he would say, always a man who lived by his own rules. "I can do with it what I please."

Pierson had always been accident prone. Once he fell into a manhole and broke his leg. Another time an airplane door came crashing down on his head, and he was out of work for six months. Still another time he got his hand caught in a machine and almost lost his thumb. He had surgery done on his knees because of his many spills on the job.

But the accident that seemed to disturb Pierson most, perhaps because by then he had already been through so much, took place just before his fortieth birthday. It was in September of 1983. Pierson and his family had just moved into the house at 293 Magnolia Drive. Both his in-laws were dead. He was in the process of building an extension. He was on the roof at the time, when he miscalculated a step and came crashing to the ground. All the bones in his feet were crushed. It was not clear whether Pierson would ever be able to walk again. His response was as frustrated and furious as when he was a teenager and lost control of his arm.

The fear, he said it himself, was that he would be like his father: confined to a wheelchair at the age of forty-five and without control.

# 9

Plea negotiations are probably the least understood but most important part of any criminal case; an intricate behind-the-scenes dance with maneuvers that are hard to put into words. Not unlike master card sharks in a high-stakes game of poker, the lawyers rely on their instincts, bravado, and ultimately the strength of their hand. It is often a game of bluff. The ante is time: how much time in jail a criminal deserves given the circumstances of a specific crime. And the stakes are never higher than with murder.

When Judge Harvey Sherman refused Paul Gianelli's defense motion to separate Cheryl's case from that of Sean, Ed Jablonski, the prosecutor, had won a major victory, and he knew it. It meant that he was now in a position to play Gianelli and Martin Efman, Sean Pica's lawyer, off against each other. Gianelli would have liked Cheryl to have been tried alone for the murder of her father. Cheryl would have been a far more sympathetic defendant seated in that courtroom alone rather than alongside the killer that she personally hired and paid. Now tried together, each would blame the other for what took place. The issue of sexual abuse would get lost. Ed Jablonski would shrug his shoulders and ask the jury to convict them both.

"I'm worried about the message, judge," Jablonski said, asserting that he believed Cheryl should be sent to a state institution for at least two years.

"Cheryl does not believe she deserves a pat on the

back for her actions,'' Gianelli countered. ''She knows what she did was wrong.''

''Fine, then she should go to jail,'' Jablonski said.

''A year's jail time makes absolutely no sense,'' Gianelli said forcefully. ''Either she is guilty or she is innocent. If she coldbloodedly ordered the execution of her father then she should be sent away for ten years, fifteen years. But if this little girl was forced to have sexual intercourse with that man from the time she was thirteen, she has been punished enough. And I cannot agree to her spending even a day in jail.''

''You're a real gambler, aren't you,'' Judge Sherman said, smiling. He had heard these kinds of arguments before.

Holding the best cards at this point, Jablonski made the following offer: Sean could plead guilty to manslaughter provided that Cheryl did as well. If Cheryl did not plead guilty, neither could Sean. It was as simple as that. Jablonski would not budge. The deal he was offering was that Sean would get six years in jail, Cheryl two—an arrangement he knew Martin Efman would be eager to grab. Without a plea, there was a good chance Sean could get convicted of murder, which in New York State meant a minimum of fifteen years in prison.

But Gianelli hung tough. He felt a jury would never convict Cheryl of murder. There was good chance she would be exonerated entirely of the charge. Efman tried to persuade him otherwise, but Gianelli's position was firm. He would not agree to allow Cheryl to go to jail even for a day.

''No jail,'' he said.

No deal.

A trial date was tentatively scheduled for January.

Valentine's Day was always an event in the Pierson household. Not unlike Christmas or New Year's or a Pierson birthday, it was a day of expectation, anticipation, the promise of presents. There were always boxes of chocolates, flowers, gifts, and perfumes. It was the kind of day that was planned for weeks. But Valentine's Day in 1984—just one month after the festivities of his fortieth birthday and two years before his murder—James Pierson had to take his wife to the doctor. She was seriously ill again. The swelling had returned. It was becoming increasingly clear that the first kidney transplant had failed, and she would need another.

It was a stressful morning. Cheryl had missed the bus to school, and Pierson drove his daughter there himself before escorting his wife into the city. He had asked Cheryl whether she was sending a Valentine's Day card to the boy she liked at school, a boy named Glenn, of whom James Pierson did not approve. Cheryl said she was not. But as she picked her books off the seat, a Valentine's Day card addressed to Glenn slipped out of her notebook. Pierson saw it, realized what it was, and exploded. In a blind rage he punched his daughter in the face.

Tom and Mary Melvin, who rented the house the Piersons owned across the street, noticed Cheryl's swollen lip when she came over to babysit. Cheryl told them what happened, but pleaded with them not to say anything. MaryAnn Sargeant, Cheryl's friend from up the street, noticed too. For years MaryAnn's mother, Grace, had worried about Cheryl's relationship with her father. She would not allow her own daughter to drive in a car with him. Now she said she wanted to call the police. But MaryAnn pleaded with her mother not to get involved. Diana Erbentraut, Cheryl's friend from school, noticed also. The Erbentrauts, too, had suspected for years that there was ''something wrong'' at the Piersons' home.

''My daughter would come home and tell me he was taping the phone conversations,'' recalled Dennis Erbentraut, an electrician. ''They were not allowed to have the bedroom door closed. They weren't allowed to go down into the basement. He always wanted to know what they were talking about. If my daughter wanted to call and talk to her she would have to call her at a neighbor's house. I keep putting all this together. I heard about the mother being sick. She's not allowed to have boyfriends. No makeup. I don't like to say things that I'm thinking myself.''

But with the Valentine's Day incident, Dennis Erbentraut could no longer hold his silence. He insisted that his daughter confront Cheryl directly and find out more.

"So I went into school and asked Cheryl is there anything going on between you and your father?'' Diana Erbentraut would recall. ''It was our class in business dynamics. And she just gave me a blank look. It was a look like she wanted to tell me but she couldn't. When I told my parents, they told me to go tell the guidance office. So the next day I went and spoke to Mrs. Weiss in the guidance office. She told me she had to go to a meeting. When I told her it was important, she asked me what it was. I told her I thought Cheryl was having a problem with her father. She told me Cheryl would have to tell her herself.''

She never did.

Cathleen Pierson received a second kidney transplant on March 30, 1984—her son's eighteenth birthday. But it was hardly a day for celebration. It was a sad day, an ordeal that seemed to spell the beginning of the end. In some ways that day was the beginning of the end for Pierson and his son as well.

James Pierson and his son, Jimmy, had been on the outs for years. Not that any one issue came between them. It was more a battle of style, identity, independence; a classic tug of war between father and son. For as overbearing and tough as James Pierson Sr. was, James, the son, aspired to be gentle, introspective, offbeat. Pierson had always wanted his son to be an athlete, to go out for baseball, to be the way he had been as a youth, to be tough. But young Pierson had other plans. He thought of himself as a poet, a flower child born a decade too late. Alone at night in his room when everyone else was asleep, he would lie awake and read Allen Ginsberg. He dreamed about becoming a rock star, of performing at heavy metal clubs in Manhattan, of recording his songs. He wore his hair long and several earrings in each ear. Nothing delighted him more than driving the streets of Selden and being whistled at by some truck driver who had mistaken him from behind for a girl. He was thrilled with the deception. It was the kind of thing that bolstered his contempt for stereotype, his love of the absurd. If James Sr. stood for everything that was macho and conventional, James Jr. had his own personal stake in just the reverse. If a waitress asked young Pierson if he had any questions about a menu, he would always reply, "Yeah, who wrote it?"

"I wanted to live for the present," Jimmy would say. "My father wanted me to live for the future."

James Pierson Sr. had wanted his son to go to college, to make something of himself. Jimmy could not imagine what a college would want with him, so after his son graduated from Newfield High School Pierson gave him a $400-a-week job in his cable television business. He wanted his son to have a curfew, to wear "respectable" clothes. He demanded that his son address him as "sir." But young Pierson had other ideas. He got speeding tickets, which his father had to pay. He ran up credit card bills and totalled a car. Driving fast was probably the only trait of his father's Jimmy sought to emulate. He too loved to dodge in and out of lanes at race-car speeds, and he liked to stay out all night. All this served only to invite his father's wrath.

"He was heartbroken about his son," recalled Kenny Zimlinghaus, Pierson's friend. "But it was his own fault. He had to live the way he wanted him to live. He had to have his hair cut the way he wanted his hair cut. He was very strict. He was just overpowering. His son got to be fourteen or fifteen. You get tired of bowing down. "Yesir. Yesir.' He wanted him to love him and be close, but he was forcing him away at the same time. He said, 'I can't get close.' But how can someone get close to you when you're at arm's length? When someone is always barking at you, how can you get close? I liked his son. I liked his son a lot. He was a good kid.''

A few months after his eighteenth birthday, young James Pierson moved out and got an apartment on his own. His father was devastated. He took Kenny Zimlinghaus to lunch and wept.

It was in August of 1984—not long after his son left home—that James Pierson took a summer's drive upstate with another friend of his named Fred Hunsucker. Pierson owned property near Oneonta, New York, where he would often walk in the woods and experiment with his guns.

On this particular visit, Hunsucker recalled, Pierson was in a bad mood. He became annoyed that some garbage had been left at the side of a road. Rather than take it up with the neighbor involved or report the incident to the police, Pierson stopped his truck, opened the back trunk, took out his Uzi submachine gun, and when no one was around, took aim at the neighbor's truck. He shattered the rear window and windshield. He shot up the radiator, the driver's door, a metal storage box mounted on the rear. Then he got back in his truck and drove home.

"He told everyone about it," Bruce Bandes, Pierson's attorney, would recall. "He took such pleasure in it. It was almost sexual.''

James Pierson and his wife were having problems. She was as distraught as he was about the departure of their son. But they dealt with it differently: Pierson by venting his anger, Cathleen by seeing her son on the sly when her husband was not around. Cathleen's health was deteriorating. She told the doctor she was seeing "men coming through the walls.'' So weak she would spend entire days on the living room couch, she increasingly relied on Cheryl to take care of the family. Pierson and his wife argued frequently. JoAnn recalled one night her mother got so angry at her father that she threw a plate of food at him in the middle of dinner.

Around this time, on a balmy Indian summer night, Cathleen got her strength together and drove to the home of her old childhood friend, who had been a bridesmaid at her wedding.

"She said, 'I'm down the road from you,' " the friend would recall. "She came over and we talked for hours. 'I want to leave him. He's always fighting with the children.' She said she was concerned about Cheryl. She didn't like how he didn't let her go to the movies with her friends and when he did let her go, he would follow her to make sure she was there. I said, 'Call home and let him know you're here.' She wouldn't do it. I said to her, 'Jimmy is a good provider. Go for counseling.' She was just being polite when she said she would think about it."

After their long conversation, Cathleen's friend wondered whether James Pierson had struck his wife. It was nothing in particular that Cathleen said, rather how she spoke. Still the friend never asked because she was too embarrassed.

But someone else did ask. The date was October 15, 1984, just four months before Cathleen Pierson would die. Cathleen Pierson had a regularly scheduled appointment with Dr. Eli Friedman, her kidney doctor.

"I asked whether anyone was 'beating up' on the patient," Dr. Friedman noted on Cathleen's medical chart for that day, adding that he had found bruises on her right and left upper arms as well as her left breast. But Dr. Friedman added that his patient denied being abused.

"Strong believable denial" was the note Dr. Friedman made on her chart. It was never mentioned again.

*Well, I think I loved her a lot more than she knew, but there was a jealousy because she didn't think me and my father should be as close as we were. She always wanted to be closer to him, but he always would rather do things more with me than with her. And then when she got upset, she'd get upset with me, but I'd try to make it up to her by doing stuff like taking care of the house and stuff.*

*She would be like: Why can't you watch TV in the living room with everybody instead of just going in the room. She'd say that to my father and so my father would say, " 'cause you don't like watching sports and stuff and Cheryl does," when I actually didn't but . . . to keep peace in the house because I don't want my father to scream at me or be in a bad mood and then take it out on someone else.*

*They fought a lot over us kids. My father would be like screaming at us and yelling at us and my mother would stick up for us and they would fight because she was sticking up for us.*

Becoming a cheerleader is almost every girl's dream at Newfield High School. To march onto the gymnasium floor in a tight-fitting red and white uniform is a statement that a girl is among the school's prettiest, most athletic, most desirable. It was what Cheryl Pierson had always wanted from the time she was a little girl. To her it was synonymous with success, with what she wanted most to be—just like her mother. For when Cathleen Pierson looked back on her life, it was being a majorette at Northport High that made her the most proud.

Pierson loved to watch Cheryl practice her cheers on the football field. Jimmy had never been athletic the way Pierson had so much wanted him to be. So he was proud that Cheryl was out there representing herself and the family.

"I never thought I could enjoy sports with my daughter," Pierson would say proudly. He would sit in the bleachers watching the girls practice and drive Cheryl home afterward. Cheryl would later say that she liked having her father there watching her, that she enjoyed how proud he was. But then she wondered that perhaps the real reason he was there was to check up on her, to make sure she was telling the truth about her whereabouts.

Pierson had become concerned about Cheryl and boys. The Valentine's Day card was just one of many lies Cheryl had told him about where she was going and what she was doing. Cheryl would arrange to meet boyfriends at her babysitting jobs; Pierson would catch her lying to him about it, lies that he did not know how to handle.

"Your mother was not a slut and I don't want you to be a slut," he would shout at his daughter. He disapproved of the clothing Cheryl would wear. He did not want her to wear bikinis in front of strangers. He disapproved of her wearing too much makeup. Her reputation, Pierson would say, was the only thing she had. Her propensity to play coquette angered him. Now with his wife ill, Cheryl seemed hard to control. He began listening in to her telephone calls, he began following her.

Seated face to face with Cheryl Pierson in Alberta Kosser's kitchen, Paul Gianelli was trying to assess what kind of witness his client would make. They began to go over the facts of the case. When did the abuse start? Why had her thoughts turned to murder? Why could she see no other way out? Gianelli listened to what she said and how she said it. He watched what she did with her hands. He kept track of when she hesitated, when her syntax was no longer her own. He tried to see her the way a jury would. Clearly there were problems.

There was a coldness to Cheryl. A seeming aloofness, particularly whenever she began to describe her physical relationship with her father. It was not a laugh exactly. But suddenly in the midst of recalling some horrifying detail like how she said her father would force himself on her in the shower, Cheryl would break into a smile as if she had just told the punch line to a joke. The expression in her voice turned hollow. A hardness took over her demeanor as if what she was describing was either trivial or amazingly funny. Her embarrassment, if that's what it was, prompted a giggle. But it was not only her manner that disturbed Gianelli but her appearance as well. In the nine months that had elapsed since the crime, Cheryl had lost much of her schoolgirl innocence. Her mannerisms had more edge. She was no longer the vulnerable little girl Gianelli would have liked a jury to see.

Gianelli, clad in tennis shorts and a polo shirt, was seated at the table in Alberta Kosser's kitchen; with its neat gingham curtains and prayer over the door, it would become the scene for many strategy sessions. Alberta sat at the table and said nothing. But every once in a while, she would refill a glass of soda or open a can of sweet peanuts.

"I don't see how a jury is going to convict you of murder," Gianelli began, reporting on his progress at the plea negotiations. Cheryl was seated next to him in a loose-fitting white jumpsuit.

"What about the manslaughter charge?" Cheryl asked, resting her face on her elbows. The words had now become familiar. *Manslaughter. Youthful offender. Probation.*

"That's a little of the reason it might go to trial, unfortunately," Gianelli said. "The prosecutor would like you to go to jail. My feeling is that—"

"The prosecutor wants me to go to jail?" Cheryl

interrupted seemingly surprised at the notion. "What would that prove?"

"That society has to respond. A life has been lost."

Cheryl made a face.

"You want to go to jail for one to three years?" Gianelli asked. "I can get you a plea tomorrow. Okay? Probably Sean could get five to fifteen. And you would get one to three. You would go to Bedford Hills. Jail."

"Not a farm or nothing like that?" Cheryl asked, punctuating the word *farm* with an ironic twist as if she had just envisioned herself milking cows.

"They've got some rough people up there," Gianelli said. "I've been there. My feeling is you don't need that. You've been hurt enough."

"He did it," Cheryl said angrily under her breath, disassociating herself from the crime. No trace of remorse in her voice, she would insist she did not believe she did anything wrong. She only mentioned it to Sean, she would say. She did not really believe he would do it. It was "just talk."

Gianelli listened.

Paul Gianelli had interviewed scores of witnesses, many of whom suspected "something" between Cheryl and her father, but no one knew for sure what it was. He kept waiting and hoping for someone to materialize who could point to a specific incident or quote a particular conversation. But as the weeks elapsed no one would.

It was becoming increasingly clear that the case would have to rely on Cheryl's word alone, what a jury thought of her, whether they believed her, whether they could understand.

Wherever he went, people talked about the Pierson case. Passions ran strong. There were those who believed Cheryl without question, those whose hearts went out to her because in their minds, her father "deserved to die." There were others, both men and women, who believed Cheryl too but could not understand her silence, why she told no one, why she saw no other way out, why if she was really all that desperate she didn't kill her father herself. Still there were others who were skeptical, who wondered if sexual abuse had taken place at all or whether it was just a convenient alibi provided by the newspapers.

Over and over, Gianelli heard the same questions about Cheryl's brother's involvement, about Cheryl's dispassionate payment to her father's assassin, about the pregnancy, about the size of her father's estate, the months of premeditation, and as he listened, he found himself thinking more and more about another high-publicity murder case. Gianelli pondered the case of Jean Harris, the notorious preparatory school headmistress serving fifteen years in jail for the murder of Scarsdale Diet Doctor Herman Tarnower.

Gianelli is a fierce advocate in the traditional sense of the word. He is a man whose convictions depend at any given moment on his client. At that moment he absolutely believed Cheryl Pierson's account of sexual abuse, and because he did, he believed she should not go to jail. But he is also a pragmatist. He was becoming concerned that this inflexibility would backfire. The problem with the Harris defense, he thought, was that her lawyer was blinded by the publicity. He made the stakes higher than they should have been. He offered the jury no way out. Either Jean Harris was guilty of murder or she was innocent. There was no middle ground. A defense of manslaughter, which carried a much more lenient prison sentence, was never pursued. From the lawyer's point of view, it made the case an exciting crap shoot, but it was a crap shoot that Jean Harris lost.

---

*I was totally confused. He yelled at me for being a liar. I was living a lie. He was telling me if I ever was in trouble, I should come to*

The Pierson family home at 293 Magnolia Drive and the driveway where James Pierson was shot on February 5, 1986. *Tony Jerome/The New York Times*

James Pierson with his daughters, Cheryl (left) and JoAnn (right), the year before the murder. *The New York Times*

James and Cathleen Pierson as young parents expecting their second child, with the two-year-old James Jr. *Photo Courtesy Virginia Pierson*

Below left: James Pierson with his mother, Virginia, and three children, Cheryl (left), JoAnn, and James Jr. in the backyard of the Pierson home. *Photo by Cathleen Pierson*

Below right: James Pierson as a choirboy with his sister, Marilyn, three years his junior, at the Pierson residence in Brooklyn. *Photo Courtesy Virginia Pierson*

James Pierson and his mother on his last birthday, January 4, 1986. *Photo by Kim Adams*

Above: Cheryl and James Pierson at JoAnn's First Communion in April 1985, two months after Cathleen's death. *Photo Courtesy Virginia Pierson*

Left: James Pierson and Cathleen at his fortieth birthday party, just three months before Cathleen's second kidney transplant. *Photo Courtesy Virginia Pierson*

Above: Cheryl and her father at her Sweet Sixteen in May 1985, six months before Cheryl offers Sean Pica $1,000 to kill him. *The New York Times*

Below: Cheryl and her boyfriend, Rob Cuccio, in the Pierson home on February 8, 1986, the day of her father's funeral. *Photo by Marion Lehning*

Opposite above: Cheryl Pierson, who has just confessed to her father's murder, under arrest and in police custody. *Dennis Caruso/The New York Daily News*

Opposite right: Cheryl Pierson and her attorney, Paul Gianelli, preparing for court. *Michael Shavel/The New York Times*

Opposite below: Sean Pica, aspiring Eagle Scout, in jail following his arrest for murder. *Dick Yarwood/Newsday*

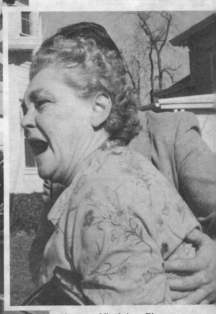

Cheryl Pierson and Alberta Kosser, the next-door neighbor who believed Cheryl and took her into her home, leaving court during the hearing, September 1987. *Thomas R. Koeniges/Newsday*

Above: Virginia Pierson, who could never believe the reason Cheryl gave for having her father murdered, en route to court. *Mary McLoughlin/The New York Post*

Left: Cheryl Pierson and her brother, James Jr., arriving for court. *Rameshwar Das/The New York Times*

Cheryl Pierson outside the courthouse, being led off to jail, still clutching the apology she had planned to read to the judge. *Ken Korotkin/The New York Daily News*

Sean Pica after serving six months of his minimum eight-year term. *Don Jacobsen/Newsday*

Cheryl Pierson, her boyfriend, Rob, and her brother, James Jr., in the white limousine on January 19, 1988, the day of Cheryl's release from jail. *Thomas R. Koeniges/Newsday*

Rob Cuccio and Cheryl show off the engagement ring he gave her the day of her release. *Thomas R. Koeniges/Newsday*

*him. How could I go to him? How could I trust
him?*

———————————————————————

"I didn't want to do that to Cheryl," Paul Gianelli
would say.

There were many lies Cheryl Pierson told. Lies she
told her father, lies she told reporters, lies she told her
friends, lies she told her lawyer, lies perhaps she told
herself.

Cathleen Oitzinger, Cheryl's psychologist, would say
that lying was one of the ways Cheryl learned to deal
with the incongruity of her life. She after all lived a
life where the rules handed down at the dinner table
were broken in the darkness of her father's bedroom.

But if there was one subject about which Cheryl
consistently lied over the years, it was about boys, and
it was this history that many of Pierson's oldest friends
thought about when they considered Cheryl's allegations about her father. Pierson was a strict disciplinar-
ian. He had firm ideas about what he wanted for his
children. Many of them were convinced that the real
reason Cheryl had her father killed was because she
found out she was pregnant.

Richard La Barbara, one of Pierson's oldest friends,
kept thinking back to a conversation he had with James
Pierson five days before he died. The two men were
seated in the basement of the house at 288 Magnolia
Drive Pierson owned across the street from his own.
La Barbara was putting in a new boiler. Cheryl had
just brought over some coffee for the men.

"How ya doing?" Pierson asked, joining his friends
at the standup bar.

"Don't ask," La Barbara replied, launching into a
tirade as he often did about problems with money.

"You call those problems?" Pierson asked.
"Money? You don't know what real problems are."

La Barbara recalled being surprised. Usually Pierson was a good listener. In fact he liked opening up

to Pierson because he was one of the few friends who actually took an interest. He looked up and was astonished to see that Pierson was crying. He had never seen the man weep before, and the images of this big man overcome with tears startled him.

"I got so many problems. Real problems," Pierson was saying, shaking his head.

"What's the matter?" La Barbara asked.

"Cheryl," Pierson said. "She can't be trusted."

"What are you talking about, Jim?" La Barbara asked, absolutely stunned. "She's such a good girl. You don't know how lucky you have it. She's as sweet as pie."

"I caught that son of a bitch humping her boyfriend on the living room couch," Pierson added.

La Barbara said nothing. He just let his friend talk. He knew how strict James Pierson was with his daughter.

"I can't take it anymore," Pierson said. "I tell you. I can't handle it. I've got to be a mother to them. I've got to be a father. I can't trust them alone. I can't even trust my own kids."

La Barbara would say he did not know what to say to his friend. He knew about Pierson's problems with his son. But Cheryl had always been his solace.

"Is there something I can do?" La Barbara asked.

"How can you help me?" Pierson demanded, sobbing. "I don't know what to do. I've had it. I've just had it."

At this point La Barbara's brother, who was helping on the boiler job, came down into the basement. Pierson turned away and walked up the stairs. La Barbara never had the chance to talk to James Pierson about it again.

# 10

It was eight months after the murder. Sean Pica was out on bail and now living with his father and step-mother in Valley Stream in a cramped two-bedroom home they had planned to sell. In fact, the morning Sean was arrested, his father had been making a final inspection on a house he and his new wife were planning to buy. It was the house of their dreams, a place where Benjamin Pica, retired early on disability from the New York City Police Department, would be able to have his own studio to make stained glass. KarenAnn, Sean's stepmother, who loved to sew, would have her own sewing room. There would be plenty of room for the large oak dining table that was too big for their present house and all the other antiques they loved to collect. But now, with Sean's legal bills, the house was no longer a reality, and the contract was cancelled.

Sean got a job driving a bread truck. He was considered a reliable and trustworthy employee. KarenAnn would look at Sean and still find it all impossible to believe. Always religious, she turned to her faith. It was a tense, awkward time. KarenAnn was a New York City policewoman. Her job for years was to arrest people like Sean. Now she tried the best she could to welcome him with love into her home. Sean had developed serious stomach problems. They never spoke of the crime. They wanted Sean to enjoy whatever precious weeks remained of his freedom.

One weekend Sean went home to visit his mother.

Ironically, their relationship had improved since the murder. They were not fighting anymore. He had started to redesign her kitchen the way she had always asked. Grey cabinets. The only argument they continued to have was about his seeing Michael Kerwick. Joanne could not understand how Sean could still want to see the boy who "sent him down the river." Sean idolized the youth.

Sean and Joanne were standing in the kitchen when the telephone rang. It was Ben. He was actually returning his wife's call. She wanted to talk about the problems she was having with her youngest son, Sean's fourteen-year-old brother, Vincent.

It was the kind of battle Joanne always had with Ben, a battle about discipline, about responsibility, about commitment. So far as Joanne was concerned, Sean killed Cheryl's father for the money because he never learned the responsibility of earning money on his own. She never lost the opportunity to remind her former husband how irresponsible he had been to leave the family and how because of him irresponsibility was their son's main problem.

Sean sat and listened to his mother and father bicker.

"Isn't it better to have a happy home life?" Sean asked seemingly out of nowhere. His mother apparently did not hear.

Sean was five when his father left the first time. The date was January 15, 1975. Not long after, little Joseph Pica came down with what Joanne thought at first was pneumonia and rushed him to the doctor.

"It's serious, Joanne," the doctor had said.

"How serious?" she asked.

"Very."

"Should he be in the hospital?"

"Yes."

Joanne tried to contact Ben, but he was nowhere to be found. Finally she tracked him down at the home of a girlfriend. He was angry she called until he heard the reason. He raced home to join her at the hospital, where the doctor broke the news.

"That's when he told us he had acute leukemia and five years to live," Joanne would recall. Ben moved back home. The two saw a marriage counselor, but it would do no good.

"I just couldn't take her," Sebastian Pica would recall. "The way she did things. The way she responded to things. Her whole demeanor. The way she was. She was driving me crazy. I called her up one night. 'I'm going to be late. I've made an arrest. I have to go to night court.' Her attitude was: 'I don't understand how you could have made an arrest. I have to go to work tonight. What am I supposed to do?' I'd say: 'Get a babysitter. Don't go to work.' 'What do you mean don't go to work?' When she had a commitment to something that was it."

He and his ex-wife fought constantly over the same subjects: discipline, money, commitment.

In 1979 Sebastian Pica served his wife with divorce papers. Out of spite, he chose Valentine's Day.

Dr. Stephen Honor met Sean Pica for the first time in jail on what turned out to be the youth's seventeenth birthday. He had been hired by Sean's mother and attorney for the purposes of evaluating Sean's state of mind and psychological functioning and to help provide a better insight into how and why Sean, who had never given even the most remote indications of a propensity for violence, could have committed a murder.

Dr. Honor's impression during those interviews was that Sean was "forthright and honest" and that there was "no indication of evasiveness." Furthermore, he found that Sean was "always oriented in time, place and person. He was rational and coherent" and there was "no overt indication of significant psychopathology." But in assessing the youth's intellectual abilities, Dr. Honor concluded that Sean had a low level of "abstract reasoning" and was otherwise unable to "appreciate the consequences of his behavior."

"Sean attempts to deal with the world on his 'own terms,' " Dr. Honor stated. "While he is clearly able to differentiate right from wrong, he is quite capable when it suits his purposes of going beyond what is typically considered to be 'right.' Under those circumstances he is not troubled by the "correctness" of his behavior, but rather by what it is that he immediately wants. In that sense it is in fact clear that he is not consequence oriented . . . Sean is not really upset about the fact that he killed a man; he is upset because he has been imprisoned for this offense."

It was a surprising statement to hear about Sean for anyone who knew him well. He had always seemed such a gentle and caring young man. Among his many preoccupations in recent years was helping a young mentally retarded boy in the Boy Scouts earn his Eagle badge. Sean personally made sure that the boy completed his special project: building a set of planters at an old age home. Every day, even in the rain, Sean was there hammering away until it was all completed.

Carmen Rosalia and her husband had been friends with Joanne and Ben Pica since 1967. Their children were the same age. They had a daughter Joseph's age. Sean was born in the same hospital room three months before her only son, John. Vincent was the same age as their triplets. The Rosalias lived across the street from the Picas in the exact same style house and they worried about the same things.

Joanne and Carmen spent so much time together they often joked they were married to each other. Both of their men were never home. So the two women entertained themselves by helping out at the church bazaar and belonging to a club called homemakers, where they learned to make quilted photograph albums and skirts that wrap around the base of Christmas trees. Joanne was particularly good at wreaths for the door, and there was not a holiday for which she didn't have an ornament of one kind or another: witches for Halloween, pilgrims for Thanksgiving.

But there were differences between the two women when it came to their children.

"If the school called me I always thought there was a reason," Carmen said. "If they said they did it, then I believed them."

Carmen recalled that when her son was thirteen she found out he was drinking beer and she "dragged" her entire family in for counseling. Once a week at 8 A.M. the entire family showed up for $65 a session, and, she said, it helped. In counseling, they devised a plan to help Carmen make each of her five children seem unique within a large family. Once a week they put their names in a hat and whoever was drawn got to go out to dinner on Friday night alone with their mother.

"Joanne's ideas were different." Carmen would say. "Joanne's boys were her boys."

Still the Picas and Rosalias were close friends. They kept an eye on each other's children. When Carmen's water broke for the triplets, Joanne was there to keep her calm. When John split his chin open, once again Joanne appeared on the scene, always the voice of reason. The two couples saw each other often, and when Ben and JoAnn separated it was difficult on the Rosalias. Like an illness or some other tragedy, the failure of the Picas' marriage reminded the Rosalias how tenuous everyone's life really is. The Rosalias stayed away. And when Joanne married Jim, Carmen felt that she and Joanne had less in common. Carmen had been fond of Ben. She had trouble understanding Joanne's attraction to Jim. She found him odd, particularly after he showed up one day at a party and, commenting on her four small daughters, announced she was raising "little whores."

"She always wanted to make it right," Carmen said, commenting on Joanne. "I'm more of a pessimist. I'm more suspicious. She's more clinical. When things are hard she protects herself. When things are hard I fall apart. I keep letting it out. I just wish she would cry. I just wish she would scream. If it's a storm and we're supposed to go somewhere, I say, 'forget it.' She says, 'let's try in an hour.' ''

When she married him, there was a lot about James DelVecchio's past Sean's mother did not know. There was a lot she never thought to ask.

''It happened so fast,'' she would say of their relationship. ''I felt guilty about sleeping with a man to whom I wasn't married.''

But it would not take long before the past would make itself known, to Joanne and her three sons, particularly Sean.

James DelVecchio as a child always thought it odd that his ''parents'' were short and he was so tall. They looked so Italian. He looked anything but. It was in 1942 when he was around four years old that a ''strange man'' showed up in his parents' living room and took him to the movies. Only in retrospect many years later did DelVecchio realize that the man was probably his real father. He was later told his father was killed in the Second World War.

''After my biological father was dead his family tried to come back,'' James DelVecchio would recall. ''I remembered all the meetings in the living room in the house in the Bronx. 'I'm your Uncle so and so.' It was strange. I must have realized then I was adopted.''

When he was thirteen or fourteen years old, James DelVecchio set out in secret to learn the truth. He did not want to hurt his adoptive parents so he never told them. But one day he traveled into Manhattan and went to the church where he was told he was baptized. From his baptismal record, he learned the name of his mother, who, as it turned out, still lived nearby in a walkup on Manhattan's Upper East Side. There he stood in front of her building for days until one day a pretty woman arrived who was tall and "fair skinned" just like him. He marveled at how "alive" she was, standing there with a bag of groceries in her arms, fumbling for her keys. He studied the lines in her back, her neatly coiffed hair. He returned and watched some more. He got to know the woman's schedule: when she left for work, when she came home, which mass she favored on Sunday. He found it fascinating that she still went to church to pray. For weeks on end, he would just stand as though in a trance in front of her building and watch this woman, his mother.

"I never went up to her," James DelVecchio would recall many years later. "I guess it was enough to know she was alive. This is what she looked like. I guess I figured she never made an effort to see me. How am I going to address this lady? Tell her I'm her son? I might have been scared she would have said 'so what?' "

At eighteen James DelVecchio married and eventually had three children of his own, two daughters three years apart and much later a son named Jamie. Not long after his namesake, Jamie, turned two, the couple split up, and James DelVecchio chose not to see his children again.

"Too much pain," he would give as explanation.

There was another marriage after that and a number of different careers. Then one day, working as an X-ray technician at a community hospital on Long Island, he was fixed up on a blind date with an intensive care nurse, Joanne Pica. The year was 1979. A recent divorcée, Joanne had three sons aged twelve, ten, and seven.

Three months later, in a small ceremony at a Southampton church, they were married. Claire Gould, Joanne's good friend from Windover Drive, was JoAnn's witness. So were Claire's husband and JoAnn's three boys.

\* \* \*

"I was happy to have someone around," Sean would recall of how he felt when James DelVecchio moved into his father's bedroom.

For the first few months Sean's house on Windover Drive was filled with promise. James DelVecchio helped the boys install a basketball hoop over the garage. He took the boys to softball games. He carried the pictures of his new sons to work with him in his wallet. They all posed for a family portrait.

But it did not take long for another side of Jim DelVecchio to emerge, a side that Joanne and the boys had never seen before, a dark side that only came to the surface when he drank. Sometimes he would sit at the dinner table and refuse to speak. At other times he would shout at the boys and ridicule them for no apparent reason. There was the day he got so angry he threw Butterscotch the dog clear across the backyard with such force he and Joanne had to take the animal to the hospital for X-rays. Another day he ripped the air conditioner out of the window and dragged it down the stairs, destroying the brand-new carpet his wife had just installed in the hall. There was the day he threw pizza against the kitchen wall. There was the day he tried to throw his wife from a moving car.

Sober, James DelVecchio was as gentle and loving a husband as one could find. But when he was drunk, he smacked his wife across the face and called her cunt, whore, slut. The children watched.

"Well, at least you're not an alcoholic," Joanne would say, asking her husband to just "cut back."

The neighbors had begun to talk, although none of them said a word to Joanne. Always in control, she was not the type to invite concern. "Everything's fine" she would say with that stoic smile of hers.

One beautiful spring day James DelVecchio put on his softball uniform, took off for the ball park, and never returned.

"What would have been the point?" he said.

* * *

In retrospect, Joanne would not recall her second husband's behavior as being all that bad.

"I'd tell him the next day and he wouldn't remember," Joanne would later say. "He'd always say he had had too much to drink and that he didn't really mean it."

Joanne would say she never thought of herself as being an abused woman. She never considered violence a feature of her home. Certainly it was not something she would ever mention to anyone else. It was a private matter, something she could handle on her own.

Anything, it seemed, would be better than getting divorced for a second time, than having to tell her parents yet again she was a failure, than having to face her friends, than having to start over.

Joanne was as surprised as anyone when Jim Del-Vecchio walked out the door. She actually thought they were doing well, that the family was happy.

"I'm a study in suppression," she would say with her nervous laugh. "That's how I survive."

In many ways, that was how she dealt with Sean.

In truth, there had been problems all along with Sean. Nothing that in and of itself would predict a major disturbance, but there were signs. There was the time after Ben left that Sean went to school with bullets and tried to sell them to his friends. There was the time Joanne came home and found her son sick to his stomach with drugs the apparent cause. Joanne thought it an isolated event. But, in fact, Sean would later say his cocaine habit cost as much as $200 a week. The year before the murder, a guidance counselor called Joanne at home and told her that her son had bragged to her during a routine interview that he was being used as a lookout in burglaries. Joanne "looked into it," she would later say, and determined it was false. The counselor told Sean's mother that he must have been trying to get attention. The truth was, Sean in fact had been a lookout in many burglaries that he had committed with Michael Kerwick. Indeed, there was little that Michael asked that Sean would not do.

"Usually if there is a problem, it's something you don't want to broadcast," Joanne DelVecchio would say of her reluctance to seek help for Sean. "If you go for outside help you are broadcasting it, which you might not be ready to do. And you start hearing from other people who have gone for help. I mean this is not an isolated situation and everybody talks about their situations. With your co-workers or whatever. I know families who have gone for assistance and the assistance has been useless. I have one friend who has four boys. One of her boys was a discipline problem in school, kicked out of school and sent to private school. They were going to a psychologist and the psychologist was giving them such impractical advice. For instance: Basically let him do whatever he wants. He doesn't have to live by the rules. And you're torn with: this is malarkey. This kid needs a kick. Maybe I'm wrong. I'm not educated in that direction and obviously I'm not doing the best job or we wouldn't be having this problem. You turn it inward. I am to blame. I am to blame. You don't know what to do. Someone has given you advice that you don't understand. Having heard these stories, I shied away from going to these outside agencies because I wasn't sure that their assistance was going to be helpful."

Besides, Joanne would say, she was proud of her son. He was the kindest and most academically driven of her three children. She never believed he was really in trouble.

"He did it for the money," she would say with dispassion, once again returning to her theory that because of his father Sean had never learned to be responsible.

Sean himself would say he did not know why he did it, but it was not for the money. Dr. Stephen Honor, the psychologist who examined him in prison, agreed with him.

"In my opinion Sean did not enter into the agreement in a coldblooded manner," Dr. Honor would write in his report. "Throughout the scenario, the situation seemed almost gamelike. Psychologically he was able to disassociate himself from both the enormity of his proposed act as well as from the appropriate affect which could have stopped him. His primary focus was on the notion that this girl needed help and that he, as a 'friend' and as a 'man' was 'duty bound' to help her."

"The concept of 'friend' occupies a central role in Sean's behavior," Dr. Honor continued. "One of the few commitments that this young man can make is in terms of his friendships. Once an individual is admitted to this status, Sean becomes extremely loyal to the person. There is a basic honesty in these relationships in the sense that for Sean they are 'pure' relationships. They are not questioned. His loyalty is such that when asked to do a favor for a friend, Sean would comply, even if the 'something' asked happened to be illegal. When combined with his gullibility, based upon his concretized way of thinking, Sean would apparently be willing to go to any lengths to help a friend."

It was an intriguing assessment. When he was a child, Sean's mother always warned him that "Someday you're going to help someone, and you're going to get in trouble. Someday you won't know when to say no."

# 11

The month of March was chilly and damp on Long Island. The flat terrain seemed all the more barren and stark beneath the slate-grey sky. A mean southeasterly breeze swept across the Long Island sound, sending fishing boats into a frenzy. The trees were still brown.

The trial had been postponed. Edward Jablonski had another murder case to try. Then Jim McCready went on a long planned family skiing vacation in Colorado. Then Paul Gianelli went with his wife to Hong Kong. Then Martin Efman took his long scheduled trip to the Caribbean. It seemed everyone was going someplace except the defendants and their families.

The case had become a prison. Wherever Marilyn Adams and her mother went they felt that they were being watched, that strangers were whispering, pointing fingers. Cheryl was working at another beauty shop now. A place called Mr. No Frills.

The trial date was set for March 24; Cheryl Pierson and Sean Pica were finally going to go to trial for the murder of James Pierson. Marilyn Adams and Virginia Pierson had been waiting months for that day. Justice would finally be served. Each had their own special fantasy for what would happen. Marilyn imagined Sean would take the stand and announce to the court something about the crime they still did not know. To Marilyn, Cheryl had been covering for her brother all along. Virginia had her own fantasy. The truth, she thought, would come from Cheryl. She would walk up to the witness stand, put her hand on a bible, and announce to the world that the real reason she had her father killed was love, love for Rob, the father of her baby.

Marilyn and Virginia arranged to take time off from work. They had already thought about clothes they would wear, what they would say, how much they would share with JoAnn, Cheryl's sister. The little girl was living with them now, and they worried what her classmates would say at school, whether they would permit her to watch the news reports on television.

It was 4 A.M. on March 24. Virginia Pierson was up, she had been unable to sleep at all. Marilyn too was busily cleaning pots before sunrise. They were dressed and ready to go when suddenly the telephone rang. Marilyn answered. It was Jim McCready, the homicide detective, on the telephone.

"She's pleading guilty," he said.

"What?" Marilyn shrieked. She had no idea what that meant.

"She and Pica are pleading guilty to manslaughter. They got cold feet," McCready said. "I'll see you there."

The steps of the flat-topped, yellow brick courthouse were crowded with journalists, photographers, and the curious when Virginia Pierson and Marilyn Adams arrived.

It was an emotional moment. The high-ceilinged courtroom was packed to capacity. The three rows of folding wooden seats were almost all filled. The brown-framed industrial clock on the rear courtroom wall read 9:55. Cheryl, in a white sweater and grey skirt, was already seated at the defense table and looking much heavier than she had the year before. She looked down at the grey fake marble tile floor. Her hands clasped her elbows. Her shoulders were up around her neck. Every once in a while a sigh emerged that was loud enough for everyone in the room to hear. She knew what was coming. Her lawyer had told her. In the end, he had said, there was no other way.

Sean, in a grey leather jacket and tie, sat beside his mother and father still amid the spectators. Virginia Pierson took a seat beside James McCready.

"Hi, Mom," McCready said, solemnly taking her arm.

The lawyers were still with the judge in chambers. When they emerged, Martin Efman, looking wan, crossed the courtroom and whispered something into Sean's ear. In a fit of rage, the youth abruptly clenched his fists and began to weep. Pale, gaunt, his fists still clenched, he followed his attorney past the swinging wooden gate and took his place at the defense table.

"What happened?" Virginia Pierson whispered.

"I don't know," McCready replied.

James DelVecchio, who sat alone in the rear, caught the eye of his former wife. She was crying too.

"All rise," the court clerk commanded as Judge Sherman walked solemnly into the packed courtroom and took his place at the bench. Everyone stood. As if at the start of a play, Cheryl followed Paul Gianelli across the courtroom, the steps of her flat shoes making sharp patter sounds against the floor. All else was silent.

She was now standing before the judge.

"How old are you?" Judge Sherman asked; his voice was soft, gentle, almost chatty, the voice of a schoolmaster the first day of class. He of course knew the answer to the question, but it was a way to begin.

"Seventeen," she replied in a whisper. Spectators leaned forward in their seats so that they could hear. She was shaking.

"Would you like to sit down?" he asked.

"No," she replied, uncertain on her feet.

"I will ask you a number of questions, and I'd like to remind you that you are testifying under oath. Is Mr. Gianelli your lawyer?"

"Sure," she said. The word, the voice, the answer, were that of a little girl.

"You heard today that you are pleading guilty."

''Sure.'' Her hands were shaking so badly it looked as though she might topple.

''And you agree that it is what you are willing to do.''

''Yes.''

''You are giving up a trial by jury.''

''Yes.'' It had been Paul Gianelli's decision. In the end, he did not want Cheryl to be another Jean Harris. In the end, he was unwilling to run the risk of having Cheryl's fate decided by a jury, of having her face the charge of murder.

''You are an eligible youthful offender,'' Judge Sherman said. ''But if you are not judged eligible it will go on your permanent record as a felony. I will order a probation report. I will consider the possibility of youthful offender. If I sentence you, the maximum will be six years with a two-year minimum. You will not get more than that.''

Until then, Cheryl—while nervous—had been composed. But with the mention of jail, she now erupted in tears. Her head was bent, her shoulders and arms quivered; the sound of her sobs filled the courtroom. Still she stood as a draft blew open the worn beige drapes that hung sadly in places off their curtain rod.

Edward Jablonski now approached the defendant. He had never before had the chance to question her. ''I would like to ask you if around November 1985 you had a conversation with Sean Pica?'' he asked, his voice official, his demeanor unmoved by her tears.

''Yes,'' she said, weeping.

''In that conversation did you ask him to kill your father?'' he asked.

''Yes.''

''Why did you want him to kill your father?''

It was the question for which everyone in the courtroom had waited. They knew the answer. They knew what she would say. Still, they wanted to hear it from Cheryl's lips, as if her tone of voice might reveal the truth. At first Cheryl could not reply. She took a deep breath and looked at the floor. She opened her mouth, but words did not come out. She was weeping, and the sounds were sharp gasps for breath.

"Do you want some water?" the judge asked. She shook her head.

"He," her voice began as she choked on the words. For a moment it looked as though Cheryl would be unable to respond. She clenched her eyes. Her arms were shaking. But at last the words came in a rush, almost a shout, a plea.

"Was . . . sexually abusing me."

The words resounded through the courtroom.

Judge Sherman said that as part of the plea, he would conduct a hearing to determine how Cheryl would be punished and that at a later time he would schedule a date for it to begin. The plea taken, Cheryl rushed to the rear of the courtroom and collapsed in her brother's arms. Her sobs echoed through the courtroom. Virginia Pierson wept too. So did Marilyn. Courtroom observers shifted uncomfortably in their seats as if they had just witnessed something so private they should not have been allowed to see it.

"She's still my granddaughter," Virginia Pierson said, wiping her face. Later Virginia Pierson would say that what she most wanted at that moment was to take Cheryl in her arms; that all she wanted from Cheryl were two words. "I'm sorry." Had she said it then, Virginia Pierson would have done anything for Cheryl.

Even forgiven her.

Sean Pica walked across the courtroom to face the judge, to proclaim his guilt. Joanne DelVecchio and Sebastian Pica solemnly followed. As Sean faced the bench, his parents stood next to him now, one on each side, the way they might if he were getting an award or taking a bride. Sebastian Pica, a large man, tried unsuccessfully to hold back his tears. Joanne, slender, stoic, briefly reached out to touch her son's arm.

"How do you plead?" Judge Sherman asked.

"Guilty," Sean replied, his voice flat.

"How old are you?"

"Eighteen," he replied.

"Is Mr. Efman your lawyer?"

"Yes."

"Did you discuss it with him?"

"Yes."

"You're here with your parents?"

"Yes."

"You understand you are giving up a trial by jury."

"Yes."

"I promised Mr. Efman that I would consider giving you youthful offender treatment, but the maximum I would give you would be twenty-five years in jail with a minimum of eight and one third."

It was the terms of the deal Jablonski had offered in the last go-round of negotiations. It seemed so much more severe than what was being offered to Cheryl, but it was still a lot better than the fifteen years he risked by going to trial. There would be no presentence hearing for Sean.

Edward Jablonski now approached the defendant. The last time he had been face to face with the young man had been more than a year before at Police Headquarters. On that day he asked Sean if he would be willing to make a videotape of his confession and Sean declined, explaining that his father was a police officer and he did not want him to see it in court. Now Sebastian Pica stood at his son's side, the tears dripping from his chin.

"Did you have a discussion in November 1985?" Jablonski asked.

"Yes."

"Did she indicate that she was being sexually abused by her father?"

"Yes."

"Sexually abused?" Jablonski asked, stressing the first word. One of the things that had always seemed so troubling about the case was that Cheryl had never told Sean the reason why she wanted her father murdered.

"Abused," he said.

"Did you give a price?"

"A thousand dollars," he said.

"Did you get a .22-caliber pump rifle?"

"Yes."

"How did you get the rifle?"

"Through a friend."

"Is that friend Michael Kerwick?"

"Yes."

"Were you asked to hold it for Kerwick because he didn't want his father to see it?"

"Yes."

"On February fourth did you contact Cheryl Pierson?"

"No."

"Did you tell her on the night before the shooting that you planned to do it?"

"I did not."

Jablonski now stopped the questioning. Cheryl had told police that Sean called her the night before the shooting and that she told him to "forget about it." It was strange. Here Sean was confessing to Pierson's murder but disputing Cheryl's claim that they had spoken. Jablonski interpreted it as a lie.

"I'm concerned about the plea," he said in disgust, throwing his notebook in a dramatic flourish onto the prosecutor's table.

"The night before the shooting," Jablonski insisted.

"No," Sean insisted. "There was nothing discussed."

As he paced, Ed Jablonski clearly decided the point was not worth winning.

"Now the next day did you load that rifle?" Jablonski continued.

"Yes."

"With how many rounds?"

"Five."

"Did you shoot him in the back of the head?"

"Yes."

"Then did you approach the body and shoot him some more?"

"Yes."

Until then not a word about the specific violence of the murder had been mentioned.

"Subsequent to that, in school the next day did you receive payment for four hundred dollars?"

"Yes."

"From whom?"

"Rob Cuccio."

"Did there come a time when you requested additional money and asked to live rent free?"

"Yes."

The plea taken, a court officer snapped handcuffs onto the youth's wrists. Although before he stepped into the courtroom he had not known it, he had already spent his last night as a free man.

As his parents watched him disappear through the back door, Joanne looked up at her former husband, but he did not notice. Judge Sherman set April 28 as the day Sean Pica was to be officially sentenced.


"It was what I felt I had to do, I guess," Sean said. "I felt hatred for a man I didn't even know based on what she fed into my mind. I was sitting in the back of the house throwing a rock through the damn window . . . saying what the hell am I doing here."

To the police, what he was doing there was no mystery at all. They pointed to Sean's purchase of gold bracelets for his girlfriend the day he was paid, his demand the night of James Pierson's funeral for additional monies, permission to live in the rental house, a motorcycle for himself and for Michael Kerwick. Then there were burglaries he committed with Michael Kerwick, his use of drugs, and his lies about where he threw the weapon.

"Sean Pica is a liar," Jim McCready would assert. "He had no interest in helping Cheryl Pierson. His only concern was money."

But the simplicity of that motive belied the facts. If Sean Pica only did it for the money, why then didn't he demand the cash up front, and why was the amount so low? Sean would say that money played no role at all.

"I felt I was the only one that could help," Sean would give as explanation.

One afternoon Sean sat with Martin Efman and tried to explain to his lawyer what drove him to go along with Cheryl's plan.

"They wanted it done before Thanksgiving," Sean would say. "Rob came right into the school. He used to go to the school so there was no trouble or nothing. I met him by the locker. He just asked if I was serious about it or not? And like that; I said. 'Yeah.' You know. He just said, 'Are you serious?' He didn't mention nothing about what I was serious about. He just asked if I was serious or not. I wasn't thinking too much about doing it. You know. Then there was another time. We went in their car. He wanted me to take a ride with him. We took a ride to Cheryl's house. And they wanted to show me the house and stuff. Rob was driving. We went in the house. They just were talking about doing it. She showed me his guns. She showed me his room. He had guns in the bedroom. Underneath the bed. In his dresser. The whole closet filled with all sorts of different guns. From Uzis down to shotguns. Automatic guns. Then Rob tried to give me one of them. The Uzi. It was in a closet in a case. He said, 'I'm going to leave it in the garbage can across the street. Then you just pick it up when you want. Tonight. Or tomorrow morning. Just take the gun tomorrow morning. 'Cause they own both houses. No one is going to collect the garbage there. Just take the gun tomorrow morning.''

"So what did you say?'' he was asked.

"Nothing,'' Sean replied. "Later that day in school, he came up to me and said: 'We decided that it's not a good idea because they could trace it back to Cheryl. So you're going to have to get your own gun.' Which I thought was fine because I still wasn't really . . . you know I was just kind of playing it off at the time.''

"What were you thinking about when they were talking about it?'' he was asked.

"I don't know,'' he said. "I was just kind of playing it off. Like it was a role.''

"Were you thinking of how you could get out of this?'' Efman asked.

"Kind of,'' Sean replied, laughing nervously.

"Like you were getting in a little deep?''

"Yeah. I wanted to get out of it without it looking like I wanted to get out of it. She'd ask me every day and like . . . I didn't want to tell her I couldn't do it. I didn't want to do it. I didn't want to let her down, kind of I guess . . . you know. Because I said I would do it from the beginning.''

Martin Efman had three psychologists prepare reports so that Judge Sherman could better understand his client's frame of mind. All three refuted the notion that Sean had done it for the money.

Dr. Honor pointed to Sean's concretized thinking, his highly defined concept of friendship, his tendency to see the world in black and white, his refusal to back out of a commitment once he made one.

Dr. Mirta T. Mulhare, who had been seeing Sean weekly for the past year, classified Sean as "someone with a Robin Hood complex, someone who had been searching for a cause, a test of his manhood, a rite of passage to enter the world of adult males.'' Dr. Mulhare said that in Sean's highly defined notion of manhood, "a man is not a coward; a man would not let his loved ones be abused; a man must demonstrate courage and strength in everything he does." She said that "at some very deep level" Sean viewed his father's departure from home as a sign of weakness and that Sean might have been making amends or indeed punishing his father by his actions.

Dr. Honor would say that "When he arrived at the girl's house he hid behind a tree for approximately half an hour. While he waited he thought about shooting the father. He states that although he had never met or even seen this man, he hated him and wanted him dead. During this time he thought of just leaving. Then as he was seriously considering running away, the father came out. Because it was still dark, he did not clearly see him; he saw the shape rather than the person himself. He raised the gun and shot him in the head. At that moment he was overwhelmed with feelings of hate towards the father; he just wanted him dead so after the initial shot he came up to him, in a 'frenzy' of hate and continued to shoot him until the gun was empty."

Both Dr. Mulhare and a third psychiatrist, Anselm A. Parlatore, had their own theory for why Sean Pica killed James Pierson.

"As Dr. Mulhare has suggested in her therapy session with Sean," Dr. Parlatore wrote, "it is most probable psychologically and psychodynamically that the classmate's father very well may have represented the negative feelings that Sean most probably had been harboring toward his father and also his stepfather, who he probably witnessed abusing his mother and also from whom he experienced abuse himself."

"Transference of anger against 'bad fathers,' " Dr. Mulhare concluded.

Their theory was that the father Sean Pica killed that cold February morning was not really that of Cheryl Pierson.

It was his own.

* * *

When Joanne DelVecchio went to see Sean in the Suffolk County jail after his guilty plea, she usually drove with Diana. Sean and Diana would sit and stare at each other and hold hands. They talked about how much fun they would have in the future, and only after she left would Diana allow herself to cry. But on this particular day, Joanne had come alone. She sat with her son on an uncomfortable bench in the prisoners' visiting area. Sean sat with his hands folded on the table.

"I'm going to marry Diana," Sean announced to his mother.

"Well, congratulations," Joanne replied to her son's news, smiling her hard-edged smile, thinking it was the only thing to say.

"How much do you think it will cost to buy a diamond ring?"

"I don't know," Joanne replied, thinking of the legal bills she still had to pay, of how Sean would probably not be free for at least eight years. "I'd guess around twenty-five hundred dollars."

"I got that saved," Sean said.

"She's a nice girl."

"Do men get diamond rings too?" Sean asked naively.

He genuinely wanted to know whether engaged men wore diamond rings on the forefinger of their left hand. Joanne tried to explain why they did not.

Joanne went home that night and had an argument with her boyfriend. It had been a tense few months, and they had been bickering all the time. Earlier in the day her boyfriend had volunteered to cook a lobster for dinner. Then just before leaving he called Joanne to tell her he was heading home.

"Well, what do you want to do about dinner?" he asked.

"I thought you were cooking lobster," she said.

"Where am I going to get a lobster?" he said with no enthusiasm.

"Waldbaum's," she replied.

Three hours later the boyfriend showed up with $40 worth of lobster, which he proceeded to throw on the kitchen table.

"You cook them," he said angrily.

"I don't know how," Joanne said with her familiar smile.

She had just gotten off the telephone with Ben and was in a bad mood. Ben had promised to take their youngest son, Vincent, for the two-week spring recess. But now he was bringing the boy home after one.

"Why?" Joanne's boyfriend wanted to know.

"I don't know."

"What do you mean you don't know?"

"I'm too busy getting yelled at by you to get yelled at by Ben," Joanne declared.

Life for Joanne continued by and large in that fashion for days leading up to Sean's sentencing.

On the night before Sean was to be sentenced, Joanne was feeling philosophical, realistic. She was no longer looking for answers or venting her rage. She had written Judge Sherman a letter on her son's behalf asking for leniency and, rereading a copy that night, she was pleased with it.

"Sean has learned his lesson," Joanne DelVecchio had said in the letter. She read it out loud. But then she looked up from the paper and wondered out loud if in fact Sean had. She still could not comprehend her son's lack of remorse, his inability to see that what he did was wrong.

En route to dinner that night, Joanne parked her car in a restaurant parking lot. A young couple emerged from the car alongside her with a small child. They bustled toward the restaurant.

"Happy family," Joanne said with contempt.

April 28 was a brilliant spring day, the kind of day on which the notion of freedom seemed all the more precious. James DelVecchio had arrived early. He took his seat, as he always did, in the back row and waited for the others. He was a striking figure. Tall, with long greying hair, a neatly cropped beard, fringe leather jacket, tan love-beads around his neck and dark glasses, he had a California surfer quality to him. He might have been a poet or a philosopher in residence at Esalen, but certainly someone who derived his aesthetics from the sixties. His movements were gentle.

As he sat there, watching the crush of observers who had come that day to court, there were many things running through his mind. Foremost among them was his one and only son; his namesake, Jamie, the boy he left when the child was two years old.

Jamie was already seventeen years old when Del-Vecchio saw him again. He had heard that his son was having problems in school. DelVecchio tracked the boy down, not unlike the way he had tracked down his biological mother so many years after she had abandoned him. He located the youth's school and one day went and asked his sons' teachers if there was anything he could do. After so long, the teachers said, it was best to just leave the boy alone. DelVecchio did. Still, he had a need to see the boy, just a glimpse to know the boy was all right, and one day DelVecchio showed up at his son's school and waited. It was early in the morning as he studied all the youngsters filing into the school building. Finally, there in the crowd, he spotted his son: tall, handsome, just the way DelVecchio himself had been as a youth. From a spot across the street DelVecchio watched, never saying a word, the way he had so many years earlier with his mother. The teenager disappeared into the school building.

It was the last time DelVecchio saw his son alive. One month after Sean was arrested for murder, nineteen-year-old Jamie committed suicide. His father would never learn why. Even as he sat in the courthouse, he was wracked with grief and guilt over his own son's death. He was still trying to understand how

Sean—sweet, lovable Sean, Joanne's middle child who was always so eager to please—could have committed a murder. He felt he was to blame for both ruined lives.

Virginia and Marilyn arrived together dressed for Sean's sentencing as if for a funeral. Virginia wore a black pants suit and Marilyn a black cotton skirt and jacket. Even their gait was slow, mournful, as if they were approaching a coffin. The two of them watched as Joanne DelVecchio entered the courtroom. She was carrying Sean's leather jacket so that he would look "right" when he approached the court. In all the many months the case dragged on, Virginia Pierson and Marilyn Adams had never said a word to Joanne DelVecchio. But both would later say that their hearts went out to her. What was worse, Virginia Pierson would muse, to have a son murdered or to have a son who is a murderer? At least Sean's mother could see her boy, Mrs. Pierson would say. Jails have rooms for visitors. All she can visit is a tombstone. Still their eyes avoided each other. Jim DelVecchio nodded as Joanne solemnly took a seat in front of him. On the other side of the courtroom Sebastian Pica sat with his wife, KarenAnn.

Sean was now brought into the courtroom in handcuffs. He looked over to his parents. His mother asked a court officer to hand her son the leather jacket. Judge Sherman took his place on the bench. It was now time for Martin Efman to address the court. He stood at the rear of the courtroom. Dead center.

"Sean wouldn't be here were it not for Cheryl Pierson," Martin Efman began. His voice had a soft-spoken, folksy quality to it, the voice not of an advocate but of a friend, a voice of reason. "She was the motivation and motivating force. It was in a classroom where the discussion was hatched. They were close acquaintances. Very innocently speaking about an article in *Newsday*. At first it was an innocent discussion, an idea hatched in the minds of two young people. I think he innocently decided to go along with it, but once the idea was set in motion, it was like a steam roller.''

He walked across the room as if he might be addressing a jury.

"Why would anyone like Sean be susceptible to an idea like this?'' he asked forcefully. "He came from a broken home with a loving relationship with two fathers but a lot of repressed anger for those fathers as well and a general problem with fathers. He had witnessed abuse in his own home.''

Efman continued as Virginia Pierson made knots with the handle of her purse and sighed out loud. Sean stood with a bent head.

"From Cheryl to Cuccio to Kerwick, no one said no. No one said this is ridiculous,'' Efman said. "Kerwick supplied the gun. Cuccio kept fostering. This was not Sean's plan. This was not his idea. Money was not the motivating force. Someone gave his word to Sean Pica and he had had that word broken to him in the past. This is not a murder for hire. This is not a murder for money. Sean made a commitment.''

It was a strange word to hear from the lips of Sean's attorney. It was the word Sean had so often heard growing up, the word that was synonymous with winning his mother's approval, with being a good father, with becoming a man.

Martin Efman asked Judge Sherman to show mercy to his client and to consider that Sean was only sixteen at the time of the crime.

"Is there anything you would like to say?'' Judge Sherman asked Sean as the young man now stood before him.

"I just want to say I'm sorry that this happened,'' he said softly.

The courtroom resounded with muffled sobs. Marilyn Adams twisted a tissue in her hands. Virginia Pierson wept audibly.

It was now time for Judge Sherman to render his

decision. It was the first time the public was going to hear what he thought of the case, whether he was moved by the events, by the backgrounds, by the facts.

"I have no messages to send to society," Judge Sherman said. "But I do have a message for you; something I hope you'll think about during the time in prison. You are not being punished for the loyal assistance to a friend. You are being punished for asking for one thousand dollars and executing him in ambush. Sean Pica, having committed manslaughter, is hereby sentenced to twenty-four years in jail with eight years of an indeterminate term."

Judge Sherman stood. Handcuffs were snapped anew on the young man's wrists. The metal echoed through the courtroom with the empty sound of finality, the same kind of sound as a prison gate closing, as dirt being thrown on a coffin.

"I feel sorry for his mother, but it won't bring back my son," Virginia Pierson said.

# 12

---

*He knew she was dying. He used to be so upset
all day sitting there at the hospital . . . Then
come home at night and do that to me. I
couldn't understand how he could do that to
me if he loved my mother so much how he was
just . . . I don't know . . . what.*

---

The Suffolk County Probation Department had begun
its inquiry into case #120045. They took into consid-
eration a wide variety of factors ranging from the
criminal's age and prior arrest record to the nature of
the crime itself, their own appraisal of the convict's
character, their sense of remorse—all to assess what a
suitable punishment would be. It is the one indepen-
dent evaluation a judge receives; a theoretically im-
partial assessment from men and women trained in
this field. Most probation reports get lost in the shuffle
of anonymity. Most are fairly straightforward.

But this report was about the highly unusual case of
Cheryl Pierson.

The interviewers spoke with many people. Ed Jablonski. Marilyn Adams. Virginia Pierson. Dr. Gary
Cox-Steiner, JoAnn Pierson's psychologist. Kim Adams, Marilyn's daughter.

But the most revealing information came from
Cheryl herself.

Cheryl was interviewed in the presence of Paul Gianelli and her brother.

She said it was during the long rides to visit her mother in the hospital that her father first began fondling her "private areas." Cheryl told them that initially she had welcomed these attentions because until then her father's interest seemed to focus on his son. So the time she and her father spent alone in the car was special time for her, and he began to pay more attention to her at home as well. Their relationship generally became more physical, and they would wrestle in a playful fashion and occasionally, Cheryl said, her father would "pinch" her breasts.

It was when she was thirteen, Cheryl told them, that she and her father had sexual intercourse for the first time. She was helping her father install insulation in the attic. She was "on a ladder." She said that as her mother's illness progressed, the sexual activity "got worse and worse" and was eventually so commonplace that they would engage in sexual relations while her mother was sleeping on the couch in the other room or even while her mother was entertaining friends. Cheryl said that she and her father had sexual relations in her parents' bedroom, where she customarily watched television in their bed. Cheryl explained to the department that until her mother died, her sexual contact with her father was primarily fondling and her masturbation of her father. After her mother's death, Cheryl told them, she had sexual intercourse with her father as many as two or three times a day. Asked about birth control, Cheryl said that her father kept track of her menstrual cycle and ejaculated inside her only when he felt it was safe. At other times, she said, he would withdraw.

"In May of 1985 she began dating Robert Cuccio," the report stated. Cheryl said that her father "liked" Rob but was also jealous of him.

"Pretend it's Rob," Cheryl said her father would tell her while she and her father had intercourse. "I would hate it." Cheryl said she began to notice that her father was becoming "closer and closer" to her sister, JoAnn. Now her father and JoAnn would "wrestle" and he would "spank her, kidding." JoAnn was now the one watching television in their father's bed. She did not, she said, want her sister "to go through that."

It was powerful testimony. Gianelli tried to persuade them to recommend probation for Cheryl.

Still the department was not moved.

"Unremorseful, totally dispassionate, self-centered, and immature" was their assessment of Cheryl Pierson.

"Although it seems likely that the defendant was abused, it cannot be substantiated," the report said.

Their recommendation for Cheryl: jail.

JoAnn Pierson was not interviewed by the Probation Department. Indeed, no one in preparation for the case was given access to the little girl. Clearly she had a story to tell. But Marilyn Adams, who was her guardian, said she did not want her to be subjected to the stresses of inquiry. Nevertheless, the little girl had something she wanted to tell the judge. She wrote him a letter. It was dated May 13, 1987. It was scrawled on notebook paper in large print complete with spelling and grammatical errors.

It said the following.

Dear Judge Sherman,

I'm the daughter of James M. Pierson, Sr. and the sister of Cheryl Pierson. My name is JoAnn Pierson. The reason I'm writing you is to let you know how I feel and so you know the truth and not lies. I was living at the house at the time and I really didn't see anything. Sometimes we would watch TV in my father's room. Sometimes we would fall asleep in my father's bed and he would go and lay on the couch. My sister often said "My father was always laying all over me." said my sister Cheryl. But she is wrong because I saw my sister always laying all over my father and sometimes she would say "oh Dad, I love you and start hugging him and start fooling around with my father. But I'll tell you right now she was a liar because I lived with her and my father always caught my sister in lies and she was a sneak. She would always lie to my father and father didn't like liars or sneaks. And my sister was both. My father would catch my sister in lies and my father knew she was a sneak. But of course my father can't speak for himself. THANKS TO MY SISTER. Sometimes my sister would get me in trouble, when I didn't do anything. If you're wondering if anybody is making me say this, your wrong. Because I am sitting on my lawn all by myself and writing how I feel.

> Thank you for understanding.
> Sincerely,
> JoAnn Pierson

Cheryl and JoAnn had the kind of sibling relationship that only accompanies family tragedy. JoAnn looked to Cheryl for love, support, security. Cheryl derived strength from the awesome demands of responsibility.

Hour after hour they were each other's source of solace, sounding board, confessional. They played with Barbie dolls. They watched television. They rented movies for the VCR and memorized the entire script of the musical, *Annie*. Cheryl tried out hair-styling techniques she learned in school on her sister. JoAnn entrusted Cheryl with her deepest secrets, she even let her read her diary. Cheryl saved JoAnn from her father's wrath and JoAnn did the same. It was a pact between sisters.

But now the pact was broken. Ever since the arrest, their contact was strained. Now that they were living in separate homes, they saw each other only four hours a week, usually on Sunday. They would walk through the mall, visit a local amusement park, try "to have fun."

"Cheryl, why did you kill Daddy?" JoAnn Pierson asked her sister one day when the two of them were alone.

"Because Daddy was abusing me," Cheryl replied. "And I didn't want him to abuse you. I wanted you, me, and Jimmy to live happily from now on."

"What do you mean happily?" JoAnn asked.

They were sitting in a darkened school parking lot. Cheryl had driven there so the two of them could be alone; so "they could have a talk." Cheryl had found out that JoAnn had written Judge Sherman a letter.

"Why did you write the letter?" Cheryl had asked.

"Because I wanted to."

"Marilyn made you write it, didn't she? I know she did. She's just fucking crazy and she's brainwashing you."

"I wrote that letter myself. I wrote it 'cause I wanted to."

"Don't you understand I did it for you?" Cheryl said, bursting into tears. "I did it to protect you, 'cause I love you and I didn't want—"

"I don't believe you, Cheryl. Daddy loved us. I loved Daddy. I hate you! He was my father too!"

The talking stopped. Cheryl drove her sister home to Marilyn. Then wept most of the night on Alberta Kosser's sofa.

It was a difficult summer. Cheryl saw her sister only on Sundays and with each visit the relationship became more strained. Cheryl continued her work at Mr. No Frills. Virginia Pierson had a stroke and almost died. Cheryl never went to see her.

Just a month before the hearing at which Judge Sherman was to decide how Cheryl was to be punished, James McCready was finishing up a night's tour of duty and having a nightcap at the Island Squire. Ironically, it was the restaurant where Cheryl's father had thrown his daughter's Sweet Sixteen, where the disc jockey had played the song "Sixteen Candles" and where so many had watched Cheryl's father take his daughter in his arms and dance with her for what was probably the last time. It was here too that Cheryl danced with Rob Cuccio to that same song one final time, and he asked her to go steady.

It was now nearly one A.M., and McCready had had a long day. He sipped a glass of Miller's and thought of that Sweet Sixteen as well as other things. It had been a long year and half since he walked up the snowy driveway of 293 Magnolia Drive and heard the name *Pierson* for the first time.

Still, as he sat there at the bar in the Island Squire, there were many things about the case that bothered him. He wondered if the loose ends would ever be resolved. Michael Kerwick still gnawed at him. He knew Kerwick was hiding something from the police, but he was not sure what. Had he driven Sean Pica home from the scene of the crime? Perhaps he had witnessed the first attempt. Perhaps he had encouraged Sean to ask for additional money. He had questions still about young Jim Pierson's involvement and felt frustrated that Cuccio would serve no time in jail.

But the thing that troubled him most that night as he sat there nursing a beer was Cheryl. Public opinion had turned against the girl. No women's groups had leapt to her cause. The entire police department was still skeptical, although now they were boxed into a corner. If they did not think she was sexually abused by her father, then they were letting her get away with murder. From the start McCready had been the only one to believe her, and now as he sat there he had begun to question himself.

It had actually been his wife, Judy, who initially raised the question the week after Cheryl's arrest. They had been talking about what should become of her and Judy asked him a question that, at the time, had seemed absurd.

"How can you be objective about this case?" Judy McCready had asked.

"Don't be ridiculous," McCready had replied.

What she was referring to was an incident that happened early in their marriage when McCready and his wife were taking care of a friend's four-year-old son. The friend had been called away on a family emergency and the McCreadys were looking after the child, who will be called Pete, until their friend could return. On this particular night the McCreadys were going to a Super Bowl party and had hired a babysitter they knew from the neighborhood who had babysat for Pete during this period once before.

"Do you have to go?" the child asked them as they walked down the stairs.

"We'll be back soon," McCready replied cheerfully. "Besides, that nice girl Ann is coming over to stay with you."

"Do I have to stay with her?" Pete asked. The question surprised them.

"You don't like Ann?"

"Do I have to play her games?"

"No, of course you don't have to play her games," McCready said, laughing as he gave the child a hug.

"Do I have to play the penis game?" Pete asked.

Jim and Judy McCready froze as if a bomb had just exploded. Judy McCready would later say she physically had to hold herself back from letting out a scream. She had already begun to cry. James McCready sat down on the steps with the little boy to make sure he had heard correctly.

"What kind of game is that?" Jim McCready asked cheerily, not wanting to frighten the child.

"That's when she pulls down my pants and makes me put my thing in her hole," the boy replied. McCready could barely contain himself. He left Pete at home with his wife and took off to confront the sitter. He felt to blame. The child was his responsibility.

All the way to Ann's parents' home, McCready remained calm. He politely knocked on the door. Ann's mother was sitting at the kitchen table with a number of her children. He told her that he needed to have a word with the woman alone.

"Oh come on in. We have no secrets in this house," the woman said lightly.

"I do think this is something we should discuss in private," McCready insisted.

"Don't be silly," the woman replied.

"Have you ever had problems with Ann?" he asked.

"No," she replied. "Why?"

"Because she molested our friend's son," McCready snapped, still maintaining his calm.

"Oh, that's ridiculous," Ann's mother said, totally unperturbed. "The child must be lying."

It was this accusation that an innocent boy had concocted this outrageous act that finally triggered McCready's rage. He stormed out the front door and slammed it behind him with such force he thought it might come out of its frame. He knew he had to leave because if he hadn't he might have done something for which he would have later been sorry. He only later learned that Ann had done a similar thing to the son of another boy they knew, but his parents had been too ashamed to warn any of the neighbors. He learned too that Ann had been sexually abused by her stepfather.

Was it because of the violation of this little boy he had promised his good friend to protect that James McCready had been so eager to believe Cheryl Pierson? As he left the Island Squire bar that night, he thought of Pete. He thought of Cheryl. It was deeply on his mind.

In the weeks before Cheryl's presentencing hearing—the hearing that would determine whether or not she would be sent to jail—letters poured continually into Judge Sherman's office, poignant correspondence from incest victims who empathized with Cheryl's case. Many pleaded with him to have mercy and not to send the teenager to jail.

* * *

"As a desperate and terrorized fourteen-year-old I seriously considered killing my father," wrote one victim. "I wanted to sneak up on him in his sleep as he did me . . . The idea that I'd be depriving my family of its source of income, and the overwhelming shame of having to explain his death made me reconsider . . . I decided that suicide was my best alternative. I tried."

"I am an incest survivor—a survivor who was silent for thirty-five years," wrote another. "Silent in words and action but not at all silent in the rage that lived inside of me—that still does. This silence, this knowing and not telling has affected every part of my life—my relationships, my self-esteem."

"The real murderer is her father who seduced, violated and betrayed his child's trust," wrote another.

"There can be no rational perception of reality because the child's experiences per se are irrational," wrote another. "The child is taught to trust no one in the adult world. There is no one and no place to turn."

"When Miss Pierson killed her father I thought as did many women I have spoken to that he was more than justly sentenced for his crime," wrote another. "He essentially murdered his own daughter. She is simply a ghost who has exacted a revenge of a sort. After what she has been through she is, you can be sure, no longer alive, physically or emotionally."

On the Thursday two weeks before the start of Cheryl's hearing, the television program "20/20" aired its segment on Cheryl. Paul Gianelli could not have scheduled it better if he had done it himself.

"20/20" directed national attention to a story that up until then had only a local following. Gianelli's hope: to create as much pressure as possible on the

District Attorney to back down from his quest to send Cheryl to jail.

The report itself was largely sympathetic and contained little new. But for the first time it showed the faces behind the names, a dramatic prelude to what was to follow at Cheryl's hearing.

It did something else too.

In a living room in Tucson, Arizona, some two thousand miles away, someone happened to be watching television that night; someone who had not seen or really spoken to the Piersons in five years. Paul Gianelli had hoped the broadcast would set off a groundswell of public opinion.

It did something far better; something that would surface in the weeks to come when it was least expected.

# 13

September 9 was a sparkling Indian summer day.
Through the second-story courtroom windows the trees
were still very green and the sky a robin's-egg blue.
Despite balmy temperatures outdoors, indoors there
was a draft that blew open the room's tattered beige
curtains.

The courtroom was packed. Friends and relatives
who had never appeared before in court made their
way past guards with metal detectors. Reporters and
sketch artists nervously waited their turn in line, hoping there would be enough room. It was a small courtroom not built to accommodate a crowd. Just three
long wooden rows. The room was abuzz with chatter,
expectation. At last Cheryl Pierson was to have her
day in court.

Virginia Pierson was there. It had only been three
weeks before that she lay on an operating table, the
left side of her body paralyzed by a stroke. She had
told her doctors then that if she could not be in court
September 9 to simply let her die. But there she was,
very much alive; somewhat pale and uncertain on her
feet, but otherwise looking fine, a white scarf around
her neck that hid the scar from the surgery that saved
her life. She had come to court that morning with the
fantasy that Cheryl would throw her arms around her
and say that she loved her and that she was sorry.

There was something familiar about the scene; the
high ceilinged courtroom was packed with people who
had seen each other over the years at Christmas parties

and funerals, now avoiding each other's glances, eventually picking their seats in accordance with what they believed to be the truth. Cheryl came dressed for the most important event of her life in a white blouse and beige skirt with a little pink ribbon around the waist. She had put on weight since her arrest. No longer the cheerleader working out every afternoon, she had developed chunkiness around the hips. Her face was more mature. There were many who said it: Cheryl Pierson was looking more and more like her father.

At precisely 9:50 A.M. everyone in the courtroom stood, and Judge Harvey W. Sherman, who alone would decide whether to send Cheryl Pierson to jail, summoned the proceeding into order.

Paul Gianelli began. An elfin figure, short, dark, with a purposeful gait and a pleasant, round face. His gestures were sharp, forceful; his hands as expressive as his speech.

"There are misstatements in the Probation Report concerning Cheryl Pierson's character," Gianelli asserted, standing at the defense table, looking down at his client, his voice somber. "The Probation Board recommended incarceration of an indeterminate nature. The witnesses will paint a rather vivid and realistic picture of the kind of life Cheryl Pierson was living several years before her father's death."

Judge Harvey W. Sherman nodded without expression.

Then it was Ed Jablonski, the prosecutor's turn. He cut a very different image in the courtroom: tall, lean, well manicured and athletic, with a formality to his demeanor. Jablonski could have been a drill sergeant in the Army. Where in anger Paul Gianelli had a penchant for moral outrage, Ed Jablonski favored sarcasm.

He stood now at the prosecutor's table and, holding a pair of wire-rimmed glasses in his right hand, announced that he would not contest Cheryl's claim that she had an incestuous relationship with her father.

"No one here can answer that," Ed Jablonski said, pausing for dramatic effect. "The only person here who knows for sure is the person who had her father killed. And you have to ask yourself: why? The situation we will hear about is a situation that is not that infrequent. As adults we know they do happen. We'll hear from the Police Department how frequently it happens in Suffolk County. But you must ask yourself: Why was it necessary for this one girl to do something that has never been done before in this county; never been done before in the history of incestuous relationships? Why did she decide to take someone's life? Why was her situation special? Why does she deserve probation, a mere pat on the head? Why was her situation different from all other incestuous situations?"

Alberta Kosser was the first to take the stand, and the drama of that moment overwhelmed her. Just the act of lifting her right arm and taking an oath brought tears to her eyes as she looked across the docket at the teenager with whom she had so frequently fought, embraced, cried. At that moment Alberta Kosser, a dark, pretty woman who had welcomed a neighbor's daughter into her home out of charity and out of love, believed that she and she alone was in a position to save Cheryl Pierson.

"How long have you lived on Magnolia Drive?" Gianelli asked Alberta. He could see how the witness was shaking. He wondered how she would hold up.

"Twenty-two years," Alberta replied.

Under questioning by Gianelli, Alberta described her relationship to Cheryl; how she and Cheryl's mother had become good friends over the years and how as a frequent visitor in the Pierson home she had developed an intimate sense of the family's life. What had always troubled her, she told the court, was the arrogance with which Cheryl's father oversaw his home. She described scenes at the dinner table in which the children were not permitted to speak and where obsequity was the rule.

"It would start with kidding," Alberta said. "He would pull them by the hair and . . . 'what do you say to me?' 'I'm sorry daddy.' "

"What else did you observe?" Paul Gianelli asked.

"Cheryl was always in the bedroom with her father watching TV," Alberta continued.

"Do you know what Cheryl and her father were doing in the bedroom?" Paul Gianelli continued.

"Cathy told me they were watching sports."

"Where was Cathy?"

"Cathy was on the couch."

Alberta said that there were many times that Cheryl's mother confided that she wanted her daughter out of the bedroom, but that she did not know how to ask her to leave. The few times Cathleen Pierson did say something to her husband, Alberta related, James Pierson would accuse his wife of being jealous. Nevertheless she and Alberta plotted one day to call Cheryl out of her father's room.

"Cheryl, you're a big girl," Alberta recalled saying one night when the girl had come into the kitchen to fetch her father something to drink. "He'll never see you as a big girl if you go to his room every night. You have a television in your room. You should watch television in your room."

Cheryl watched television in her room for a night or two, Alberta recalled on the stand, but then returned to be with her father.

"But if her own mother—" Alberta said, cutting herself off. "This is her house. I'm not going to say anything."

There was a limit, she said, to what she as a neighbor could say. After all she had discussed it with Cheryl's mother, now it was up to her. But there had been other things that disturbed Alberta Kosser as well. She recalled an openly sexual conversation that she overheard between Jim Pierson and his daughter about how the boys at school would want to get their "squantz in her." She also thought it odd how Cheryl would fre-

quently want to sit on her father's lap and in front of
company would rub his bare chest at the kitchen table.

Asked to put this behavior into some chronological
framework, Alberta said that the year must have been
1984, just before Cathleen Pierson's last transplant.
Alberta recalled how Cheryl's mother spoke about dying and how "it had to be beautiful compared to living
in this hell." It was the worst period in everyone's life,
Alberta said, because no one knew from one day to
the next whether Cathy was going to live. It was also
just about this time, Alberta recalled, that Jim Pierson
Jr. moved out of the house because he could no longer
"take his father."

Cathy was still alive and in the hospital, Alberta
recalled, when one night Cheryl and JoAnn came over
for dinner and JoAnn announced "Cheryl slept with
Daddy last night." It was a comment that was hard to
gauge. Alberta told Cheryl's mother about it the next
time she went to see her in the hospital and left it at
that. What else could she do? Occasionally she asked
Cheryl directly if there was something wrong. She
looked as though she had something on her mind. But
Cheryl would simply reply she was worried about her
mother.

"Did there come a time when you began to suspect
that there was sexual contact between Cheryl and her
father?" Paul Gianelli asked.

"Yes," she replied.

"Did you go to the authorities?"

"I did not," she said sadly. "I was afraid of Jimmy.
Always he was with a remark. I was tense. He got to
me."

Alberta described how during this time she had begun to see a psychiatrist. Although she did not fully
elaborate in court, there had been many stresses in
Alberta's life in that previous year. Her own thirty-
five-year-old sister died unexpectedly, and Alberta was
diagnosed to be a serious diabetic. She was so concerned at the time about Cheryl, she told the court,

she told her psychiatrist, who encouraged her to notify the authorities.

"Did you ever tell any authority?" Judge Sherman asked at this point with interest.

"No," Alberta replied.

"Did you ever mention your concerns to any member of your family?"

"I told my sister," Alberta replied. "I didn't think intercourse. But I'd seen the petting."

"Did you suspect intercourse?" Judge Sherman asked.

"I'd never seen it," Alberta replied, clearly uncomfortable with the question. "Maybe I blocked it out of my mind. To think that such a thing could go on. I didn't want to."

Alberta's anxiety with the entire subject was palpable and made the spectators uncomfortable. They shifted nervously in their seats. Paul Gianelli would later say she was not as strong a witness as he had hoped.

Now it was Edward Jablonski's turn. Just the way he stood and cocked his head, he was a natural performer. His diction was precise. Once again he twirled his wire-rimmed glasses with his fingers.

"Do you feel there were options open to Cheryl Pierson?" Jablonski asked with great formality.

"I don't understand," Alberta replied, shivering, brushing her dark, wavy hair out of her eyes.

"If Cheryl Pierson had told you that her father was abusing her sexually, would you have done something to help her?" he asked. His voice was soft and polite. He would save his theatrics for later.

"Yes," she said.

"How frequently would you say you were at the Pierson home?"

"Just about every day."

"Do you know what James Pierson thought of you?"

"I was polite to him."

"Did you ever ask him why Cheryl came to his bedroom at night?"

"Yes. And he told me because she had nightmares. I was quiet. I didn't say much. He didn't like people telling him how to run his house."

"When Cheryl would come over to your house for dinner, did you talk to her about things?" Jablonski asked.

"No," Alberta replied somewhat foolishly. It was hard to imagine she did not speak to the girl.

"When you went to the funeral, did you hear that speech that Cheryl wrote about her father?"

"Yes," Alberta replied.

"What did you think of Cheryl at that funeral?" It was clear where he was leading.

"I was just busy consoling her. She hugged me and kissed me."

"You had a lot to say to the family over the years, didn't you?" Jablonski began, his voice hinting at the sarcasm that would follow. But before he could continue, the judge interrupted.

"Did you see Cheryl in bed with her father?" Judge Sherman wanted to know.

"Yes," Alberta replied.

"Was the door open?" the judge asked.

"Yes," Alberta replied.

"Did they jump when you came into the room?" Jablonski joined in, seeing an opportunity to express the sarcasm.

"No," Alberta replied.

"They were wearing clothing," the judge stated.

"Yes," she said.

Now the prosecutor was interested in hearing what Alberta had to say about Cheryl Pierson's character.

"Is there anything bad you can say about Cheryl?" the prosecutor asked.

"No," Alberta replied. She wondered what he knew about the arguments the two had had; how they had argued in particular about her seeing Rob.

"Other than having her father killed, is there anything bad you can say about her?"

"No," Alberta said.

"I thought you might say that. Did you ever have a conversation with her about what she did and how she set it up?"

"I took her in," Alberta said in response. "I wanted it to be a normal household."

"If Cheryl had told you she slept with him, what would you have done?"

"Told my husband," Alberta said. "Take her away where she would have been safe."

"If Cheryl had said to you, I'm having a problem at home. Please help me. Would you have helped her?"

"I would have seeked help, yes."

"Did Cathleen Pierson look to you as a good friend?"

"That was a secretive household," Alberta Kosser said. "They never told their feelings. Here's the mother telling me these things and she doesn't know what's going on? Maybe I have the deviant mind."

"Was there any adult excluding the mother who had a closer relationship than you?" Judge Sherman asked.

"No."

"How many times would you say you had conversations with Cheryl Pierson about her leaving home when she was eighteen?"

"I can't say."

"Many?"

"Yes."

"And in all those conversations, did she ever say to you that she had sexual contact with her father?"

"No."

"No more questions," Ed Jablonski said, making the point he would make time and again. Cheryl could have told Alberta. She could have told so many people.

Michael Kosser, Alberta's husband, was the next to take the stand. He was dressed very differently from the way he was that icy morning he discovered James Pierson lying in the driveway. He wore a grey pin-striped suit, the same suit he had worn to James Pierson's funeral. He told the court he had been an auto mechanic for the Brookhaven Highway Department for twenty-six years and that he had known Cathleen and her parents—John and Helen Fleckenstein—since he was a boy. He was a tall, striking figure with a stringy mane of grey hair. His face was lined and expressive. His tone of voice was firm and self-confident.

"What did you think of James Pierson?" Paul Gianelli asked.

"I thought he was very crude. He was always smacking the children. Pulling their hair, punching them. To me there was no reason for it."

"Are you against hitting kids?"

"No, I am not."

"What upset you about the kind of physical violence?"

"I wouldn't want to be punched the way he punched his son."

"Did you ever talk to James Pierson about it?"

"Yes I did, and he told me it was none of my fucking business."

"Did anything happen that caused you to look more closely?"

"In 1981 John Fleckenstein came to my house," Kosser replied, referring to Cathleen Pierson's stepfather. "He looked upset, and I asked what was the matter. And he said, 'I hope I'm wrong. I think Jimmy and Cheryl—something is going on.' He said he had walked in on them. Cheryl was under the covers lying on top of her father. I made a purpose of watching after that."

"And what did you see?" Paul Gianelli asked.

"He was always pinching, pulling her hair, fondling her, making remarks like 'doesn't she have a nice pair of tits?' He was rubbing her bottom."

"How old was she at this time?" Gianelli asked.

"Fifteen or sixteen."

"And what did you do?"

"I was disgusted," Michael Kosser said. "I shied away. At first I thought I had the evil mind. But the more I looked, the more I saw."

"Did you ever consider contacting the authorities?"

"I didn't feel I had enough proof." Over and over proof is what the neighbors said they wanted; something tangible, something they could point to other than suspicion, something they could see.

Court broke for lunch, and reporters met with Gianelli in the hall. These late-morning conversations would become routine. It was when the television cameras got their "story" for the day, when the radio reporters went "live from Riverhead" over the all-news radio stations. The questions that day pertained to strategy and what was ahead.

"Silence goes hand in hand with incest," Paul Gianelli said as Cheryl was whisked across the hall into a small room where she could take refuge from the press until court resumed again. Reporters fired questions at her, but she only looked to the floor. Ed Jablonski had disappeared through a back door.


Judy Ozarowski took the stand. She identified herself as a friend of Cheryl's mother and spoke about how she, Cathleen Pierson, and Alberta Kosser would often get together as neighborhood friends to chat.

"I said, 'Cathy, that's not a normal relationship,' " Judy Ozarowski recalled she had told Cheryl's mother.

"What had made you think that?" Paul Gianelli asked, and Judy Ozarowski described a Fourth of July party in which she heard James Pierson summon his daughter.

"You! You little cunt, get over here," Judy Ozarowski recalled he said.

There was silence in the courtroom. Gianelli let it sink in.

"When you say that it was not normal, what were you thinking?"

"I was thinking that Jimmy is sexually abusing Cheryl. If I go to the police, what am I going to say? I think she's being abused? I let it go at that. What do you do? We had never come across a situation like that."

"You've heard of the Police Department?" Ed Jablonski asked.

"How do you go to the police with the assumption that you think a child is being abused?"

"Wouldn't it simply have been easier to have asked Cheryl whether she was abused?" Jablonski asked rhetorically. "If you had done something, if anyone had done something, maybe we wouldn't be here today."

He threw down his notebook.

MaryAnn Sargeant, Cheryl's friend from Magnolia Drive who had been on the school bus when she had seen James Pierson bleeding in the driveway, took the stand next. She was Cheryl's age, a plump young girl who expressed her anxiety about being in court with nervous, dramatic gestures. She told the judge she had known Cheryl since the eighth grade and that as a cheerleader she was very popular and that a lot of people liked her. But there was something always different about Cheryl Pierson. She was never allowed out. She was afraid to talk. One time, she recalled, she was on the telephone with Cheryl when all of a sudden Cheryl said she had to hang up.

"She said she had to take a nap with her father," MaryAnn would recall. "I told my mother and my mother wanted to call the police, but I didn't want her to."

Ed Jablonski asked MaryAnn if she ever asked Cheryl outright if she was having a problem with her father. She said she had not. He asked her if she ever went to enlist the assistance of a teacher or school principal to get to the bottom of the matter.

"No," she said apologetically.

Now Grace Sargeant, MaryAnn's mother, took the stand. A heavyset woman, she moved slowly up to the witness stand. There was something direct about her. Devoid of pretense, she was a woman who, before she even opened her mouth, seemed as though she could be believed.

"Did you ever think of notifying the authorities?" Paul Gianelli asked her.

"Yes. Once Cheryl had a black eye because she sent a Valentine to a boy. I really wanted to call the authorities but I let it ride."

"Were there any other times?"

"There were two other times. But I let my daughter talk me out of it. My daughter was over at Cheryl's house. They were spending the afternoon together and she came home and I asked her what are you doing back so early and she told me Mr. Pierson came home. And I said, 'So what?' And she said Cheryl had to take a nap with her father. And then I said, 'That's it!' I feel bad I never did anything. That bothers me more than anything."

"When did you first hear about James Pierson being killed?"

"It was at a quarter to eight that morning. My daughter called. She said Mr. Pierson was dead. I ran down there. There were two police officers. A man and a woman. And when I saw them I thought: Please God don't let it be Cheryl because he went after JoAnn."

"You thought it might be Cheryl?" Ed Jablonski asked, his voice booming.

The witness nodded.

"The police were there. As a good citizen did you consider telling the police a possible motive? Hey. I think I know who was behind this?"

"That was my own thing," Mrs. Sargeant replied firmly.

"Do you have an aversion to calling the police?"

"No."

"Have you heard of an anonymous report?"

"Yes. Sure I have."

"Did you ask Cheryl about the nap with her father?"

"No."

"And yet your first reaction when you saw her father lying in the driveway was that Cheryl had killed him."

"I know it's unbelievable."

"You must have had strong feelings."

"I did."

"And yet you never said anything to police," he said. He turned on his heels, shrugged his shoulders, and resumed his seat.

Lois Hunsucker, a friend of Cheryl's parents and the wife of the man who frequently went hunting with Pierson in upstate New York, was next. She spoke of her friendship with the Pierson family over the years.

"What was James Pierson like?" Paul Gianelli asked.

"He was like two different people," she replied. "He'd be sweet and pleasant and then bam, he'd go off the deep end." She said over the years she had become concerned about Cathleen Pierson's safety.

"Do you have reason to believe that James Pierson was beating Cathleen Pierson?" Judge Sherman asked.

"I saw black and blue marks," Lois Hunsucker replied somberly.

"Yet you remained friends with this man," Paul Gianelli said.

"Yes," she replied. "We loved his family."

Then Paul Gianelli asked Lois Hunsucker about the kinds of gifts James Pierson used to give his wife and daughter.

"Do you recall the Christmas before Cathleen died?" he asked. She nodded.

"Cheryl got a diamond bracelet," Lois Hunsucker replied. "Cathleen got a carriage for her Cabbage Patch doll."

It was just the kind of role reversal Gianelli was trying to establish.

Fred Hunsucker, Lois's husband, followed. He described an incident in which he tried to play a practical joke on James Pierson. Pierson was taking a shower, and from the basement, Hunsucker shut off what he thought was the hot water. In fact, he shut off the cold, and Pierson was scalded. Pierson got so angry he came out of the shower, got his gun, and put it to his friend's head.

"If you're going to shoot, shoot," Fred Hunsucker told his friend.

Barbara Pallas, Cheryl's godmother, next recounted how Cheryl's mother once confided in her how upset she was because a neighbor once asked "who's the wife. You or Cheryl?"

"I feel like there's something wrong," Barbara Pallas recalled Cathleen Pierson told her, referring to Cheryl's relationship with her father, but Barbara Pallas said she never pressed to find out just what that "something" was.

"My brother is on trial here," Marilyn Adams told a friend with disgust as court began its second day.

Marilyn had known it was not going to be easy sitting there. But funerals aren't easy either. She had wanted a trial. A trial, she thought, would finally uncover truth.

Marilyn Adams still could not believe that her brother sexually abused his daughter. There were scenarios she could envision. She could imagine him being crude with his daughter or even touching her sexual organs as part of a game. But she still could not accept that her brother would actually engage in intercourse with Cheryl and risk a pregnancy. He was too cautious for risk, too obsessed with consequence. She could see Cheryl as the seductress, going after her father's attentions in exchange for presents. Marilyn knew that he was strict and at times mean, but he was also vulnerable and devoted. She thought back to their last Christmas together, the Christmas during which Cheryl had asked her brother to find a hit man. Marilyn and James Pierson had had an argument that was so typical of her brother. He barked. He shouted. He threatened. He criticized. But then he broke down and cried. Marilyn Adams wondered whether Judge Sherman would hear about those tears, all those tears he shed while he watched his wife die. If he was in fact doing this to Cheryl, then didn't he deserve the opportunity to get help? Did he deserve to die? Didn't he deserve the same mercy from the court for which Cheryl was now asking?

"Cheryl ain't right in the mind," Marilyn Adams said. "She should get more than Pica. This child acted so lovey dovey with this father. You tell me this is a sexually abused child?"

Toni-Ann Macaluso testified next. She was a striking young woman in a short powder-blue dress that matched her eyes and accentuated her voluptuous figure. Had this been a televised trial, she might well have stolen the show. She wore spiked high-heeled shoes that showed off her legs, and her gait suggested a woman who knew her worth. She was far flashier than Cheryl. If she was feeling nervous that day, then it translated itself into bravado, because the way she sauntered up to the witness stand was more like she had just been elected to office than about to tell why she believed James Pierson had sexually abused his daughter.

Toni-Ann Macaluso announced that she was twenty-one years old, graduated from Newfield High School, worked as a teller at Northstar Bank, and was a former girlfriend of Cheryl's brother. She had had dinner with Pierson and his family several times. She described the Piersons as being "very different."

"His arrogant personality was intimidating," she said. "Mrs. Pierson was a very nice person. She was sweet and sentimental. Mr. Pierson was strong and overpowering. She took a lot."

She described how young Jim Pierson would always complain about how "nasty" his father treated him and how "he couldn't wait until he was eighteen and could move out of the house."

"When Mr. Pierson picked a fight with his son, what reaction did Jimmy have?" Gianelli asked.

"He did nothing," she said. At this point she locked eyes with young Jim Pierson in the rear of the courtroom and smiled.

Paul Gianelli now introduced a photograph into evidence. It was taken at a birthday party. It showed James Pierson holding a red bandana around his son's neck.

"Does this photograph represent the nature of the physical contact between Jimmy and his father?"

Ed Jablonski objected to the photograph's admission, but he was overruled. Toni-Ann Macaluso said that it did. She described how frequently James Pierson liked to tease his children and how the teasing often escalated into a kind of competition for control that made her uncomfortable.

"One time I was at the house," she said. "Mr. Pierson was a strong, very macho man. And he was smacking Cheryl. 'What's a matter. What's a matter,' he kept saying. 'You can't take it? You can't take it?' The only way he would stop was for her to give him a big hug and say, Ah Daddy, I love you and be all over him."

"Did you witness any contact between Mr. Pierson and Cheryl?" Paul Gianelli asked.

"Yes," she replied. "He would lift her over his head and his hands would go between her legs."

"In the vagina area?"

"Yes," she said.

Virginia Pierson gasped.

"I did speak to my parents," Toni-Ann continued. "I was uncomfortable with the situation."

"What did your mother do about it?"

"Nothing," she replied.

"Did you fear Mr. Pierson?"

"I was intimidated by him. His presence made me uncomfortable. He'd joke around and punch you."

"Just one other thing. What kind of relationship did Cheryl have with her sister?"

"Close," Toni-Ann replied.

Mrs. Pierson let out a sarcastic laugh.

"And why didn't you go for help?" Paul Gianelli asked.

"I didn't want to take a chance of becoming involved," she replied. "I don't know if I would have had any regrets."

"In all the times you were there, did Mr. Pierson ever make sexual advances to you?" Judge Sherman interrupted. It was an obvious question. Toni-Ann was an attractive young lady.

"No," she replied. He nodded.

The next witness Paul Gianelli called to the stand was Thomas Melvin, who at one time was Pierson's tenant at 288 Magnolia Drive, the house across the street where Pica had made his first attempt. He described himself as being thirty-three and a telephone installer. Formerly he worked for Pierson repairing cable boxes when Pierson was still in the cable television business with Kenny Zimlinghaus.

"He was always hitting his son," Thomas Melvin recalled. "He told me one story when he beat the hell out of him. It seemed like he lost control."

He then described how Cheryl often was the Melvins' babysitter.

"We knew JoAnn," he said. "She would come over and play. After the mother's death, Cheryl wasn't allowed to do too much. She wasn't allowed out of the house."

"Did you see physical contact between Mr. Pierson and Cheryl?"

"I saw the results," Thomas Melvin replied. "Bruises. A swollen eye."

"Did you ask her what happened?"

"She told us her father hit her because a card fell out of a book."

It was a point Ed Jablonski did not miss.

"She told you it was her father?" he asked, seeming to suggest that when something was wrong, Cheryl had no problem talking about it.

"All I remember she kept on saying it was nothing," Thomas Melvin replied.

Mary Melvin, Tom's wife, took the stand next and spoke of her observations.

"During the two years you lived at 288 Magnolia Drive did you observe what kind of person James Pierson was?"

"Yes. He was loud, vulgar, and abusive with his mouth and his hands."

"Were there times when he was also loving and caring?"

"Yes he was."

"Did his moods change radically?"

"They just changed."

"Did you and Cathleen ever have the chance to discuss her relationship with her husband?"

"She said she wanted to leave but was afraid what would happen to the children if she did."

"Did you ever see him strike JoAnn?"

"Yes. He struck JoAnn and Cathy said, 'What are you crazy?' We all were standing there. There was no reason for him to have hit her except she interrupted him while he was talking."

"Were there other times?"

"He'd like to punch her in the arm. 'Hit me back. Hit me back.' "

On June 30, 1985—about four months after Cheryl's mother died and a month after Cheryl's Sweet Sixteen—

Mary Melvin held a christening for one of her children. Mary Melvin's own mother was there and seemingly out of nowhere pointed to James Pierson across the yard and declared, "That man is having sex with his daughter."

Mary Melvin told the court she was shocked.

"And when your mother said that to you did you go to Cheryl and ask her about that?" Ed Jablonski wanted to know. It seemed a legitimate question.

"No," Mary Melvin replied.

"When you saw the black eye, you asked her about that, but after what your mother said you did not ask about the sexual abuse?"

"No," she said. She was not asked why.

Barbara Manowitz was next. A wiry woman, birdlike and intellectual in manner, she looked more like an archeology student than a resident of Selden. Analytical, directed, observant, she said she had known the Piersons for years—ever since her mother married Cathleen Pierson's uncle, Joe Nazar, after his wife Anna died.

She did not tell the court that day about the folklore that surrounded her stepfather. She did not mention for example that there were many who believed that Joe was Cathleen Pierson's real father; that when he discovered that his own wife could not have children, he decided to have them with her sister, Helen.

Instead she confined her remarks to her opinion of James Pierson and what she observed during the many times she babysat for the children at the Pierson home.

"Jimmy had a terrible temper," she said, describing how she watched him smack his daughter and send her flying into a wall.

"What did Mrs. Pierson do?" Paul Gianelli asked her.

"Cathy was a quiet person," she replied. "She sat there gritting her teeth but didn't go after him in any way." The image was a haunting reminder of Cathleen

Pierson's behavior as a little girl watching her mother attack her brother John.

"Did you ever have a discussion with him?" Gianelli asked.

"He made a lot of comments. About my body, what I might be doing with my body. He felt free to grab my behind. I didn't like it. He scared me. On a sexual level. He had no real regard for women."

She described how once when she was eighteen James Pierson drove her home after she had been babysitting for the children.

" 'You're a big girl,' " she recalled that James Pierson told her. " 'You're in college. You must have gotten laid by now. How does it feel?' He was intimidating. He enjoyed using his power as a big person. He felt he could get away with everything."

Ed Jablonski had only one question for this witness.

"Did he touch you?" he asked, picking up on the earlier question by the judge of Toni-Ann Macaluso.

"No," she replied.

Probably the most dramatic witness of the day was Cheryl's young friend Diana Erbentraut, the one who had gone to elementary and junior high schools with Cheryl and had gone to share her concerns with the guidance counselor at school.

"Is there anything going on between you and your father?" Diana told the court she asked her.

"What did she respond?" Paul Gianelli asked.

"She looked at me," Diana said. "And the look. To me she looked scared. It was kind of like, help."

"What did you do after this encounter?"

"I went to the guidance counselor. I went to see my guidance counselor. I said it was important. And she said, 'I don't have time for you now.' I went home. And my father said to go and speak to the guidance counselor again. I did. I said I think something serious is going on. Cheryl was beaten. I think something is going on between her and her father. Her response was, 'I cannot take your word for it. Cheryl will have to tell me about it.' ''

Ed Jablonski was hard on Diana Erbentraut, perhaps because she was such a powerful witness. Through his questions, he sought to show that one physical beating does not connote sexual abuse.

''Why did you assume something sexual was going on from the incident involving the Valentine's Day card?''

''The way her father was.''

''How was he?''

''Possessive. She could not stay on the telephone. He tore her room apart until he found a note she wrote. He would watch her at school. He bought her a lot of jewelry.''

''Tell me other things that delineated something sexual was going on.''

''Just the way they were in general. I thought it was abnormal.''

''A girl was beaten, therefore we know sex was going on?'' Jablonski said, his voice brimming with sarcasm.

Now Judge Sherman interceded. He asked the question in a less threatening and provocative way.

''Why in your mind did you think it was sex?''

''To me it wasn't normal,'' Diana replied, turning to the judge. ''Cheryl was never a bad kid. The door to her bedroom always had to be open.''

Judge Sherman complimented Diana for her courage.

''Of the fourteen adults who have spoken here in this courtroom, most of whom had suspicions, you are the only one who attempted to go to the authorities. I understand you are the only one who took some steps.''

She was.

# 14

On day three Paul Gianelli introduced a photograph into evidence. It was a huge blow-up picture of Cheryl and her father on a sofa. Mr. Pierson was barechested and clad only in sweatpants. He was lying on his back. Cheryl, clad in thermal underwear, was seated on top of his stomach. Without knowing what preceded the incident or what followed, it was ultimately ambiguous and inconclusive, more dramatic in size than content.

Then Cheryl's attorney called his next witness: a seventeen-year-old former neighbor of Cheryl's, Jennifer Budner.

Jennifer Budner lived two houses from Cheryl off Magnolia Drive. A pretty, dark-haired girl, she and Cheryl had been friends since junior high school. She told Judge Sherman about what happened in the Pierson home during the autumn of 1983 when, dressing to go to a pep rally at school, Cheryl had laced a sash through the belt buckles of her trousers.

" 'You know you're not supposed to wear that,' " Jennifer recalled James Pierson telling Cheryl. "Then he punched her in the face."

"Were there any other times when you saw him strike her?" Paul Gianelli asked.

"No."

"Were there any other times when you saw bruises?"

"A couple of times on her face and legs."

"Did you ever speak to her about it?"

"Yes, I did. I asked her, and she told me her father hit her for different reasons."

"When you knew Cheryl and you were friends what kind of health was James Pierson in?"

"He had broken his heels," she said. James Pierson broke his heels that day he fell from the roof in September 1983. It was about three months before his fortieth birthday and two months after his wife's mother died. Cheryl was fourteen. It was during the time the Piersons and the Adamses were not speaking because John Adams had refused to cancel his vacation in order to attend his mother's funeral.

"Did there ever come a time when Cheryl came to your home?"

"Yes. When my mother cut her hair. She'd come over for a certain amount of time for a haircut and then have to come home. She always felt someone was watching her."

"Did there ever come a time when you discussed the situation with your mother?"

"Yes. One morning Cheryl came on the bus and she was crying and telling me about an incident with her father. Her mother was ill. I talked to my mother about it. She seemed so scared. I didn't know whether I should say something or not and I never did."

"What did you think was going on?" Paul Gianelli asked.

"I did suspect something more than physical abuse by the way he treated her. I think he was always wrestling with her, smacking her on the behind and tickling her."

"Was there any experience that you had that would make you sensitive to Cheryl's situation?" Gianelli asked the girl. It was a pointed, leading question.

Jennifer Budner paused. She looked with pain over to the windows. It was as though she were about to reveal something very important, very private, very painful.

"My mother's ex-boyfriend," she said, her voice breaking. "Came on to me."

Jennifer Budner then turned to Judge Sherman. She explained that she too had said nothing until her mother and the boyfriend had split up.

"But did you seek someone to kill this person?" Ed Jablonski asked with sarcasm.

She shook her head.

"Did you ever tell Cheryl?" Judge Sherman wanted to know.

"No."

"You suspected it was sexual with Cheryl?" Judge Sherman asked.

"I was young and didn't understand what was happening," she replied sadly.

Donna Paccione, who had known James and Cathleen Pierson for years from the local bowling alley, testified next.

"I liked him as a person," Donna Paccione said of Cheryl's father.

She said she knew how dedicated he was as a father, how much he cared about his family. But sometimes, she said, that commitment to family bothered her as if it somehow could provide a rationalization for just about everything else. She remembered calling once and asking to speak to Cheryl and being told by Cheryl's younger sister, JoAnn, that Cheryl was "taking a nap" with her father. She thought it odd. She also thought the physical component to their affection strange.

"Cheryl always seemed as though she had to please her father," Donna Paccione recalled. "She was always leaning over his shoulder and caressing his chest. He was twirling his fingers through her hair. I didn't want to think it was evil."

"Did she do it spontaneously or did he request it?" Judge Sherman wanted to know.

"It was like: 'Come here by Daddy.' It was odd. You had to see it. It was like a routine."

It was an intriguing remark, as if the relationship were an accommodation, a quiet, almost comfortable arrangement.

"Did there ever come a time when you thought that something terrible might be happening?" Paul Gianelli asked the witness.

She said she did not.

"I don't see the worst until it hits me in the face," she said.

James Pierson Jr. was next. He was a witness from whom many had waited to hear. After all, he had been told of the murder plot by his sister. He lived in the house where Cheryl said the sexual abuse had occurred, but had never once gone to the police to report what he knew. Clearly he would have a lot of say.

He was a gaunt youth. As he walked to the witness stand, his long blond hair cascaded down the back of a neatly pressed grey suit. His voice was quiet, his diction refined. It was not what one would expect from the son of James Pierson Sr.

"You have heard testimony about your father and mother," Paul Gianelli began. It was true, he had. Although in a trial he would not have been permitted to listen to testimony if he planned to be a witness, he was permitted to do so here. As with many other aspects of this presentence hearing to determine whether or not Cheryl should be sent to jail, Judge Sherman cared less about rules governing procedure than obtaining information.

"Yes," young Jim Pierson replied, squinting as if to help him concentrate.

Gianelli asked Cheryl's brother about his father, and the youth replied that his earliest memory of the man was when he was five years old and it was "report card time." No matter how complimentary his teachers were, he said, it was never good enough. It was a "feared period," he said. If he came home with a B+, he would be physically beaten. Asked about his earliest recollection of his mother, young Pierson replied it was when he was about three years old and she bought him an ice cream cone.

"We'd play baseball together," James Pierson said of his relationship with his father. "He'd hit the balls over my head and watch me chase them." Cheryl's brother spoke without emotion. In fact, his voice was remarkable for its total lack of intonation. It could have been one of those mechanical voices from a computer. His manner was sincere. He gestured often with his shoulders and neck. But the voice itself was vacant.

"What was your physical relationship?" Gianelli asked.

"He hit me and I got hit."

"Did he ever show you physical affection?" Paul Gianelli asked.

Young Pierson paused.

"The only time I ever received a hug from my father was when my mother passed away," he said sadly with what was the first indication of emotion. He and Cheryl had been with their father in their mother's hospital room the afternoon she died.

Young Pierson said that he perpetually tried to please his father. But he never did.

"I wasn't what he wanted," young Pierson said. "No matter what I did, it wasn't enough."

"How about your mother? Could you please her?"

"Yes," he said. "By not upsetting my father."

Young Pierson described mealtime in the Pierson household in a way that was hauntingly reminiscent of his father's own childhood. The children, young Pierson said, were not allowed to drink until all their food was eaten. They were required to eat a little bit of everything on their plate in even proportion. They were carefully watched by their father as they consumed their meals. He studied them at the table. They were not allowed to speak. Frequently they were slapped.

"I still eat a little of everything on my plate," James Pierson Jr. said.

Young Pierson told Judge Sherman that when his mother took ill, she often fell asleep on the living room sofa. His sister Cheryl, he said, often fell asleep in her father's room. His father had a special security system installed that permitted him to lie in bed and know exactly where someone in a different part of the house was walking.

"How old was Cheryl when the system was installed?" Judge Sherman asked with interest.

"Fourteen or fifteen," young Pierson replied, turning to face the judge, his answer polite and direct.

Gianelli resumed his questioning.

"What if anything do you know about your parents' sexual relationship?" he asked.

"I don't know," young Pierson replied.

"What did you do when Cheryl told you she wanted your father killed? What was your response?"

"I told her. I went through it. Hang in there."

"Was JoAnn brought up?"

"Yes. Cheryl said that she couldn't leave JoAnn behind. I told her I went through the abuse. She went through the abuse and it would be JoAnn's turn."

"What kind of abuse did you mean?"

"Physical abuse."

"What did Cheryl say?"

"She would never leave JoAnn behind. She would take JoAnn with her."

"Who were you living with?"

"Several friends."

"From the day you had the conversation Christmastime and told Cheryl to hang in there. Between Christmas and New Year's, did you have other conversations with Cheryl?"

"Yes."

"Did you get concerned?"

"No. I just figured things were tense around the house. I went through the same thing. A few times I also wanted him dead."

Gianelli concluded on that note. Pierson had been a strong witness, stronger than Gianelli expected.

Later, on cross-examination, Ed Jablonski turned to the conversation Jim Pierson had had with Rob Cuccio about killing his father.

"Did you think he was being silly?" Ed Jablonski asked, his voice characteristically arch. "Now it wasn't just your sister but a college-age person. Didn't you think he might be serious?"

"No," Jim Pierson said calmly. "No sir. Not for the excuse they gave."

"When did you learn about your sister's other plan. The one with the rock?"

"On my father's birthday. January fourth." So, as James Pierson was slicing into the birthday cake, Cheryl was telling her brother how Sean Pica had tried to kill their father with a knife by setting off a burglar alarm in the house across the street.

"Here she is telling you about an aborted plan. At this point did you think it was serious?"

"She had been let out New Year's Eve. She went out, the plan failed," Pierson replied.

Now Judge Sherman had a question.

"Were you surprised there had been an attempt?"

"I thought they were just kids," Pierson replied, looking up to the judge.

"Did you know your father was intending to cut you out of the will?" Jablonski continued, his voice now booming from the rear of the courtroom.

"Yes I did. I told him I didn't care."

"You didn't say, 'Do that quick 'cause Cheryl's planning to kill you,' " Jablonski shouted sarcastically. The youth did not reply.

Now Ed Jablonski asked Jim Pierson to elaborate on the value of his father's various assets. He complied: The house at 293 Magnolia Drive, he said, was worth

$140,000. The one at 288, where the rock had been thrown, was valued at $110,000. The residence in upstate New York had a value of $25,000. The bank accounts, most of which were in the names of his sisters, were worth more than $200,000 in cash. The eight life insurance policies amounted to more than $130,000. The estate as a whole, he said, was valued at $600,000.

"Have you promised Cheryl she will get her share of the estate?"

"More than equal to mine," he replied.

"Will you pay the legal expenses?"

"Yes."

"Out of money from the estate."

"Yes."

Jablonski turned on his heels and resumed his seat at the prosecutor's table, but not until after he had made the point that with all Jim Pierson knew both before the crime and after, he never once went to the police.

If there was a moment that the spectators were awaiting it was a moment that happened without fanfare. It was out of order and sequence. It came on Monday morning at 9:50 A.M., the start of the hearing's second week. Everyone imagined Gianelli was going to call to the stand yet another neighbor; another witness who suspected something but never did anything because they never knew "for sure."

"I now call to the stand Cheryl Pierson," Paul Gianelli said simply, and this mysterious girl, not quite child, not quite adult, stood. Her white pleated blouse was neatly tucked into a grey skirt, the cross around her neck was neatly in view. It was Paul Gianelli's wife, Linda, who had selected the wardrobe. For months she had been sending Cheryl clippings from magazines and catalogues, circling A-line skirts and button-down shirts, boxy cardigan sweaters, flat pastel-colored shoes. The teenager's hair was pulled back with white barettes. Her complexion was pale. She had been instructed by her attorney not to wear even a dusting of powder.

A hush fell over the courtroom as Cheryl Pierson stood at her place at the defense table, walked swiftly to the witness stand, and for the first time looked out at the crowd—a motley group of spectators who had been anxiously awaiting her story. What she would have to say about her father, about why she could never tell anyone, about her building rage, about the inevitability of the murder.

As Cheryl sat there in the witness box, glancing first at the judge and then her lawyer, it was as if she knew it was her most important moment; the moment for which she had been waiting and preparing for more than a year. She had rehearsed it with her lawyer. She had gone over it with her boyfriend. She had stood in front of the mirror in Alberta's bathroom and rehearsed it on her own. But oddly there was one thing for which she was not prepared. The sight of her grandmother.

Virginia Pierson sat in the middle row as she always did, a kerchief still around her neck from surgery. Cheryl looked at Virginia Pierson. Their eyes locked for perhaps a second. Virginia Pierson was impassive. Cheryl bit her lower lip, and then her eyes fell to the floor.

"What is your earliest memory of your father?" Paul Gianelli asked. Cheryl sat up in the chair. Her eyes focused on him.

"I'm on a black minibike and he's teaching me how to ride."

"How old were you?"

"Nine or ten." It seemed late for an earliest memory. Had she no others?

"What was your mother's health like when you were young?"

"Okay."

"Did there come a time when her health subsequently changed?"

"Yes. When I was about eleven."

"What happened then to your family?"

"We grew closer together," she said, her voice muted but audible. "My mother was hospitalized from time to time at Mather Hospital and at Downstate."

"What happened when you went to visit her?"

"When we visited her in the hospital on the way there my father and I, we'd talk and stuff," Cheryl said, shifting in her chair. "My head was on his lap and he'd stroke my back and rear end. It started off like that. We'd go every day. He started putting his arm around me and had me sit close to him and he'd be rubbing my legs and chest."

"How did that make you feel?" Gianelli asked. He had approached Cheryl from the rear of the courtroom and was now standing directly in front of her.

"I just thought he was showing me affection, and I was just happy," she said.

Cheryl had to be reminded by the judge to speak up. Her syntax and accent were twangy New York, not as polished or precise as her brother. At this point, she seemed neither particularly vulnerable nor scared.

"What was your relationship like with your brother, Jimmy?" her attorney asked.

"Close," Cheryl replied.

"What was your relationship like with your sister?"

"JoAnn was like a little doll to me," Cheryl said. "I'd clean her room, make her bed, give her a bath, tuck her in at night. Wherever I went, she came with me." She spoke in what was almost a monotone, the same hollow voice she had had with her attorney in Alberta's kitchen.

"When your mother came home from the hospital, where did she sleep?"

"On the couch in the living room."

"Do you know why?"

"I would fall asleep in my father's room. She'd wake

me. And my father would say: Just leave me alone. I fell asleep. There's no sense to wake me up.'' Cheryl's nervous laugh was gone. Instead, she sounded wooden.

"How would you find yourself in your father's room?"

"He would call me: 'Aren't you going to watch TV with me? You have to learn the sport,' if I wanted to go to baseball games, if I wanted him to take me. I thought we had grown closer and that he wanted me around."

She looked down and now spoke in a soft, pensive voice.

"During the trips to the hospital when your father was doing those things to you, did you speak to anyone?"

"No, I didn't think anything was wrong."

"Tell the judge," Gianelli instructed. Clearly, he thought this point important.

"My father started paying attention to me, and when he started touching me I thought it was affection," Cheryl said with confidence. "I trusted him."

Gianelli studied Judge Sherman's impassive nod and immediately shot back his next question.

"Did you ever consider asking him to stop what he was doing?"

"Yes," she said. "I asked him why he was touching me, and he told me he touched me because he loved me and to never let any other person touch me."

"As you got older did the situation change?"

"The older I got, the more possessive he got. I wasn't . . . he went through my drawers and my pocketbook. He would start I'd have 'better things to do than write letters.' I had to go over to him and tell him I was sorry and have to lay there." She paused briefly. It was her first reference to their actually having sexual relations in bed. She sighed. "If I didn't do that he'd become tense. Just to make him happy I would do what he wanted me to do."

''What would he do if you didn't do what he wanted you to do?'' Gianelli asked.

''He'd pick a fight with my mother or get angry and take his frustrations out. He'd pick a fight,'' she said with disgust.

''And when you did let him do what he wanted to do?''

She hesitated for a moment.

''He was calm,'' she said, letting out a sigh. ''He was normal.'' She sat back in her chair as if she knew what was to come.

''How did you deal with the situation?'' Gianelli asked, his voice low as if he were a psychiatrist waiting for an explosion.

''Just lay there,'' Cheryl said, bursting into tears as if re-creating the horror. ''He'd breathe in my face . . . He'd look at me. I'd put a pillow over my face,'' she said, shouting as she choked on the words. ''I'd block it out . . . until it was over.''

Gianelli paused to allow the image to sink in: Cheryl having sexual intercourse with her father, a pillow over her face so she would not have to see his face. It was a point to which he would undoubtedly return. Everything Cheryl had said to this point smacked of such complexity. Her early acceptance of her father's tenderness, her mistaking pleasure and sexual awakening for normal parental affection. Her sense of betrayal. Even her depiction of her father: The sexual frustrations of a man watching his wife die being soothed by the affections of his loving daughter; perhaps losing himself in them and coming to expect them as her duty to him. Her own sense of obligation to satisfy her father and to keep the family's peace. It all had, as Gianelli would describe it, ''the ring of truth.''

Virginia Pierson and Marilyn Adams sat stonefaced.

Paul Gianelli continued.

''You sat here as Alberta described how she spoke to you about your relationship with your father,'' he said. "Do you recall that conversation and what happened?"

Cheryl nodded.

"I'd come out to get my father some club soda. And she said, 'You're getting to be a big girl. You should start watching TV in your own room.' So I did, and he began getting really mean. 'What's a matter, I'm not good enough to watch TV with?' There was so much tension in the house. I just went back."

"Do you remember Valentine's Day?" Gianelli said, referring to that February day in 1984 Cheryl's father punched her in the face. She nodded.

"I liked this kid, Glenn," Cheryl explained. "My father asked me, 'Did you get a Valentine's Day card for Glenn?' We were having a fight and I said 'no.' "

"Had you gotten your father a card?" Paul Gianelli asked.

"Yeah. I got him candy too," Cheryl replied with resentment. She then tried to explain that since the time of that first conversation with her father, she and Glenn had reconciled and she went out and bought him a card after all.

"He told me I was lying," Cheryl said. "And I was a slut. I explained that I would throw it out. All the way home, he was hitting me hard. I fell down and he told me to get back in the car. He told my mother that I lied."

Paul Gianelli then asked Cheryl about her conversations on the telephone, and she told about how her father used to listen in on them with a special blue telephone he kept in the basement.

"Do you have any recollection of your mother's last illness?" Gianelli asked, referring to the period in January of 1985 when Cathleen Pierson was admitted to Downstate Medical Center with pneumonia.

"Yes," Cheryl replied. "She couldn't breathe. My father called Alberta. Me and Alberta dressed. She was crying. She was in pain."

Not long after she fell into a coma, and died on

February 13 at the age of thirty-eight. The day before Valentine's Day.

"When your mother was alive and your father was touching you, do you in any way feel that your mother knew what was going on?"

Cheryl leaned back in the chair.

"I knew that she had arguments sometimes with him that me and my father were too close," Cheryl said. Her voice was pensive.

"And after your mother's death?"

"I really didn't think she knew until . . ." Cheryl's voice trailed off as if the thought she was about to express was so private it was unfair to be required to say it out loud. "When she was sick and in a coma, when he'd start touching me. I said, 'I don't believe you! Your wife's in the hospital and she's in a coma and you're touching me!' And he's like: 'Don't you ever play a guilt trip on me!' "

She paused then finally blurted the answer.

"I figured if she was in heaven, she would be watching us." Cheryl was sobbing now.

The courtroom observers were mesmerized by the testimony. So it was not until her mother died that Cheryl thought her mother knew what was going on. With each question, another layer of Cheryl's tortured mind was being exposed. Cheryl said that when she lay in bed with her father, she always lay on her mother's side and that after her mother died, she became convinced that her mother was looking down at the two of them.

"I felt she was mad at me," Cheryl said as she lapsed into an imitation of her father. " 'What's a matter you afraid she's watching?' I felt she was watching and I had to care after my sister. I had to make it up to her.' "

At this point the judge asked a question. Until now he had listened intently to what Cheryl had to say. But did not so much as nod.

"Do you think your father felt guilty touching you?" Judge Sherman asked.

"Yes, I personally think that," Cheryl replied. The formality of her reply seemed incongruous.

Judge Sherman nodded.

Gianelli kept up the momentum. By now it was clear his strategy was to demonstrate the growing pressures on Cheryl to defend her younger sister.

"After your mother died, did you meet a new boy?"

"Yes," Cheryl replied proudly. "Rob Cuccio."

"Did your father meet Rob?"

"Rob came up and asked me to be square dance partners in gym. I asked him to my Sweet Sixteen."

"How did your father and Rob get along?"

"Good. Because my father didn't like Glenn," Cheryl said.

"The night of my Sweet Sixteen Rob asked me to go steady. That night I told my father. And he's like: 'what are you going to say?' But every time I had a date with Rob, my father tried to start a fight."

"After your mother died did you and your father have sex more or less frequently?"

"A lot more," she said.

"More frequently?" Judge Sherman asked.

"Could you tell the judge how often your father touched you?" Gianelli asked. He could tell the judge was listening closely.

"After my mother died at first it wasn't that much," Cheryl said, turning to face Judge Sherman directly. "We had a lot of company. He made me stay home from school. But then when the company left, it was a couple of times a day. I was afraid to go into the shower by myself. He used to try to prove . . ." Once again she was about to lapse into an imitation. " 'Be more affectionate with me. Tell me you love me.' "

It was time once again to shift gears. Gianelli was now about to lay the groundwork for the mounting motivation for the crime.

"In September 1985 did Jimmy come back home to live for a while?"

"Yes. At first I was happy he was home because my father did not have sex with me as much, but then he got a job from 9 P.M. until 7 A.M. He worked and he would be sleeping all day."

"In September 1985 were you still having a relationship with Rob?"

"From August to September I didn't see him, but in October he came up to me in school and we started seeing each other again."

Cheryl told the judge that when Rob returned to her life, her father called Rob aside one night and told him that if he ever touched his daughter he would "break both his legs." It was the kind of statement many men of a certain generation and style would make to protect their daughters. However, she then described an evening when Rob, her sister, and her father were eating ice cream in the Pierson living room and watching television.

"My father said, 'Get us napkins,' and I gave Rob his napkin first. He punched me in the face because I didn't give him his napkin first. Rob just left."

"In September 1985 when you went back to school, what was the situation between you and your father at home?" Gianelli asked, once again directing the narrative to express Cheryl's growing rage.

"For him to be nice to Rob I had to be nice to my father."

"Did you have to pay a price?"

"Yes."

"Was Rob the first boy you were allowed to go out with?"

"Yes."

"Now going back to your childhood," Gianelli said. "Had your father ever touched you before the trips to the hospital? Before the trips to the hospital did the two of you wrestle?"

"Yes," Cheryl declared.

"Before or after your mother got sick?"

"Before."

"What were the wrestling maneuvers like?"

"My father would punch me and I would punch him back. He threw me around, and when I got older he'd pinch my chest."

"What was your father's relationship with JoAnn after your mother died?"

"As I went back to school and made the cheerleading team and went to games I came home and found her with her head on his chest and they were watching TV like I used to do."

"When you saw your father and JoAnn becoming closer, what did you think about?" Gianelli asked.

"At first I was mad she was sitting there. I remember thinking 'no need.' I would tell her to get ready for bed. Then I would go to his room."

Here Cheryl sounded almost like a rejected lover, wanting to reassert herself. Or was it the role of protective mother she had assumed; the role her own mother never played for her.

Paul Gianelli now asked Cheryl to tell Judge Sherman about that fateful day in November 1985—just nine months after her mother died—that day Cheryl found herself in her homeroom at Newfield High School discussing a story in that morning's newspaper, a story in fact she herself had never read.

"I was in my homeroom and Sean Pica right in front of me was talking about the Beverly Wallace case, who hired someone to kill her husband because he sexually abused her," Cheryl began, launching into a reenactment of their conversation. " 'Who would do that?' 'I would if the money was right.' 'Well, how much money would you want?' 'One thousand dollars.' And we left it at that. I told him I knew someone who wanted it done for one thousand dollars. A couple of days later I told him it was me."

It was strange hearing Cheryl's description. It was almost verbatim how she described it more than a year before. Was it that she recalled it so vividly, or was it so well rehearsed that the expressions, inflections were unchanged?

"Did you think about what you were asking Sean to do?" Gianelli asked.

"I thought my father wouldn't have sex with me anymore, that it would end," she replied, her voice even, almost cold, its robotlike quality bespeaking a chilling pragmatism. "It didn't seem serious. It was more like a game. I was crying. I told him he could set an alarm off."

"Did you tell him why?" the judge asked.

"No."

"Did you ever feel that the game was getting more serious?"

"One day Sean came up to me. 'I have to talk to you. I threw a brick through the window, and the alarm didn't go off.' And I said, 'Do me a favor and forget it.' I thought my father would kill him." So Cheryl was saying to him it was only "a game." She never believed Sean would do it and in the end she was more concerned that Sean would get killed than her father. Gianelli made no mention of Cheryl taking Sean Pica home with her one day and showing him her father's guns. Nor did Cheryl Pierson volunteer this information.

"In December did you have a conversation with Rob Cuccio?"

At this point Judge Sherman interrupted. He had another question he wanted answered first.

"Remember Beverly Wallace? Had you talked to Rob about it at all?"

"No," Cheryl replied. Then Cheryl replied to her lawyer's question and told Judge Sherman about how one day in December Rob called her and said he wanted to speak to her.

"I have to talk to you," Cheryl recalled Rob told her. "Oh God. He's going to break up with me again. 'Is it all right if I go over to Rob's house for a couple of hours. He's breaking up with me again.' " Cheryl recalled she told her father. "My father drove me over there," she added, pausing briefly as if to allow the judge time to consider the strange image of her father driving her over to the home of his rival.

"He sat me down. 'Sit down,' " Cheryl said, imitating Rob, " 'I have something to tell you. I don't want you to be mad at me. But remember the time I kissed you?' He surprised me from behind once. 'Who else did you think that was? All the time your father listens on the phone. You say you take naps in your father's room. All those instances I remember. Is your father sexually abusing you?' "

The term *sexually abusing* sounded awkward on her tongue. It was hard imagining that Rob would use such a phrase unless he too had read the article about Beverly Wallace.

"I said, 'What are you crazy?' I started to cry. He gave me a hug. That's when I told him about Sean. I wanted to see if Sean was serious. That's when he said to forget about Sean. That's when he said he would talk to Jimmy." Clearly these facts were inconsistent with the fact that Rob Cuccio had told the police he knew about Cheryl's plans with Sean long before he had learned about Cheryl's sexual involvement with her father.

Judge Sherman was interested in Cheryl's relationship with Rob.

"Was he having sex with you?" Judge Sherman asked Cheryl.

"No," she said. "He would try but . . ." Her voice trailed off. Her tone was matter of fact.

"What happened between you and your father between January and February?" Paul Gianelli asked, referring to the weeks preceding the murder.

"My father was concerned I was pregnant," Cheryl said sadly.

"How did you know he was concerned?"

"He knew when I had my menstrual cycle," she

replied. "He started looking for a clinic far away so no one would know."

"Did he actually call a clinic?" Judge Sherman suddenly asked.

It was a question for which Cheryl was not prepared.

"No," she said. But her manner was suddenly hesitant, anxious. "The one in Islip I think he said was best." Even the words she used were awkward.

"Do you know if he contacted them?"

She hesitated. Was she concerned that a record of such a call would have been kept?

"I don't think so," she said in such a way that sounded as though it were false.

"In February 1986 did you speak with Sean?"

"He said I should call him. I called his home. 'What do you want?' 'I'm going to kill your father tomorrow.' 'I told you to stop. Drop it.' 'No. Don't worry about it.' He said to me he's still going to do it. I called Rob at work. I was really upset. 'He said he would before so forget it. Don't worry about it. He's just trying to get your attention.' "

"What happened the next day?" Gianelli asked.

"My father woke me up. I was late the day before. I fell back asleep. I was making my bed. The dog was crying. I opened the blinds of the screen door and I saw him. I got my sweat jacket. There was blood all over. I started banging on the door. Everyone came running out. He was laying there, and I didn't know what happened. And they said he just slipped. I have to tell my sister. I woke up my sister. 'Relax. He's going to be okay.' The police officer told us our father had died. My sister hugged me. She asked, 'Does this mean I can wear nail polish?' My aunt was shaking me. 'Who did this?' Then I hear this walkie-talkie 'gunned down in his driveway.' "

Cheryl said that a week later she was arrested and taken to the Riverhead County jail. She was then released initially into the custody of her aunt and then moved into the home of Alberta Kosser. She told Judge Sherman that she had been seeing a therapist twice a week and was now working as a beautician.

"Do you remember your father's funeral?" Paul Gianelli asked. His voice was quiet, as if it were building to a powerful crescendo.

"I remember."

"Do you remember what you wrote five minutes before the mass?"

"Yes." He was referring to Cheryl's eulogy; the words about her father that had made so many that day weep, the words that so many had thought true, words that spoke of his being a mother and father, about his being his children's "best friend."

"What you wrote. Was it the truth or was it something else?"

"It is what I wished my father would have been," Cheryl said.

# 15

Cheryl's cross-examination would wait to accommodate the schedule of Dr. Jean Goodwin, who flew in from Milwaukee to testify on Cheryl's behalf. A Harvard-trained psychiatrist and professor of psychiatry at the Medical College of Wisconsin, Dr. Goodwin was a nationally renowned expert on child sexual abuse and the author of a widely respected textbook entitled *Sexual Abuse, Incest Victims, and Their Families*. She had interviewed Cheryl and her brother, spoken at length with Cheryl's therapist, and had been hired by the defense to share her impressions.

She was a petite woman with blunt-cut shoulder-length hair and wide, intelligent eyes. She had a small, nonthreatening voice that made technical terms sound almost friendly. Her polite, informative manner exuded precision.

"In my opinion," Dr. Goodwin began in her quiet schoolgirl voice, "Cheryl was subjected to emotional, physical, and sexual abuse."

If Cheryl's testimony was raw data for the judge to digest, Dr. Jean Goodwin's would present an analysis; a lesson in the intricate psychodynamics of incest and what it does to the mind. Dr. Goodwin had also submitted a psychological report to the court discussing her findings.

It was Cheryl's psychological state at the time of the crime that Dr. Goodwin addressed first and what drove the teenager to thoughts of murder.

"My diagnosis is posttraumatic stress syndrome,"

Dr. Goodwin said, explaining that it is a psychological condition that results from experiencing stress outside the range of normal experience. Its symptoms, she said, include fear, flashbacks, coping mechanisms, anger, isolation, and sleep disorders.

"And were those symptoms present?" Judge Sherman asked.

"Oh, yes," Dr. Goodwin replied with conviction, sliding back in her chair. "One thing apparent is how easy it is to startle Cheryl. It happened, for example, when a roommate touched her while she was sleeping. Cheryl hit her. I had given her a self-report questionnaire and it was high on anxiety, depression, hostility."

"Was there anxiety because she was under indictment for murder?" Judge Sherman wanted to know.

"Sure," Dr. Goodwin replied cheerfully, but then without missing a beat resumed her highly clinical description of Cheryl's symptoms.

"The easy-startle response," she said. "And specific phobias were consistent with the diagnosis. She is terrified of being in the shower still. She has to force herself to do it. She was often bent over the toilet or in the shower when he would penetrate her. She remains afraid to be alone in the dark. There were many things she backed away from: She has difficulty making friends, although it is hard to distinguish whether this stemmed from childhood abuse or her legal situation. She had difficulty having an orgasm until after her father's death. Anger control is another aspect. She complains that she is chronically angry. She has had episodic loss of controls. Temper tantrums. The repetitions of trauma she had in nightmares and flashbacks."

Dr. Goodwin now cited one of Cheryl's flashbacks. "She reports: 'My mother started watching while my father is doing sexual things. I ask for forgiveness but she never wants to see me again.' "

Judge Sherman seemed fascinated with the information. Paul Gianelli let his witness continue.

The next concept Dr. Goodwin introduced was in some ways the most illuminating with respect to what precisely was going on in Cheryl's mind when she asked Sean to kill her father. The words Dr. Goodwin used were *depersonalization* and *derealization*, highly complex coping mechanisms that she said Cheryl, like so many victims of incest, developed to emotionally distance herself from what was going on in her daily life.

"She tried to numb out by not being present in her own body," Dr. Goodwin said. "She would do this when she put a pillow over her head. The derealization is not being able to feel reality; not being able to tell what was really real, what people really mean. That explains her perplexity about the murder plot. Was it something she and Sean thought was really going to happen or just something they were talking about and the talking made her feel better?"

It was an intriguing notion: that just talking about her father's murder provided a release for Cheryl. It appeared to bolster the teenager's own contention that her overtures to Sean Pica were all "just talk" and she did not "really believe" he would kill her father.

"Did she have a hard time understanding the consequences?" Paul Gianelli asked, now interrupting his witness for the first time.

"Many things to her are not really real," Dr. Goodwin replied, once again underscoring Cheryl's rich fantasy life.

Dr. Goodwin explained that Cheryl's cognitive and emotional development was trapped at a young developmental age and that she only had limited capacity for empathy, good judgment, and being able to abstract. The only thing that concerned Cheryl and what helped permit her to function was "what am I feeling now?"

"When one is under extreme degree of emotional

distress,'' Dr. Goodwin explained, ''such as when one has a toothache or is in labor, the attention narrows and it is difficult to plan. One is concerned about how to get through the next hour or next night. Her sense of consequentiality was limited.''

''Consequentiality is a problem for judges dealing with young people,'' Judge Sherman said, interrupting the witness, but clearly intrigued by what Dr. Goodwin had to say. ''What was Cheryl's ability to abstract?''

''It was limited,'' Dr. Goodwin replied.

''Was Cheryl having flashbacks?'' Paul Gianelli asked, returning again to the specific symptoms of posttraumatic stress.

''Yes,'' Dr. Goodwin said. ''The first was with her mother. She heard her mother's voice. She talked to her mother. She felt her mother's presence. She felt her mother was observing her. There was one episode in jail. It was not a psychotic experience but an intense flashback experience.''

Dr. Goodwin elaborated on this and other symptoms in her psychiatric report. She mentioned, for example, how after the death of her mother, Cheryl developed an ''imaginary companionship'' with the image of her dead mother and told Dr. Goodwin that ''I used to pray to her . . . tell her I was sorry for what me and my father were doing . . . and scream at her . . . and throw things.'' ''After her father's death,'' Dr. Goodwin wrote in her report, ''Cheryl had several 'flashbacks' in which she believed she saw him. She had difficulty integrating her own feelings ('One minute I'd . . . hate him. Next minute I'd stick up for him.'). She felt she was losing control of her hostility and had rage outbursts with her sister.''

''She slept only four hours a day,'' Dr. Goodwin continued. ''She was busy cheerleading and taking care of JoAnn. She was also trying to contend with and control her father's depression and anger.''

''As a result of the condition Cheryl Pierson was

suffering, what was her level of participation in her conversations with Rob Cuccio and Sean Pica?'' Paul Gianelli asked. At last there would be some professional assessment of Cheryl's frame of mind at the time she was devising the murder plot. Clearly, it was his intention to show that her participation was minimal.

''I think it is important to understand that revenge fantasies are almost universal to victims of posttraumatic stress disorder,'' Dr. Goodwin replied. ''And that is part of the internal armament that is developed to help go through this emotional disturbance. Whenever incest victims are asked specifically about revenge, everyone always will have thought about what they would have done to strike back.''

''Are these waking fantasies?'' Judge Sherman asked.

''Yeah,'' Dr. Goodwin replied politely, informally as if she were addressing a student in class. Then she quickly resumed her response to Gianelli's question. ''Because of the fears of physical retaliation. And her fears of her sister becoming involved and the kind of commandment Cheryl was left with to protect her sister, a safe release for Cheryl was being able to talk about revenge fantasies obliquely without recalling the facts of her situation.''

''What was her level of participation as an accomplice or coconspirator?'' Gianelli asked.

''Objection!'' shouted Jablonski, who up until now had said nothing. He complained that Dr. Goodwin was only in a position to give her medical opinion, not her legal opinion. Still Judge Sherman, clearly taken with what the witness had to say, permitted Dr. Goodwin to reply.

''Severe posttraumatic symptoms would have interfered with her ability to understand during her conversations with Pica, Cuccio, and her brother.''

''This desire for revenge—is that a motivation for actions?'' Judge Sherman asked.

"Yes," she replied.

"Is this unique or is it present with other incest victims?"

"Universal," Dr. Goodwin replied with authority.

"Do you have an opinion about her mental capacity to pursue other options and her fears about the sexual abuse of her sister?" Gianelli asked.

"As a means of self-protection, there is a learned helplessness," Dr. Goodwin replied, now introducing yet another concept about the interfamily dynamic between an incest victim and her father. She cited the research of Dr. Roland Summit, a nationally renowned psychiatrist who has written extensively about posttraumatic stress syndrome and a victim's inability to see alternatives. She said that Dr. Summit had coined the phrase *incest accommodating syndrome*, in which a victim of sexual abuse is taught by the abuser "first to minimize" the horror of the experience and then "to see herself as being responsible" for the behavior. Dr. Goodwin said that the child victim of sexual abuse no longer sees herself as "being compliant," but as being "totally responsible." She feels entirely to blame.

"To ask for help," Dr. Goodwin said, explaining why it is so difficult for a victim to come forward, why so many remain silent, "is to indict herself."

"There is a narrowing of options," Dr. Goodwin continued. "In infant victims of child abuse, they develop a response of frozen watchfulness. The child watches in an immobile state. Their world narrows to themselves and the perpetrators, keeping the next hit from happening or the next sexual encounter from happening. They don't have the resources to look outward. Many perpetrators fit the paranoid pattern. They see the rest of the world out to get them. People who grew up in an environment tend to develop that view as well. They see the perpetrator as more powerful than he really is and see the rest of the world as more hostile and less easy to communicate with."

"Did you hear the options that Cheryl Pierson did consider?"

"The options she considered are typical," Dr. Goodwin replied. "It is not clear what percentage of incest victims report the abuse. Of the twenty-five victims I now see, two did report and those victims were removed from the home temporarily. Cheryl did consider suicide, although she would have had to kill him too to protect her sister."

Dr. Goodwin's observations sounded so matter-of-fact.

"Was the fear of potential sexual abuse of her sister a real fear or one brought about by the posttraumatic stress syndrome?" Paul Gianelli asked.

"The image of her sister sitting beside her father in the car set off her own intrusive memories," Dr. Goodwin replied. "But statistically, in forty percent of the cases the perpetrator will start abusing the younger sister."

The court now broke for lunch. It had been an exhausting morning. As she had been from the start, Cheryl was led into the small room where she could be alone with her brother. After side-stepping the crush of cameras, Gianelli closed the door.

A camaraderie had developed among the press corps. Lunchtime usually meant rushing for telephones, buttonholing Cheryl's attorney for a quote on camera, going over difficult-to-hear testimony, comparing impressions. For the first time since the hearing started, a sympathy was building for Cheryl, particularly among some of the women reporters. But still the question remained: Did incest justify murder? Should Cheryl be punished?

When court reconvened at precisely 2:10 P.M., Dr. Goodwin took the stand once again.

"Was Cheryl Pierson the engineer of this crime?" Paul Gianelli asked. Time and again Cheryl had said that she was never serious; that she had told Sean to "forget it," that their talk was "just a game."

"It is important to understand her degree of control," Dr. Goodwin replied in her little-girl but very analytical voice. "She had difficulty functioning as a daughter, as a sister, as a cheerleader, as a girlfriend. It is probable she had difficulty functioning in the context of these discussions. To characterize her as an 'engineer of this crime' is to misunderstand her basic sense of unreality."

"The probation report characterized Cheryl as being unremorseful," Gianelli said. "Is that accurate?"

"It is partially accurate," Dr. Goodwin replied. "She continues to feel she had to do something to prove to her dead mother that she did not enjoy sexual relations with her father. She continues to see that she did not have many other alternatives around for her father to exit the house. She continues to be terribly guilty about the sexual abuse and yet regrets the absence of her father. She is terribly guilty. So guilty of having survived."

"Is she 'totally dispassionate, self-centered, and immature' as the probation report states?" Gianelli asked.

"This dispassion is bravado," Dr. Goodwin said. "The self-centeredness is associated with a high degree of emotional distress. Her immaturity? She is immature. It relates in part to the development progress having been halted at age twelve when the sexual abuse began."

Judge Sherman now asked Dr. Goodwin a question that clearly reflected his own doubts about Cheryl's account.

"Are there cases you have handled where there has not been incest?" he asked. "Where the charge of child abuse was a fantasy? Have there been anywhere you concluded that the abuse never took place?"

Dr. Goodwin replied by saying that every evaluation is different but that in her professional opinion, with all her years of experience, she was convinced Cheryl Pierson was sexually abused by her father.

It was now Ed Jablonski's chance to cross-examine the witness, and he did not lose the opportunity to follow up Judge Sherman's skepticism.

"How many cases of father-daughter incest are you familiar with?" he began, his voice curt but polite.

Dr. Goodwin replied it was hard for her to estimate but somewhere around six hundred.

"How many cases resulted in a victim of the case committing an act of violence?"

Dr. Goodwin said she did not know.

"How many cases right after the sexual act did they grab a weapon?"

"I really can't think of a situation in which a female child victim fought her father."

"Any leading to death?" Jablonski was on a roll. His back was now to the witness. He was facing the gallery of spectators. There was pleasure in his voice.

"No," she said. "One girl burned her home. One girl's brother beat his father to death. I've never heard of a case like this."

"I guess you might say this is one for the textbooks?" Ed Jablonski said, emphasizing the last word, showing his sarcasm.

"You are here to assist me in coming to a decision," Judge Sherman said after a time. "A number of witnesses have testified that the father was a loud, boisterous, gross, vulgar, and intimidating man who exercised a lot of discipline. But my one concern is, was that not the explanation in this case without the sexual context?"

He had intimated before that he wondered whether psychological and physical abuse might have precipitated Cheryl's desire to kill her father and that her extraordinary capacity to fantasize might have invented the sexual dimension to her relationship with her father.

"If the question is, can one experience posttraumatic stress from physical and not sexual abuse? The answer is yes.''

"But the only ingredient is Cheryl's statements," Judge Sherman continued, underscoring his doubt.

"I look at five factors," Dr. Goodwin replied in explaining how she arrived at a determination. "The physical state, witness data, photographs, the profile of the alleged perpetrator; the fifth factor is the child's account of the pattern of the symptoms. And in this case they are fifty percent or better that the child was sexually abused.''

"So it is not identical to the physical and emotional abuse profile?'' he asked. "Have you heard anything here today that would change your opinion with regard to the fantasy and disreality such as the disclosure following the incident that Cheryl gave Mr. Pica four hundred dollars taken from the safe. Does that indicate disreality?''

It was the question that still concerned many. That Cheryl was so much in command of the situation that she thought of going to her father's safe just hours after his body was removed from the driveway to pay his killer.

"What I was seeing was a youngster who made a decision as rationally as she could," Dr. Goodwin said. "The death of her father was the only way out. She was so symptomatic that she was not able to act on that decision. So she was engaging moment to moment in tension-releasing communication rather than something that someone would describe as an engineer of a conspiracy. The plan was an abstraction, a concept. It is interesting that her brother regarded it not as a request but rather as a cry for help. She asked two people to kill her father. In November she asked Sean Pica. In December she asked her brother. It is the same girl, and her brother knows her best. And he knows she's just letting off steam.''

"Had she been luckier about asking someone else,

perhaps it might have turned out differently,'' Gianelli said. Dr. Goodwin agreed.

It was a staggering idea. That Cheryl's plot was just a strange, convoluted fantasy she had the passing need to articulate. Had Cheryl been seated next to someone else, who did not have his own need to seize her fantasy and make it concrete, the murder might never have happened.

# 16

Riverhead is about a forty-minute drive from Selden.
By the time court was over for the day, everyone was
so exhausted all they could think of was having some
pizza on the way home, going to bed, and starting
over.

Virginia Pierson said she could hardly sleep at all
during the hearing. Night after night, she would lie
awake and play back so many things about her son,
about Cheryl. She kept thinking of the two of them
going off to a baseball game, raking leaves on the lawn,
how attentive Cheryl was to her father, how "jealous"
she seemed those Saturday mornings Virginia Pierson
went over to the house to iron, the fights the teenager
had with her younger sister. The more she thought
about Cheryl and her claims the more she realized the
girl's responses "were strange" and that she was
probably psychologically disturbed and "in need of
help."

But there was no way, she would say, that she could
believe that what Cheryl was claiming was true.

"I raised him," she would say. "I should know. If
Mother Mary came down and told me he was doing
that, I would say, 'Mother Mary, I do not believe
you.' "

But there was another reason Virginia Pierson said
she could not believe her granddaughter. It was a reason Virginia Pierson never meant to advertise. Indeed,
it was something she had never before discussed. But
it had come out in a moment of rage; a moment when

she could no longer contain her thoughts. It was the real reason Virginia Pierson did not believe her granddaughter and never would.

"I was sexually abused as a child," she said, referring to her childhood in a foster home. "And I didn't kill anyone."

Ed Jablonski stood at the prosecutor's table. He had his list of things scrawled on a yellow legal pad. He walked up to the witness. Cheryl, dressed like a schoolgirl in a white skirt, blue and white striped blouse, and blue jacket, sat with her hands folded in her lap. She sucked in her breath and closed her eyes.

"When was the first time you asked anyone to kill your father?" Ed Jablonski asked.

"I think it was in the beginning of November," Cheryl replied, looking at him directly. Her voice was soft but steady.

"Did you ever indicate in any fashion on any other occasion when you were with Rob Cuccio, did you ever say, I wish he would drop dead? Did you ever say I wish he would be shot?"

"No," Cheryl replied, shaking her head but quickly adding that "after my father hit me in front of him I might have said I wish he would drop dead."

"Did you read that article? The one Sean Pica was talking about to the girl? Who said what to whom first?"

"Well, I asked what they were talking about and he says that a woman hired a police officer to kill her husband and I asked, 'Who would be crazy enough to do that?' And he's like: 'I would if the money was right.'" It was odd that Cheryl had thought a police officer had been hired to kill the woman. Is that what Sean had told her? Is that what she had heard?

"You thought that was crazy?" Jablonski asked, approaching the witness as he emphasized the last word.

"Not really, but I didn't want to admit it," Cheryl replied curtly.

"When you say something is crazy, does that mean you don't feel it was proper conduct?" Jablonski asked calmly.

"I don't know," Cheryl replied. She was pensive, tense. She leaned forward.

"At the time you said it, did you think it was wrong and against the law to kill another person?" he asked, standing directly in front of the girl.

"I guess it depends on the circumstance," Cheryl replied somewhat arrogantly.

"Do you feel it was wrong to have hired Sean Pica?"

"I do now. With a lot of counseling," Cheryl said. Clearly, it was a lawyer's response, a response she had rehearsed.

"Did you then?"

"I guess not."

Cross-examination continued.

"Tell us about February Fourth," Jablonski invited, shifting now to the night before James Pierson was murdered.

"Sean came up to me while I was leaving. I said: 'What?' Only please call him. I did. I was at the basketball game. I got him on the phone: 'What's the problem? I told you not to do anything.' He told me he had a gun. I hung up."

"Before the first attempt did you ever call his home?"

"I called him two times before the first attempt."

"You only called his house two times," Jablonski said, sounding incredulous.

"Yes."

"Did you tell Pica that your father drove a truck?"

Cheryl nodded.

"Now the next morning when you saw your father lying in the driveway, did you know he had been shot?"

"No." It was a fact that seemed astonishing, given her conversation the night before.

"Did it dawn on you that it might have been Sean Pica?"

"No."

"It never occurred to you?" Jablonski's soft, un-threatening tone had now turned sarcastic.

"No," she whispered.

"Did you go up to your father?"

"Yes," Cheryl said.

"Was he lying on his stomach?"

"Yes."

"Did you see four bullet holes in his back?"

"No."

"Were you standing over him?"

"Yes."

"Close to him."

"Yes."

"At no point, even given your prior conversations, did you think he was shot dead."

"No, I was worrying about getting him help."

"You did not want him dead."

"Not at that moment, no."

It was a dramatic exchange. Marilyn was weeping. Her arms were around her mother as the questioning continued.

"When you were told that your father was dead, did you smile?"

"I don't remember," Cheryl said. "I smile some-times when I get nervous."

"Did there come a time when Robert Cuccio arrived on the scene?"

"Yes."

"And at the point when they were lifting the body into the ambulance were you with Cuccio in front of the house kissing, embracing, and laughing?"

"No," Cheryl said.

Jablonski now shifted his line of questioning.

"The day after. Did you go to school?"

"Yes."

"Why?"

"To get some jewelry from my locker. And to find out if Sean really did it."

"Did you have money with you?"

"Yes."

"Where did you give Sean the money?"

"In school."

"Now you have sat here and listened how many people asked you if something was wrong. And each time they asked you, what did you tell them?"

"I said there was nothing wrong."

"There were at least two times when people asked about marks on you and to each of those people you said that it was your father who had done that. To either of those people did you ever say to them that you were being sexually abused?"

"No," Cheryl said.

"When you told them about the physical abuse, did you ask them not to say anything?"

"Yes. But I didn't want to tell anyone."

"So you figured it would be better or easier to kill your father than to tell," Jablonski said, raising his voice.

"I figured if I wouldn't get caught no one would ever know I was abused," Cheryl said with conviction.

"Now that you're caught you just don't want to go to prison," Ed Jablonski said sarcastically.

"I don't know," Cheryl said, breaking down for the first time. She was sobbing.

"Now did there come a time when you became pregnant?" Jablonski asked.

Gianelli said that he wanted to stipulate that he would have no objections to discussions about the pregnancy, but that he would not permit discussions about prior boyfriends.

Judge Sherman now turned to Cheryl.

"I need some clarification about when the abuse began," he said. "When did you and your father first have sexual intercourse? Before your mother died or after?''

"Before,'' Cheryl stated.

"How old were you when you began to have sexual intercourse with your father?''

"I was fourteen,'' Cheryl said, looking at the judge.

"You were a prisoner in your own home but you made time for Chris Marabito and for Glenn Schmidt,'' Jablonski said under his breath, referring to two former boyfriends.

Paul Gianelli objected.

Ed Jablonski took a walk in the courtroom. He ambled slowly toward the rear and leaned against the back wall. It was a careful gesture. Now he raised his voice.

"Did you sometimes leave school during the day and go to Rob's home?''

"Yes.''

"At the time when you first felt you were pregnant, had you been sexually intimate with Rob Cuccio?''

"Not until I thought I was pregnant. Rob tried to be with me sexually.''

"You're telling us that it was not until you thought you were pregnant by your father that you had intercourse with Rob Cuccio.'' It was hard to believe.

"Yes. I was two weeks late.''

"So it was not until you were two weeks late that you had intercourse with Rob Cuccio?'' Given Cheryl's lack of information about sex, it seemed unlikely that would have been her logic at the time.

"And during this time you talked with your father about going to an abortion clinic?''

"Yes.''

"You are aware that Robert Cuccio is the person who impregnated you?''

Gianelli objected.

"Have you been told it was Robert Cuccio's baby?''

"I was told it was not by my father. I was never told it was Rob Cuccio's; I read it in the papers.'' It seemed an odd distinction.

* * *

Day after day Kenny Zimlinghaus had come to court with one purpose: to stand up for his friend. It bothered him that with all the friends James Pierson had, he, his wife and just two other friends were the only ones who were there. To be absent, he reasoned, was to remain uninvolved. To remain silent was to accept the version of events as the defense had painted them. He was tired of hearing only bad things about James Pierson. Every day he was there and with every day he only grew more incensed. He told Virginia Pierson at lunch that day that he was going to try to talk to Ed Jablonski. He was going to tell him he wanted to testify for the prosecution. He wanted Judge Sherman to hear some of the good things about James Pierson; some of the things that his friends all knew and loved about him, things that his children had loved as well.

"I want to get up there," Kenny Zimlinghaus said.

But Ed Jablonski was noncommittal.

"We'll see how it goes," he said politely. At this point Jablonski only planned to present the police officer who first responded to the scene and Cheryl's boyfriend, Rob Cuccio.

Paul Gianelli's strategy for redirect examination was to explain why Cheryl couldn't speak up, why she couldn't tell someone, why for so long she kept her silence.

"You told us that you were questioned the night you got arrested," Gianelli began slowly, walking across the courtroom.

"Yes," Cheryl said.

"How long were you at Police Headquarters?"

"From twelve to two-thirty."

"That night during the two and one half hours, did you share your secret with anyone else?"

"Two police officers and my brother."

"Was that sharing of your secret . . . what was going through you?"

"That everyone would . . ." Her voice trailed off.

"What were you feeling," he said, pausing, "when the police officer said he knew you had been sexually abused and asked for details?"

"Ashamed and embarrassed," she said, hesitating. "And it all came out."

"Why was it so important prior to February to keep the sexual intercourse secret?"

"I was ashamed and didn't know what everyone would say."

"Since February you have learned to deal with that shame?"

"I've learned to walk into stores . . . people I don't know, deal with it. I have ups and downs."

"When people point or whisper, are you ashamed about the abuse or because you're the one who hired someone to kill her father?"

Cheryl was now weeping.

"Even if my father weren't murdered, they would still point and whisper about the sexual abuse," she said breathlessly through her sobs.

It was more than a week into Cheryl's hearing, and the patience of Judge Sherman was beginning to wear thin.

"We have already heard from seventeen witnesses," he said with obvious displeasure. "We've heard about the vulgarities, the gross and abusive conduct, his method of intimidation. How much more do we have to listen to?"

"My sense is there is not a readiness by the court or the prosecutor to accept that my client was sexually abused by her father," Paul Gianelli said with great formality.

But then a tall, dark-haired man in a blue pinstriped suit and wire-rimmed glasses took the stand and suddenly all that was about to change.

His name was a name almost no one in the courtroom had ever heard before; a man who until about a month before had virtually had no contact with the

Piersons for more than five years. He had read about James Pierson's murder. He had heard about his daughter's arrest. But it was not until the television broadcast of "20/20" just two weeks before the pre-sentence hearing that he decided to break his silence of many years and finally speak up. He had written Paul Gianelli a letter.

"I would like to come forward to say something that Cheryl's mom once told me," he had said. "I realize that this can be considered hearsay and is late in coming, but after seeing the "20/20" program about Cheryl, I feel it must be said."

His name was Jay Fleckenstein, and he flew all the way to Long Island from Tucson, Arizona, to make his declaration.

"Tell us what if any relation you are to Cheryl," Paul Gianelli asked the witness.

"I am Cathleen Pierson's brother by marriage," the witness replied. "An uncle by marriage."

"So Fleck was your father."

"Yes," he said.

"What was the age difference between you and Cathleen?" Gianelli asked.

"Six or seven years. During the time Cathleen was in her teens we lived in the same house. Our relationship was good. That's where I met for the first time Jim Pierson."

Jay Fleckenstein gave his age as thirty-three and said he had a five-year-old daughter. He spoke with a clear, loud voice.

"Did there come a time when you left Long Island?"

"Yes. When I joined the Air Force in 1975." In 1975 Cathleen had been married ten years. Cheryl was six years old.

"When was the last time you saw Cathleen?"

"It was in December 1982," he replied. "My father died. I came for the funeral."

"How long did you spend?"

"Exactly one week. I stayed at 293 Magnolia Drive. The Piersons at the time were living across the street."

"When you were here in 1982 what happened?"

"I went with Cathleen to the doctor's office. Cathy's mom asked me to. During the ride that day I engaged Cathy in conversation. You know, chit chat. I asked Cathy why all of a sudden with her kidney transplant. Why was she having problems with that."

"What did Cathy say to you?"

"She said they had deteriorated because of the beatings James Pierson had given her."

The charge echoed through the courtroom. It was an accusation of murder.

"Did you say anything to her about that?"

In his letter Jay Fleckenstein had said, "I asked her why the hell he did that. She went on to say that Jimmy was screwing around with their daughter Cheryl, and she confronted him about it. When I asked her what she meant by screwing around, she told me that Jimmy had been molesting Cheryl when he thought Cathy was asleep. She further went on to say that Jimmy said she better not say anything about it or the next time the beating would get worse. I asked if there was anything I could do and she asked me not to do anything because it would destroy her mom, Helen. She made me promise that I would not say anything to anyone. I felt she feared for Cheryl's, hers, and my safety."

In court his comments were more terse.

"Yes," he replied to Paul Gianelli's question. "I asked her why she was getting beaten, and she said that while James thought she was asleep, he was going into Cheryl's room."

It was the most spellbinding revelation of the hearing. It meant for the first time that there was someone else who knew of the abuse.

Cheryl's mother.

# 17

"When a young girl's father is behaving in a non-violent manner in his sexual contact with her, although the sexual behavior is inappropriate, it can serve to make the victim feel close and loved. Her needs for human contact and warmth become translated into the specific sexual form of her father's stroking and fondling. In a home in which the only love and tenderness a girl receives takes the form of sexual play, the child's slowly growing sense of wrongness of such intimacy takes years to surface and when it does is coupled with her own incorporated feelings of guilt and responsibility for having let it go on."

—*Conspiracy of Silence: The Trauma of Incest*
by Sandra Butler

"Incest," Dr. Kathleen Oitzinger was saying, "has been referred to as the murder of the soul."

Cheryl's psychotherapist for more than a year, Dr. Oitzinger, probably knew Cheryl Pierson better than anyone. There was a sense when she took the stand that things would be revealed about Cheryl's mind that never had been before.

"In many ways these children die inside," Dr. Oitzinger said, following up her earlier point. "And what you have left is a shell. In order to survive they literally split themselves into different people. When they feel helpless and hopeless, they stuff those feelings down. They develop an inner emptiness and an outer self that presents itself to the public as if nothing is wrong. There is a psychic numbing. They feel nothing.''

"Could you tell the judge what you mean?'' Paul Gianelli asked.

"The first time I saw Cheryl, in a flat voice she spoke about the horrendous things that had happened to her.''

"Unemotionally?'' Judge Sherman asked.

"She would laugh and smile,'' Dr. Oitzinger replied. "It sent chills down my back. I asked her about that, about why she laughed about things that sounded so terrible, and she said it was a nervous habit that would get her into trouble.''

Dr. Oitzinger now spoke about the dynamics of Cheryl's immediate family and how it was a prototype for the setting in which sexual abuse occurred. She cited a body of psychiatric literature on the subject.

"Is there a profile of an abuser?'' Gianelli asked. "Does Cheryl's father fit a profile?''

"Most definitely,'' Dr. Oitzinger replied, adding that Mr. Pierson's personality was that of a type known as "the tyrant.''

She elaborated.

"He is like a general in the household,'' she said. "He is usually a proud patriarch, who likes to present himself as an all-giving father with the wife and children in debt for how much he has provided.''

She was, in fact, paraphrasing a section of a book entitled *The Broken Taboo: Sex in the Family* by Blair and Rita Justice.

> The patriarch will go to great lengths to hide any problem at home and to preserve an image of competence. He sees his wife and children as being in his debt and his daughter as owing him sex on demand. . . . The tyrant may use bullying tactics to engage his daughter in sex, but he also has affection for her, which she recognizes and responds to. He often has little to do with his wife, who has

long since retreated from him sexually and emotionally and has tacitly moved the daughter into the role of wife. . . . Many tyrants disguise their needs for closeness and intimacy through strong macho attitudes toward sex. Sex is the only way they permit themselves to get close to anyone. . . . Beneath the bark and the bite, a tyrant develops deeply tender feelings for his daughter, who may well reciprocate.

With an incestuous father . . . three things usually stand out in his developmental history:

1. He never got over a fixation with his own mother.
2. He never identified with his father.
3. He was encouraged to be "the little man of the house" or to take care of his parents' emotional needs.

For a person to be fixated with his mother does not mean he has a close relationship with her. . . . Often the mother is emotionally distant but implies that if he pleases her enough or does enough for her, then she will allow him to become close. He remains hungry, then, for closeness and keeps seeking it in a woman. . . . In reality, many of the fathers got very little love and nurturing from their mothers and this is a basic reason that they become symbiotic personalities and want someone to satisfy their needs as adults. . . . Erroneously he fantasizes that his mother embodies all-embracing, unlimited love if only he could possess her and this is the fantasy he pursues with his daughter, whom he believes he can possess . . .

Just as incestuous fathers remain emotionally tied to their mothers or to a fantasy of one, similar dynamics are at work in the mother. . . . The collusive mother often had a father who abandoned her. Her mother was generally stern and unloving but she was all there was to cling to. . . . When her daughter came along, she made her into the image of her own unloving mother. Meanwhile she continued to try to get her own mother to love her and give her the nurturing she never got as a child. She would either move in with the mother or keep in close contact.

Another well-regarded expert in the field, Dr. Alvin A. Rosenfeld, while not cited specifically at the hearing, has also described such a family.

> The family has for many years seemed unremarkable socially. There is little history of deviance, criminality, asocial behavior, school difficulty and so on. It therefore comes as a complete surprise when it becomes known that incest has been a regular part of family life for a long time. This "concealment" is the hallmark of the . . . family. All of the very serious family pathology remains within the confines of the home.
>
> Parents in . . . [such] families are immature and their lives are filled with personal losses, actual and psychological. They often seem unable to "mother" or to protect their children because of deficits in their own early experience. Since all family members fear separation intensely, they tacitly or unconsciously agree to maintain the appearance of an intact, "normal" family, using incest as a "tension-reducing" factor that helps maintain the family's tenuous stability by satisfying sexual needs within it.
>
> The child, sensitive to the precarious balance, is played on and struggles to sustain the situation, sacrificing personal desires and developmental needs. The child is "exploited" since she/he is not appreciated as an individual but rather is valued only as serving as a psychological "cement" for the . . . incestuous family's system.
>
> Force is rarely used. Incest is not a one-time "rape" but constitutes a protracted relationship evolved over time, often beginning with fondling and progressing to intercourse years later in some cases. The relationship is distorted and "unfair" because of the power differential between the adult and child. It exerts a continuously distorting influence on personality growth . . .

Fathers, whether their external behavior is domineering or submissive, are usually defending internally against gross immaturity, fears of homosexuality, strong unmet dependency needs, and an inability to deal with grown women. They tend to see their wives as threatening and rejecting and they are sexually estranged from them, but they are unwilling to look to women outside of the family for sexual satisfaction because they fear adult women. Their separation fears and unmet dependency needs also make them very fearful of divorce. Some fathers then rationalize the incest by saying that adultery is more reprehensible, while others point out that their need for sex is intense beyond that of ordinary males, or that they simply want to give their child a good introduction to sexuality. Some continue the incest compulsively though they claim they no longer enjoy it. These men obviously have a deficit in their ability or willingness to suppress their incestuous desires, though their impulse control is otherwise intact with little or no acting out in the community.

The mother is quite likely to be a needful woman, insecure in her worth and femininity. She often seems less interested in sex than her husband is. Some literature and clinical experiences strongly suggest that despite her own parenthood, the mother often remains immature and tied to her own mother, pursuing her in a futile search for approval. Since the mother is absorbed in her own infantile needs, she easily slips into a pattern of abdicating the duties appropriate to her role in traditional families to one daughter, usually the eldest. This daughter takes over the nurturing, caretaking, housekeeping and childbearing roles of mother, becoming a parent to the family. While the mother overtly supports the daughter's acquiring the social role of mother, she may also encourage the daughter to assume the sexual aspects of that role.

The child is also needful and deprived. . . . In many cases, the sexual aspects are but one part of an important relationship for the child. The "molesting" parent in [such] . . . families is often interested in the child not only as a sexual object but also in other aspects of the child's life, such as her artwork or school performance. The parent may take the child on trips and may buy her presents. In other cases, subtle or gross intimidation may be used. However, the adult is often loved, albeit ambivalently, trusted and may, some ways, be the more nurturant of the two parents. Furthermore, the sexual activities are usually at the child's psychosexual level of development—touching, kissing, fondling, rarely with penetration in prepubertal children. Therefore, the child may find the activity ambivalent, pleasurable on the one hand since it is a "special" activity with an admired adult, but not right since it often must be kept clandestine and secretive. Even when the genitals are involved in the sexual activity, the psychological meaning of the relationships is more elementary, embodying a search for the safety, comfort, and nurturance of the good protective mothering figure that neither the parents nor the child ever had.

The similarities to the description of Cheryl's family were indeed remarkable.

"Is there the possibility of seduction by a child who ultimately becomes the victim?" Judge Sherman asked Dr. Oitzinger.

"Yes. I'm sure she was acting in seductive ways," Dr. Oitzinger replied. "Flirting with parents is common." Indeed some psychiatrists say children of incestuous parents are taught to be seductive. Seduction is one of the things for which they receive positive reinforcement. The line between approval and seduction becomes blurred. When Cheryl seductively asked Lieutenant Dunn about his cologne that morning of her father's murder, was she demonstrating that confusion?

Dr. Oitzinger was now asked about the mounting

tension in the Pierson home that eventually led to Cheryl's thoughts of murder.

"What impact did Cheryl's relationship with Rob have on the household?" Gianelli asked.

"It increased James Pierson's fears of losing Cheryl," Dr. Oitzinger replied. "Every time she would come back from seeing Rob, he would insist on having sex with her. The father was starting to give her more freedom. He would let her go to the movies and then would follow her and sit two rows behind them. Although he was giving her more freedom, part of the process of lengthening the leash with Cheryl, he was spending more and more time with JoAnn. JoAnn and her father would follow in the car. It was if they were keeping a leash on Cheryl together. Up until then JoAnn was recognized by the father as Cheryl's child. Suddenly JoAnn was getting his attention. Cheryl started to become more concerned that similar behavior was developing. One day she found them wrestling. JoAnn started to spend time under the sheets in bed with her father. Cheryl was caught in a tremendous bind between wanting to spend more time with Rob but wanting to protect JoAnn. The way she looked at it, JoAnn was really her child. Cheryl started wishing her father dead. Meanwhile she became more and more isolated."

"What were her thoughts with respect to Sean Pica and the house across the street?"

"When Sean first brought up the Wallace killing, Cheryl saw it as a possible way out. She became involved taking him to the house. Most of it was on a fantasy level. Life is hell. Death is a relief. If you think about how to get a hit man, it takes the pressure off."

"But doing," Judge Sherman interrupted. "Doesn't that overstep the line between fantasy and reality?"

"That line was blurred. Once she had talked about it with Sean, she was capable of going through the elaborate details and plan without thoughts about what that really meant, without what the effect would be, without what the consequences would be.''

''When Cheryl revealed the fact that she was having sexual intercourse with her father to Robert Cuccio, did that add or subtract from her emotional state?'' Gianelli asked.

''There are two phases. The first is denial. When something happens that causes the feelings to surface, now there is more agitation. What happens when the incest is discussed is the second stage is released. The feelings are agitated. Now it is being talked about as a reality. The suppression of the incest is now a reality. Cheryl had told no one. When she was lying there with her father, she was detaching.''

Cheryl sat in the chair at the defense table as if she were in a trance. Her head was leaning on the armrest of the chair. If her eyes had not been open, it would have looked as though she were not conscious.

''In what ways did she manifest disassociative symptoms?'' Gianelli asked.

''In November, December, January it affected her ability to consider other options to stop the incest. The blurring of fantasy and reality turned into the line between what it was people knew and what they didn't know. If people didn't know about it, then it wasn't real.''

''Did her condition play a role in rejecting options?''

''Absolutely. The shame. The guilt. Prevented her from reaching out.''

''Does a person suffering posttraumatic stress syndrome manifest feelings of helplessness?''

''Incest is more damaging because one is consenting to being helpless and one feels more guilty.''

Judge Sherman now gave some insight into his feelings about Cheryl and what he was considering for a possible sentence.

''The nightmare of this court,'' Judge Sherman said, ''is that somewhere in another homeroom, some fifteen- or sixteen-year-old is going to read about this case and think that this can be done.''

''My nightmare is that the victim of an incestuous relationship is going to think that it is better not to tell,'' Dr. Oitzinger replied dramatically, to which Ed Jablonski shouted, ''If Cheryl Pierson goes to jail, we're saying it is the wrong thing to kill the abuser.''

''My feeling is that there is another child out there who has been abused,'' Dr. Oitzinger declared. ''And that child is JoAnn and she's afraid to come forward.''

Marilyn gasped. Cheryl began to sob. It was an explosive charge.

Every night after court Marilyn and her mother returned to their Selden home where Kim already had dinner in the works and JoAnn, who by then was ten years old, had done her homework. By six o'clock all of them were there in the kitchen glued to the television evening news.

JoAnn, in particular, was mesmerized. She could not wait to see the report. Not a day would pass in court without some mention of the little girl. Even in her absence JoAnn Pierson was a powerful presence, as powerful in many ways as James Pierson. She, according to the defense, was Cheryl's motive. Feeling guilt for having betrayed her mother, Cheryl Pierson felt a mandate to protect JoAnn. Once Rob came into her life, Cheryl feared her father would turn to her younger sister.

Although only in the fourth grade, JoAnn had definite ideas about her sister's case, which she usually reserved for her biweekly meetings with Dr. Gary Cox-Steiner.

''I loved my father,'' declared JoAnn Pierson. ''He liked doing things with us. He took us shopping. He helped us when my mother was sick and stuff. He tried to cook for us and stuff. Jimmy was Mommy's boy and Cheryl was Daddy's girl and first I became Mommy's girl and then Daddy's girl when Mommy got sick and stuff. We all had Daddy's attention, really."

JoAnn Pierson denied that her father was cruel to his children. She said that her father was strict and had certain rules around the house, but that he only smacked his children when they deserved it. Family, she said, was the most important thing in her father's life. He was a good father. He did all that he could for his wife and children.

"She got everything she wanted," JoAnn Pierson said of her sister Cheryl.

"Do you think Cheryl is lying?" a visitor to one of JoAnn's sessions with her therapist asked of Cheryl's allegations about sexual abuse.

"In a way yes . . . in a way no. Because nobody really knows. But I don't think it happened. My father wasn't that kind of man."

"Do you think Cheryl came on to your father?" she was asked.

JoAnn hesitated.

"Not really," she said. "She would always sit on his lap or something."

"But you don't remember her sleeping in his bed?"

"Well, she would fall asleep in his bed. Watch hockey games and stuff like that, and Daddy would go lie on the couch. And I would go in my room and fall asleep. Or Daddy would go in her room and sleep."

"But they never slept together?"

"No."

"And you never heard Cheryl go into your father's bedroom?"

"Nope, and I was right next to Cheryl's bedroom and my father's bedroom. When we slept he always wanted the doors open."

JoAnn said she was filled with rage at her sister for having had her father killed. She believed that Cheryl had other reasons to kill their father and that before she can forgive her she needs to know what they are. Still, she said, she missed Cheryl a great deal.

"Why do you think Cheryl hated your father?" she was asked.

"I don't know."

"Did she love him?"

"She acted like it," she said. "She'd hug him and go 'Oh Daddy, I love you.' "

"Did she ever get angry at him?"

"Yeah," JoAnn said. "If Daddy said 'No.' She couldn't go somewhere. She'd go . . . 'But Dad!' Then she'd go in her room and say, 'I wish Daddy would die already.' " According to JoAnn, Cheryl had expressed that thought often. Once, JoAnn said, she herself got so angry at her father that she, too, said she wished he were dead. She didn't really mean it, she said, and the day he died she initially felt so guilty about the remark she felt responsible.

Dr. Cox-Steiner said that in all the sessions he had had with JoAnn Pierson, he never got the impression that she had witnessed any sexual activity between Cheryl and her father. Nor, he said, did he ever get the impression that JoAnn had ever been approached sexually by her father.

JoAnn was adamant on that subject as well. She insisted her father had never done anything inappropriate or even remotely sexual. She said her father was always clothed around the house and that when they watched television together in bed, the only thing she would do is lie on his stomach. They often wrestled, she said, but she did not think there was anything wrong with that.

"He'd tickle us and stuff," she said, adding that she felt that too was normal.

Still Dr. Oitzinger would defend her charge. She would quote statistics that in forty percent of incest cases, fathers turned to their younger daughters, and she would point to things that Cheryl had told her.

"Wrestling was how Cheryl's father showed his affection to her," Dr. Oitzinger would say. "That was the beginning of the sex play. That was the first stage.

That is what Cheryl was responding to with JoAnn. He was starting to wrestle with JoAnn. It's the mixed sex and aggression. In a family that is dysfunctional, there is a lack of boundaries, the inability to set appropriate limits for yourself. One of the issues is the line between sex and aggression. Rape is not a sexual act, it is an aggressive act. For Cheryl, the boundary between sex and aggression was blurred from the beginning. When he would tickle her and make her helpless and make her submit, she would not find it pleasant, and yet at the same time she would provoke it because it was a way of getting affection from him, of getting attention. She was very unclear, as are most, where the line is appropriate. Lots of fathers will roughhouse and tickle. But there is a line at which it is no longer father, daughter. There are stages of abuse. It's beginning . . . There is a feeling. She would see JoAnn more secretive or withdrawn from her, with her father, and again JoAnn would need to deny it. There's no way JoAnn would be able to admit that suddenly her father who has ignored her all these years is suddenly starting to give her attention. And how nice that feels and he's playing with me and watching TV in bed with me and of course after all of this comes out and sees what has happened to Cheryl. No way is JoAnn going to say this happened to me.''

Robert Cuccio Sr. was the last to take the stand for the defense. He was a tall, husky man with dark, wavy hair and a beard. He nodded to Cheryl as he walked past the defense table en route to the witness stand. She smiled and nodded back.

A former New York City police detective, Cuccio was about to tell the court that it was not long after that Christmas Eve dinner that his son had tried to tell him about Cheryl's problem.

''It was after Christmas,'' Robert Cuccio Sr. recalled. ''Between Christmas and New Year's. We were startled. Robert said, 'I don't think I'll ever be able to marry Cheryl.' I asked him why. He told me, 'I think her father wants her for himself.' And I said, 'That's such a silly thing to say.' I turned a deaf ear."

"After Cheryl's arrest, did you confront your son?" Paul Gianelli wanted to know.

Robert Cuccio Sr. nodded.

"I asked him, 'Why didn't you come to me?' " he replied sadly. "He looked at me. He said, 'You didn't believe me about Brian. Why would you believe me now?' "

"Who is Brian?" Gianelli asked.

"In 1984 Rob's best friend, who was a foster child, was very unhappy with his home life. In June 1984 Brain came to me knowing who I am and what I am and told me that the person with whom he was living was making homosexual advances to him. I said, 'Brian, don't be absurd. If you think I am going to get involved in that you are crazy.' You have to understand that Brian at the time was trying to make me his foster father. I thought this is just another ploy. I dismissed it as such. In October 1984 he came to live with us, and we were assigned a case worker. Well a year and a half later lo and behold Angelo Patrissi, the case worker, said, 'I have something to discuss with you.' "

What he had to discuss was that there had been reports of sexual abuse in the home of Brian's previous foster parents.

"That was the first time I turned a deaf ear to my son," Robert Cuccio said sadly. "Just after Christmas was the second. Perhaps it was a cry of help."

# 18

It was the last day of hearings to decide Cheryl's fate, and Robert Cuccio was brought in as the prosecution's main witness. Under the terms of his arrangement with the District Attorney's office, Cuccio had to testify against Cheryl, the girl he said he loved and planned to marry. He had to explain how she got him involved in planning the murder of her father.

Of all the defendants in this case, Rob had been the least public. He never gave an interview to the press. For that reason his role had remained the most mysterious and least comprehensible.

Rob Cuccio, a tall, lean youth with dark, curly hair and a neatly trimmed mustache, walked slowly from the rear of the courtroom to the witness stand. Neatly dressed in a blue suit and tie, he scrupulously avoided looking at Cheryl.

"Could you tell the judge when you started seeing Cheryl Pierson?" Ed Jablonski began. Tina Cuccio, looking wan in a blue pinstriped suit, sat in the last row of the courtroom. She held on to her husband's arm. Cheryl, seated at the defense table, was biting her nails.

"May 1985," he replied in a loud voice. He sat in the witness box, his back straight and hands folded in front of him the way children are instructed to do in school.

"Did there come a time when Cheryl Pierson indicated she would like her father shot?"

"Not shot," he replied, leaning forward in his chair, his hands still neatly folded.

"Killed?"

"Yes."

"Was it in May or June?"

"Yes." The question and answer seemed to imply a loose time period, some time around Cheryl's Sweet Sixteen. Cuccio's eyes never left the prosecutor.

"Did she indicate how?"

"No, she didn't."

"Did you discuss the way it would be done?"

"I didn't think she meant really anything by it," Cuccio said, for the first time leaning back in his chair.

"How many times did she tell you?"

"Once," he said softly.

"Let's go now to November 1985. Did there come a time when you went to pick up Cheryl Pierson, and did you meet Sean Pica?"

"Yes."

"Could you tell the judge about that meeting?"

"I go to pick up Cheryl from school and there was a male with her. She introduced me. She said she had his book, and we drove back to her house. Cheryl and Sean went out of the car and I remained in the driveway." This is in direct contradiction to Sean's account of the incident. Sean had said Rob accompanied Cheryl inside the house with him.

"My note states that you went in the house with them," Ed Jablonski asserted, quoting from his initial interview with Cuccio when he was promised that he would not be sent to jail.

"I do believe I stayed in the car," Rob Cuccio replied.

"Did you learn that Mr. Pica wanted to use the Uzi? Did you say you didn't think it was a good idea?"

"I did say I didn't think it was a good idea to use the Uzi."

"Where did that conversation take place?"

"In the school parking lot."

"How did that come about?"

"She had told me she wanted to use the Uzi and I said it was not a good idea. When we got back in the car, we drove to school and at the parking lot we stayed and Sean got out. Then she told me who he was and what he wanted to do. And I said I do not think using the Uzi was a good idea."

With this statement Rob unknowingly had just made a liar out of Cheryl. In her testimony Cheryl told the court that she had not told Rob about the murder plot until after Sean's first attempt in December.

"How did this come about?" Jabłonski pressed.

"After Sean got out of the car, she said who Sean was. She had told me she was talking with someone. I put two and two together."

"She had been talking about what?"

"Finding someone to kill her father. After reading an article in the newspaper maybe it would be a good idea for her to . . . She spoke to someone who had done it before and would do it again if the price was right."

"What did you tell her?"

"I told her it was crazy. It shouldn't be done."

"Tell us about that first conversation when she tells you."

"I told her it was crazy. No one in the tenth grade would do it."

"Did you ask her why she wanted her father killed?"

"There was no need to," he said.

"The next time you talked to Cheryl Pierson about doing it, you drove her to her home and then in the parking lot what was discussed?"

"I asked her who Sean was. She told me and I laughed. I didn't believe Sean was going to do it."

"Did you ask her what she was doing at the house?"

"I thought she was looking for a book."

"How did the conversation about the Uzi come about?"

"I asked her is that the real reason you were in the house and she told me about the gun and I told her I don't think that's a good idea. The gun could be traced back to Sean or Cheryl." So Rob was not objecting to the murder but rather the method.

"Did she tell you why else she was there?"

"No."

"Did she tell you of any plan?"

"No."

"Did you come to learn of the plan?"

"Yes."

"How long after the incident did you learn there was a plan?"

"I can't recall."

"Was it weeks, months, days?"

"It was after Thanksgiving."

"How long after the plan failed?"

"A couple of days."

"Tell us what she told you about the plan."

"They were going to use the other house."

"So you knew about the plan!" Jablonski charged, catching Cuccio in another contradiction. He said nothing, but seemed unperturbed. He looked off to the windows. Now Judge Sherman addressed young Cuccio.

"Before the brick was thrown, did you know that would be the plan?" Judge Sherman asked, his voice grandfatherly, nonjudgmental.

"No," young Cuccio said, turning to face the judge. "There was speculation about it."

"Tell us about the plan as you knew it," Jablonski said with disgust.

"I thought Sean was going to stab Mr. Pierson."

"Cheryl told you Pica was going to stab her father."

"Yes."

"What did she tell you about what happened?"

"That a brick was thrown through the window. I didn't know whether he was going to be shot or stabbed, but it didn't work."

"Did you tell me of the original plan: 'A knife? A little guy like that?' "

"I did laugh. I didn't think he could stab Mr. Pierson."

"Did there come a time when you again met Sean Pica?"

"Yes, at Newfield High School when I went to see Cheryl."

"How did that come about?"

"After the first attempt we bumped into each other."

"Did you ask Pica 'are you going to do it?' "

"I do believe he said he was going to."

"Did he try to tell you he was trying to get a gun?"

"I don't recall."

"Prior to December twenty-third when you found out Cheryl's father was sexually abusing her, did you talk about the killing and Sean Pica? Did you discuss that Pica would do it?"

"He always said he would, but he never did. It made me believe he was not going to." So Cuccio was conceding that he was aware of a murder plot even before he said he knew Cheryl was sexually abused by her father.

"Did you meet him a third time?"

"Yes."

"Did he say he had a weapon?"

"He said he had an animal gun. He asked me if I wanted to use it. I told him I'm late. I have to go."

"Did you tell Cheryl?"

"No, I never did. I never told Cheryl."

"Let me read from my notes. Perhaps that will refresh your memory. 'Rob tells Cheryl: Pica offered gun to Rob.' Did you tell Cheryl? Yes. Are you now saying . . .'"

"I don't recall it." It was clear Rob was doing everything he could to limit Cheryl's involvement in the murder.

"Subsequent to December twenty-third did you say

you didn't want Pica, 'I didn't want a tenth-grader.' Did you tell her you wanted a professional?''

"Yes." Ed Jablonski had said all along that it was his impression that once Rob's suspicions about sexual abuse were confirmed by Cheryl in the kitchen of his parents' home, he started looking into ways to hire a professional killer. Sean Pica had said that Rob told him he had inquired to hire someone "in the Mafia" but that this person had told him that he was too young.

"Subsequent to that did you ask Jimmy to find someone?''

"No. I didn't ask him to find someone. I found out through Cheryl that she had talked to him. I asked Jimmy if he had talked to Cheryl."

"What did you say to Jimmy?''

"Jimmy, let's look at this logically. She's filling the role of mother. Two females. He didn't pick up. I couldn't tell him."

"You talked to a person about whether or not he had found someone to kill his father but not why?'' Jablonski said forcefully.

"I gave Cheryl my word. I never go back on my word.''

"You were having a conversation about killing another person!'' Ed Jablonski shouted. Tina Cuccio shifted nervously in her chair.

Rob Cuccio was silent. Now Ed Jablonski shifted gears to the day of the murder itself.

"The day of the killing. Did there come a time around three P.M. when you and Cheryl were at her father's safe?''

"No," he said.

"Are you saying that you were not at the safe?'' Jablonski's voice was now incredulous.

"That is correct.''

At this point Ed Jablonski turned to George Hughes, Cuccio's attorney, who was also seated at the defense table. "Have you talked to him about truthful testimony?'' he asked angrily. The three lawyers—Hughes,

Gianelli, and Jablonski—rushed to confer with Judge Sherman privately at the bench.

Ed Jablonski referred once again to his notes, which indicated that Rob accompanied Cheryl to her father's safe and then opened it.

"Did you open the safe?" Jablonski asked the witness.

"No, sir."

"Was the lawyer in the house at this point? Where are you telling us now you were?"

"On the couch outside to where the safe was," Cuccio replied. Jablonski's impatience was palpable. Ed Jablonski left it at that. But it was clear it contradicted what Cuccio had told him during their previous meeting.

"When you saw Sean in school the next day, did you say to him 'nice shot'?" The coldness of that remark had a chilling effect on the courtroom.

"Yes," Cuccio replied.

"Did you say, 'keep cool'?"

"Yes I did."

"Did you say here's four hundred dollars now, we'll give the six hundred dollars later?"

"Yes I did."

"On the night she told you the allegations about her father, December twenty-third, did you say go to the police?"

"I do not recall."

"After the murder, did you say back to Sean at that point, 'be smart'?"

"Yes I did."

"What did you mean by that?"

"Be smart. Don't tell anyone about doing it."

"In carpentry class, did you say, 'Stay cool. Keep your mouth shut'?"

"I kept saying, keep cool."

"Did you say this to him: 'There's a lot of money being thrown around and you'll get the rest later'?"

"I said a lot of money is being thrown around."

''Did Jim Pierson ask whether the two of you were involved and you said no?''

''Yes.''

''Did there come a time the night of the funeral, I think it was a Saturday, that Cheryl talked to Pica?''

''Yes.''

''She came to you.''

''Yes.''

''She was upset about that.''

''Yes.''

''The two of you went to the pizza place.''

''Yes.''

''The three of you were in Pica's car. Did Cheryl ask details of how he killed her father?''

''Yes.''

''Did he say he hid behind a tree, shot him, and went up and pumped four more into him?''

''Yes.''

''Did there come a time when you were picked up by police and brought back to the Pierson home?''

''Yes.''

''Was Cheryl asked if she had something to tell her grandmother and she said, 'No.' And you said, 'I'm arrested. They know.' And you told her to tell the police that two hundred dollars of the four hundred dollars was yours. You wanted to get involved.''

''I didn't want her to take the rap alone. I was nervous,'' Cuccio replied.

''Did it ever cross your mind that after the killing of Mr. Pierson, with all you knew about him, to go to the police and tell them what happened?''

''Yes. It crossed my mind for a brief moment. Yes.''

''And you decided not. Because if you did tell the police what would happen?''

''We would get arrested.''

''Did you think that as the plan was going down you would get arrested?''

''Yes I did. But I never believed Sean Pica was going to kill Mr. Pierson.''

"You were there when he had been to the house. You knew he had been talking about using the Uzi. You knew about the attempt. You knew he had obtained an animal gun."

"So far so good," Cuccio said flippantly.

"And you're telling this court you didn't think he was going to do it?" Jablonski asked, his voice again sarcastic and arch.

"Correct. I had never seen the gun and in November he kept saying he was going to do it and he never did it."

"You thought it was all talk," Judge Sherman said.

"Yes," Rob Cuccio replied.

"But then you asked for a professional killer," Jablonski interjected.

"Yes," Rob Cuccio replied, not appreciating that this response contradicted what he had just said.

"No further questions," Ed Jablonski said, taking his seat.

Paul Gianelli now stepped to the center of the courtroom for cross-examination of the witness, and as he did Cuccio looked suddenly relieved. The young man sat back in his chair. He unfolded his hands. He relaxed his shoulders.

"Does Mr. Jablonski know how you feel about Cheryl?" he asked.

"Yes."

"That you care about her very much?"

"Yes."

"That you care about her very deeply?"

"Yes."

"Getting back to May or June of 1985, did you see anything about the relationship between Cheryl and her father that gave you cause for concern?"

"When me and Brian and she was washing the car, the way her father leaned over and gave her a hug and kiss wasn't the way my father would kiss my sister," Rob Cuccio replied.

"Did you have dinner at her house?"

"Yes."

"Did you have any man-to-man conversations with Cheryl's father?"

"I had asked Cheryl's father if he liked me. And he said, 'I'll like you only if you don't touch my daughter and if you only go to the places you say you're going to.'"

Gianelli now turned to Rob's conversations with Cheryl about the murder.

"When Cheryl would talk about doing something to get back at her father, was she calm or nervous?"

"She seemed calm when she actually talked about her father being terminated. Yes." *Terminated.* It seemed like such an awful choice of words.

"When Cheryl told you about having sexual intercourse with her father, did she tell you about her fears for her sister?"

"Not that day," he said. "But she saw JoAnn wrestling around on the floor and became concerned that the same pattern would start occurring."

"After Cheryl told you what was going on, were you getting angry inside?"

"Yes I was." His response now, however, seemed almost removed.

"At Christmas did Cheryl tell you she spoke to her brother?"

"Yes."

"Did you know Jimmy Pierson before?"

"No." Therefore, Rob Cuccio's first conversation with Cheryl's brother was about the murder.

"Did Cheryl, JoAnn, and James Pierson go to Orlando?"

"Yes."

"When they came back, did you ask whether there had been any sexual contact?"

"Yes I did, and she said she did in the bathroom when JoAnn was sleeping." Again Rob's tone of voice was devoid of emotion. He looked up at Judge Sherman, then returned his gaze in the direction of Cheryl's lawyer.

"What did you do?" Gianelli asked.

"Nothing."

"Were you getting angrier?"

"A lot." Cuccio's voice for the first time hinted at that anger. He clasped his hands together and stretched his fingers.

"How did you hide the anger from Cheryl?"

"I tried to hide it but I couldn't."

"Did Cheryl contact you the night before the killing?" Paul Gianelli now asked.

"Yes. I was working at Waldbaum's bakery. Sean told her he would do it the next day or so and I said, 'Don't worry.' "

Clearly Judge Sherman had lost all patience with Rob.

"Then you ran right home and told your father," Judge Sherman suddenly interjected with disgust.

"No I didn't," Rob Cuccio said, in what was yet another indication that day on the stand that Rob was someone who could not grasp even the most blatant sarcasm.

"The following day did you get a phone call from Cheryl?" Paul Gianelli asked, quickly trying to resume his line of questioning.

"Yes."

"Did Cheryl know her father had died?"

"No. I found out because my father told me that Mr. Pierson didn't slip on the ice. He was shot."

"What were you thinking about when Mr. Pierson's body was being wheeled away?"

"I can't remember."

"Did you or Cheryl discuss the fact that her father had a lot of money and she would get it?"

"No. I would have said money was never an issue."

"Your father has testified that you and Cheryl will probably get married."

"I do hope so."

"Have you told any lies to help Cheryl?"

"No. I have been truthful."

Ed Jablonski spoke with great formality.

"Cheryl Pierson was indicted for murder in the second degree," he began in what were to be his closing remarks. "The District Attorney agreed that it would not agree to treat the defendant as a youthful offender but to allow a plea of Manslaughter One. We also indicated that we would not recommend serving the maximum but rather would make a recommendation for the minimum of two years to six years and would oppose youth offender status. Cheryl Pierson knew that if she pleaded guilty she would serve no more than the minimum period of two to six years. This hearing is a hearing on what sentence she should receive based on the facts. This was not a trial over whether she was sexually abused or how James Pierson was as a father or as a human being."

To all those assembled in the courtroom and to many, many more who had followed this case with interest, whether Cheryl was sexually abused and how James Pierson was as a father was exactly what this hearing was all about.

"The District Attorney's office said and still says that Cheryl Pierson fits the profile of a sexually abused girl," Jablonski continued, standing at the prosecutor's table and looking directly at the judge. "Which is why we didn't try her for murder. It is why we did not ask for the maximum under Man One. Because the nature of this case is so different. We feel, we implore Your Honor to consider the bottom line that people remembering this case remember that Cheryl Pierson did not receive probation. If she took the time and effort to bring Sean Pica to her home, tell him the hours her father left for work, the merits of which weapon to use, the plan with the burglar alarm. That conduct cannot be condoned by giving her probation. If she receives probation, the public will perceive this as condoning her conduct. Probation is not a punishment. I hope that in this case there is a message to the people and to other people who are abused: If you take the law into your own hands, you will receive state incarceration. The amount will not be recalled nor the fact that she receives y.o. [youthful offender] or has no criminal record. What will be remembered is that she received state incarceration. The biggest fear is that there is another person being abused right this minute. We fear a woman who is a victim of rape, unhappy by how she may be treated in a courtroom, might take the law into her own hands if all she receives is probation.''

Ed Jablonski spoke with conviction. His voice was loud, clear, precise. He glanced for a moment in Cheryl's direction, then toward the rear of the courtroom. Then he shifted his gaze anew in the direction of the judge.

''Where are we to stop, judge?'' he asked, pausing for dramatic effect. ''If we look at this tree in the forest, our heart goes out to her and the terrible life she has had. And we don't see the forest and the potential is that it will continue. The people would not contest that Cheryl Pierson was abused by her father. During the hearing we asked questions. No one can say to you they know for sure she was a victim of incest. So not knowing if it happened, for her sentence to be probation is even worse. We don't know if it happened, judge.''

Now the judge interrupted.

''If there was doubt, why didn't we let it go to a jury?''

''She fit the profile. The last thing the D.A. wants is to convict her of murder and have to give her fifteen years to life. It was our decision. The bottom line is James Pierson was a terrible father. I would have loved to prosecute James Pierson for that conduct. The problem is . . . we at the D.A.'s office never got that opportunity and a jury never got that opportunity. We didn't because Cheryl Pierson was the prosecutor, the judge, and jury. She decided by herself. She and the other people. She arranged for another life to be taken. So for her now to receive probation would perpetuate more conduct like this. That is why we are asking that you sentence her as an adult. If you take the law into your own hands, you will receive state incarceration."

It was an emotional appeal, and when it was over Cheryl put her head in her hands and sobbed.

Paul Gianelli had been planning this summation for months. And indeed it was his finest hour. Slowly, eloquently, with a soft-spoken elegance, Gianelli mapped out why his client should not be sent to jail.

"Cheryl Pierson, it should be remembered," he began quietly as he stood in the rear of the courtroom, "pleaded guilty. She is not saying she is not guilty."

He walked in the direction of the empty jury box as if he were going to address comments there.

"Mr. Jablonski talks about no one being able to say whether she was abused. Cheryl Pierson told you she was abused. Is she not to be believed? You've listened to witnesses. Don't they have the ring of truth . . ."

Gianelli's voice was soft. He let the words themselves evoke the drama.

"Cheryl Pierson has given a firsthand account of being verbally and physically abused in her home. It boggles the mind that someone should live in that sort of home. She committed a wrong, an unspeakable wrong, but should not the court examine who taught her the difference between right and wrong?"

Paul Gianelli compared Cheryl's case to that of Kitty Genovese, a Queens woman who was slain in front of her apartment building while hundreds watched.

"In a sense the community is in a small part responsible," Gianelli said. "What happened in Selden is not that different from Forest Hills. This case reflects a failure on all avenues of exposure. Everyone failed Cheryl Pierson."

"Yes, but Kitty Genovese screamed out for help," Judge Sherman said, underscoring what appeared to be the judge's biggest reservation about the case—that Cheryl never reached out, never told anyone.

"Think about why Cheryl Pierson didn't scream out," Gianelli countered with confidence. "Think of the shame she must suffer. Her ability to scream was impeded by the duress she was suffering. If you believe she was in fear, if you believe she was a mother to her sister, can you understand this is what propelled her silence? Think of the protective feeling a mother has for her young. A mother-daughter relationship Cheryl had with her sister. Is not the taking of a parent's life the most shocking thing a person can do? Why are not events leading up to it not the shock? The most shocking silence was the silence of Cathleen Pierson. She went to the grave with her secret with Cheryl left behind to live a life of hell. That is shocking. The anger Cheryl felt in learning of her mother's silence was expressed by her on the witness stand."

Paul Gianelli charged that the incest was about to begin with Cheryl's younger sister, JoAnn.

"When Cheryl's brother said to her, 'JoAnn's turn is next,' he did not realize what he was really saying to her. She was not going to let that happen. She had deep feelings of protection for JoAnn. Mr. Jablonski talks about absence of proof, but neither of the psychiatrists preparing reports nor the probation authorities were permitted to speak to JoAnn."

Paul Gianelli now walked slowly before the judge.

"The fact that James Pierson was killed by Sean Pica was the result of chance and luck and that Cheryl Pierson's name begins with *P-i-e*. Pierson and Pica. She did not put up a note. As lucky or unlucky as it was, her name began with the same letter of the alphabet. If your honor accepts that all incest victims universally have revenge fantasies, both Robert Cuccio and Cheryl Pierson did not take Sean Pica seriously. Think about the last year in James Pierson's life for Cheryl. The mixed signals. Including more freedom for Cheryl, more contact between Cheryl's father and

JoAnn. The pressure of Cuccio now knowing she was having sex with her father. All this on a sixteen-year-old girl on Magnolia Drive in Selden.''

"But the one thing most difficult for this court is all the avenues of available help," Judge Sherman interrupted, restating his concern that Cheryl never told anyone. "It would have taken very little.''

"Cheryl could have found refuge by disclosing it if she was concerned with only her own self-protection," Paul Gianelli responded forcefully.

"If Mr. Cuccio Sr. had listened and believed Cheryl," Judge Sherman began.

"Yes. But someone like Mr. Jablonski wouldn't have believed him," Paul Gianelli said. "He would have wanted proof. These other options must be considered in light of the fact that in 1987 there was not one case in the three hundred fifty-six reported cases of incest in Suffolk County of self-reported incest in the situation of a single-parent home. Think of the reasons why Cheryl Pierson did not self-report. I don't think the people of Suffolk County will remember the sentence. The cases are not read as closely as we would like to believe. I'd like you to consider the kind of girl she is. Consider what simple incarceration will do to her. She's not a street-wise kid. She is an immature, shy, sheltered girl from the suburbs. At some point in her life she has to put this behind her and live a normal life. If she lived through the hell of Magnolia Drive, she will learn to live through the hell of prison. But I ask you to be merciful.''

In three weeks Cheryl Pierson would have her answer.

# 19

Holy Sepulchre Cemetery is sandwiched between Route 112 and Granny Road, two busy thoroughfares that cut across central Long Island in the form of a neat triangular wedge. *Serene* is probably the last word anyone would use to describe this graveyard. It sits across from a popular discount auto repair shop. Down the street is an outlet of the neon-lit fast food chain Nathan's. A multiplex movie theater is just around the block. The sounds of traffic echo day and night. It is here that Cheryl's grandparents are buried and here too that she had come to bury her parents.

During the weeks and months that followed her father's death, Cheryl had come often to lay flowers on her parents' common grave, to have words with her mother, to pray. She believed her mother could hear her, see her from her place in heaven. But Cheryl's notion of her father was different. She did not speak to him directly after his death. Cheryl believed he was in hell and that he could still control her fate. "A lot of bad things are happening that I think he is making happen," Cheryl would say of her father.

In the days following the hearing Cheryl visited her mother's grave. But now, she would say, she had only questions. How could her mother have stood silently by knowing what she knew? How could she have permitted it to continue?

Cheryl Pierson spent her days and nights during those stressful days following the hearing preparing for what she called "the worst"—packing her clothes, her toys, the new collection of dolls Alberta Kosser had given her for Christmas, the kind her mother would have liked to collect: sweet little porcelain figurines with tiny button noses and dewdrop eyes from a Hallmark line called Precious Moments.

All night long Cheryl lay awake, worrying, wondering.

"I still feel guilt," Cheryl Pierson would say. "I still feel ashamed."


"I pray to Jimmy," Kenny Zimlinghaus said. "Before this is over. Let me know."

Kenny Zimlinghaus had been James Pierson's staunchest supporter. He had been in the courtroom every day. He granted interviews to the press about the "real" James Pierson. But now with the hearing over, he was seated with his wife in the living room of their home and about to reveal something that had been haunting him for weeks.

Tears came to his eyes as he was about to admit something that only recently he had begun to remember. It was a conversation he had once had with James Pierson. Kenny Zimlinghaus could not pinpoint exactly when it was, but now suddenly he could see it clearly as if it happened just the other day. The two of them were seated at Bennigan's, a popular lunch place off the Long Island Expressway. They were talking the way they often did—about work, about their families—when all of a sudden James Pierson broke into tears. It must have been late 1983 or early 1984. It was after he had taken the fall from the roof and during the time when he was not speaking to his sister. He was saying something about being angry at his wife for "giving up the will to live."

Then James Pierson began to tell Kenny Zimlinghaus something else.

"Some people are saying it's not normal," Pierson said, his eyes filling with tears.

"What?" Zimlinghaus asked.

''The way I am with Cheryl. They're trying to change it into a perverted thing.''

''They're just jealous,'' Zimlinghaus told his friend, dismissing the thought as foolish, absurd. ''I wish I was that way with my daughter.''

But now, thinking back to the exchange, Kenny Zimlinghaus wondered whether his good friend James Pierson in his own clumsy way may have been reaching out, trying to break the silence, trying to reveal a terrible truth about himself that Kenny Zimlinghaus simply had not wanted to hear. He never asked the question. He never pursued what he dared not believe.

''I loved the guy,'' Zimlinghaus said, leaving the room.

''I still don't believe it,'' Cathy Zimlinghaus said. ''But if he did do it, didn't he deserve some mercy too?''

Virginia Pierson would never admit that she believed Cheryl's story. All during the hearing she remained silent. However, after it was over, she composed a letter and sent it to the local newspapers. She finally needed, she said, to be heard.

> Everyone has asked me why I have not spoken out in defense of my son, James Pierson Sr. This is very difficult for me to do. James Pierson was my son and Cheryl Pierson is my granddaughter. I know in my heart that my son could not have done this. Although people have made him sound as though he was an animal, those who knew him knew he was generous, a good provider, and dedicated to his family. He did not deserve to die.
>
> These same people are accusing Cathy of knowing all and doing nothing. Her friends should be proud of the way they have disgraced her memory. Cathy would not have stood by and allowed anyone to harm her children. She was a fighter and proved it by fighting her own death long and hard.
>
> I still love Cheryl and my grandson, Jimmy, al-

though they treat me as if I have done something wrong. Guilt does strange things to people.

When Cheryl was released from jail, my daughter and I did everything we could to help her. She rejected our attempts and as she told us, we were not her bosses, her bosses were dead.

I sat through every day of the presentencing hearing through twenty-three defense witnesses, and heard many lies. These lies became apparent when the prosecutor cross-examined these witnesses. Cheryl claims she did not have sex with Rob until two weeks after she was pregnant. However tests concluded my son was not the father. Will someone please explain to me how she became pregnant with Rob's baby.

The presentencing hearing was not a hearing on Cheryl's character. But rather the trial of a dead man, who could not defend himself.

Cheryl claims she did this to protect her sister. I say, put the guilt where it belongs and not on a ten-year-old who has done nothing except to lose her father.

I am trying my best to make sense. I have difficulty putting my thoughts together since my stroke. I am trying to show people that my son was not evil. He had bad points, as everyone does. But he had many good qualities. He did not deserve to be murdered. If you draw a conclusion, you can take any action out of context and make it fit to substantiate that conclusion.

My grandson, Jimmy, accuses me of being mean and abusive to Cheryl. I have not said a word to her or to any of the press about her. Cheryl does not even acknowledge me. She acts as though I do not exist. Perhaps she wishes I did not. I still love Cheryl and Jimmy but I also loved my son very much. And I am entitled to my own thoughts and opinions.

No matter how I try, I will always be the one who is wrong in Jimmy and Cheryl's eyes because I grieve for the loss of my son. However, I am strong and I will overcome this tragedy. Whatever happens to Cheryl for her crime lies in the hands of Judge Sherman. I will live with it.

I know a lot of people sympathize with Cheryl. Put yourself in my position and tell me how you would feel if your son was murdered, your grand-daughter was responsible and now your son is being made out to be the terrible evil monster and is not here to defend himself. Am I not supposed to grieve? Am I not supposed to miss him? I am his mother. He will always be my son.

Virginia Pierson

Sean Pica kept up with the case from prison. His friends and family sent him news clippings. When he was able, he watched news reports on television. Oddly, he harbored no bad feelings toward Cheryl. All he wanted to know was "how she feels, how she's doing. I care about her," he would tell a reporter from his cellblock at a maximum security prison in Elmira, New York, where his days were spent mopping floors and carrying hot water to other inmates. He had acquired the name Angel and put on forty pounds—all muscle—from lifting weights. He had grown a mustache. On his arm was a green tattoo.

Sean seemed to be adjusting well to prison. His job for a time was in the kitchen. He liked it there because he could snack while helping to prepare meals. It entitled him to take two showers a day, which he always took. He studied drafting during the day at the prison's school, and by the time of his release he hoped to have a college diploma. Still, he said, he suffered nightmares. He also felt as though he had been "used."

"I wish I had it to do over again," he would say. "I wouldn't have done what I did. Cheryl asked me to kill her father and I did. I felt sorry for her. I thought it would help her. I guess it helped her—if nobody else."

Judge Sherman worked on his decision. The plea precluded a jury, so he alone would decide Cheryl Pierson's fate.

"I have to live with this," Judge Sherman would say.

October 5 began as a crisp fall morning. A cold Arctic air mass hovered over Long Island. Seemingly overnight the leaves had lost their color. Long before dawn, the lights at the Kosser home were ablaze. Cheryl, Alberta, and Mike were up, dressed, and seated at the kitchen table.

On the other side of the Selden, Virginia Pierson and Marilyn Adams had also spent a sleepless night. They, too, were at the kitchen table. Each had on black trousers and a black jacket, the garments they had worn to Sean Pica's sentencing, the clothes from James Pierson's funeral.

There was a sense of moment, a sense of anticipation about this day that could be felt all over Selden. The local radio stations blasted the news in between contests for the new Bruce Springsteen album. It was whispered about at the supermarkets and post office, the high school parking lot and shops along the Selden mall. The fate of Cheryl Pierson was on people's lips. It had been a year and a half since James Pierson's murder.

As expected, the courthouse was jammed. Not only the local television stations were there; the networks had sent reporters too. The ordeal of Cheryl Pierson had become a national story. Never had there been so much excitement in that small courthouse. Court officers frisked spectators at the door. Cheryl left the Kossers' residence that day just after 8 A.M. and took the long drive to Riverhead from Selden one last time. Alberta, Mike, and her brother were with her. Cheryl wept continually. When she arrived, she held on to her brother as she climbed the steps to the courthouse. She took refuge once again in the small room across from Judge Sherman's Part X courtroom and shut the door. One by one, members of Cheryl's circle took their places in the courtroom. Rob Cuccio and his family were among the first to arrive. Diana Erbentraut, the one friend of Cheryl's who had tried to speak out, showed up with her father. By the time Alberta and Mike appeared at the courtroom door to take their places, all thirty-five seats in the small courtroom were taken. Robert Cuccio's sister stood and offered Alberta Kosser her place. Robert Cuccio Sr. surrendered his seat to Michael Kosser. Kenny and Cathy Zimlinghaus gave up their seats so that Marilyn Adams and Virginia Pierson could witness the event.

After a time the door opened and in walked Cheryl Pierson, her face ashen and stained with tears. She was wearing the same white and grey dress she had worn on the very first day the hearing began, a pink sash around her waist and flat white shoes with little straps around the ankles. She took her seat at the defense table. Paul Gianelli, who sat beside her, whispered in his client's ear that before he announced sentence, the judge would ask her if she had anything to say. Cheryl immediately reached for a pen and began writing on a paper towel.

''Mr. Gianelli, Mr. Jablonski,'' the judge's clerk said aloud. The two attorneys stood and walked to the rear of the courtroom, past a swinging wooden gate, and into the judge's chambers. The heavy wooden door was closed shut. It was impossible to hear them. Cheryl, alone at the defense table, kept writing. She did not look up. Her head was bent, almost touching the table, as she scribbled furiously. The wait for the lawyers seemed endless. When the door to the judge's chambers finally opened, the noise was magnified by the stillness, the anticipation and the muffled sounds of Alberta Kosser's tears. Both attorneys carried a nine-page document in their hands, the judge's decision. They hurriedly took their places at two separate long wooden tables. Ed Jablonski, seated up front, affixed his glasses and immediately began to study the pages as everyone in the room watched. Meanwhile Paul Gianelli rolled his copy into a cone and whispered something in Cheryl's ear.

"No," she cried out breathlessly. "No. Oh no." Her voice echoed through the room, staccato breathes of disappointment and horror. Cheryl turned briefly and caught the eye of Alberta Kosser, who was seated in the front row. The expression on Cheryl's face was almost not human. It was the kind of look that was impossible to forget, an expression of raw fear. It was perhaps the only time in all those many days and months that the public got a glimpse of the real Cheryl Pierson: the scared, vulnerable, terrified Cheryl whose fragile protective shell had finally cracked for a brief public moment.

The judge appeared.

"All rise, please," the clerk announced, as the spectators stood one final time.

Cheryl Pierson was summoned to stand before the judge, the same spot where months before she had publicly admitted hiring someone to kill her father because he had been sexually abusing her. Now she stood there again to hear the judgment of the court, but almost immediately her knees buckled. Two court officers whisked a maroon leather armchair under her.

"Is there anything that you would like to say?" Judge Sherman asked, looking down at the girl, his voice somber. The spectators leaned forward in their seats.

Cheryl attempted to speak. Her mouth was open, but at first no words came out.

"I," she gasped, leaning back in her chair. She held on to the arms of her chair. Her voice was thick with tears. She started to read from the paper towel.

"I realize that what I did was wrong," she said, struggling on each word. Her mouth was still open. The judge waited. "And I . . ." She took a deep breath. The judge looked at her. He waited.

"I'm . . ." Cheryl finally said, her voice filled with pain. "Sorry."

The judge waited.

"Is that all?" the judge asked gently. She nodded.

"There are some things I want to say," Judge Sherman said, looking down at the girl. "During the time this proceeding has been going on I have received more than one hundred letters from people urging me to be lenient with you. Most of these letters are from victims and survivors of domestic violence, including sexual abuse and incest. Many letters exhibit great understanding and sympathy for the suffering you endured and your need to escape, although none of these correspondents condoned the method you used to end your plight nor do I. But it is also encouraging to observe that a number of these victims overcame their suffering to become productive members of society. Some of them have become physicians, dentists, attorneys, authors, and entertainment personalities. This is what I hope for in your case."

His voice was loud, clear, but largely without expression, as if he were reading aloud some annual report. Cheryl looked straight ahead and at the floor.

"Finally the publicity and interest engendered by your misfortune," Judge Sherman continued, "may produce some benefit for other victims who seek a way out of their unhappiness. They have been made aware of the—"

Cheryl suddenly fell forward and slid onto the floor. Two guards grabbed her arms and lifted her onto the chair. One guard cracked open a vial of smelling salts. Cheryl jolted into consciousness.

The judge kept talking.

". . . many agencies, both public and private, who are pledged to protect the innocent and obtain justice for them. Perhaps victims such as yourself and friends of victims who are aware of their conditions will thereby be encouraged to report to these agencies and thus avoid the consequences of the actions which you took."

Cheryl's deep sobs resounded through the courtroom. She remained seated.

"Cheryl Pierson," Judge Sherman said, "I hereby

sentence you to five years' probation. As part of that sentence you are to serve six months in the county jail.''

Two court officers supported Cheryl at each arm and led her through a back door, up a short flight of stairs, and over an outside bridge that led to another exit. Cheryl looked at no one. The handcuffs came just before she reached the parking lot. A white Suffolk County Sheriff's Office car waited. Staring straight ahead as though she were in a trance, her hands locked in front of her, still clutching the paper towel, Cheryl Pierson was taken away.

# 20

"Substantial circumstantial evidence and the direct testimony of [the] defendant leads this court to conclude that Cheryl Pierson was subjected to sexual contact by her father," Judge Sherman wrote in his decision, stating that he at last believed the teenager's story. "Moreover . . . she was the object of frequent, repeated acts of sexual intercourse by her father."

In determining his sentence, Judge Sherman had researched what other judges had done in similar situations. More than twenty years ago another Long Island teenager shot and killed her father because she said he was sexually abusing her. She, too, was sixteen years old. It was Valentine's Day 1964.

"Just a minute, Pops," the girl had said when her father called her into the bedroom as he often did before she went to school. The girl's mother, who was a nurse, had just left for work. The girl returned with a shotgun and fired. She pleaded guilty to manslaughter, the way Cheryl did. The judge in that case excused her with a suspended sentence. In a more recent case in upstate New York, a judge sentenced a girl to up to seven years in jail for taking a rifle from beneath her bed and fatally shooting her father for the same reason, but an appeals court found the sentence too harsh. In both cases, however, the girls had killed their fathers themselves under the immediate threat of another sexual encounter. They also quickly reported themselves to the police. No money changed hands.

Judge Sherman was bothered by Cheryl's premeditation and the fact she had hired someone for the job. It was not his role to conclude—the way a jury would have been asked to do at a trial—whether her actions were justified. Yet it was from the concept of justification under Hebraic criminal law that Judge Sherman finally found his guidance. There, he discovered, a daughter was justified in killing her father to prevent incest from taking place, but not after the fact. If, instead of bringing him to a court of law, the girl killed her father, she too would have to stand trial and face a possible sentence of death.

"I was troubled by all the circumstances involved," Judge Sherman told a reporter after Cheryl's sentence. "Is this the only way that you can solve this problem? . . . No, it's not and that's why I sentenced her to this kind of jail term."

Cheryl was in jail now over a month. Her six- by eight-foot cell was equipped with a sink and toilet. She was permitted to use a communal shower. A television set was affixed to a wall. The yellow metal bars were locked at 11 P.M. and opened again at 7 A.M., during which time she had access to a narrow seventy-foot-long "day area" furnished with four cots and two metal tables, where Cheryl and seven other inmates ate their meals. She was assigned to kitchen duty, among other chores, and also had access to the prison library. Inside her cell, she was restricted to writing letters and listening to cassette tapes. The only clothing she was permitted to wear was the dark green shirt and trousers worn by other inmates. Cologne and makeup were not allowed. She was permitted one telephone call a day. The only gifts she could receive were magazines and sealed music cassettes for her Walkman. She was not permitted to decorate her cell except for several photographs. Breakfast was served at 7 A.M. The lights were shut off at 11 P.M. Visitors were restricted to one hour per day.

Paul Gianelli, who visited Cheryl occasionally, found her adjusting poorly to prison life. She was frequently sick with colds and not eating, he said. Cheryl had less faith than ever before in the criminal justice system.

"I feel I'm being made an example of for no reason," Cheryl would tell a reporter in a telephone interview she granted from jail. "I want to be home on Thanksgiving and Christmas. They're family holidays. I need my family, and my being in here is not proving any point."

During the initial weeks of her stay, Cheryl received many letters. Other sexually abused women held a candlelight vigil outside the prison gates. Some interested groups banded together to see if they could get Cheryl released early. New York's Mayor Koch decried Cheryl's sentence as being "heartless."

Cheryl could not understand Judge Sherman's decision. She told her lawyer she understood even less why it could not be overturned. She wrote a letter to New York State Governor Mario Cuomo requesting that he set her free.

"I'm sitting in jail being made to be an example to other abused people," she said. "If only I was on the outside being able to tell these people about getting help. I'm not doing any good sitting here."

Cheryl's request for clemency would be denied.

Perhaps because it was cold out again and shops were getting ready for the holidays, perhaps because it was what she always did anyway, Virginia Pierson found herself thinking about her son. Photographs and daydreams were the only things she had left. She missed him. She would have liked to have been able to sit down and pour her heart out to him about everything that had happened.

Virginia Pierson liked to believe that she and her son had a close relationship. Of her two children, James had been her favorite, just as Marilyn had favored her father. Indeed James's wife, Cathleen, was often jealous, Virginia thought, of how close the two of them were; how Pierson preferred his mother's cooking, the way she ironed his shirts. Virginia Pierson used to stop by the house Saturday mornings after Cathleen died, and her son would keep her company in the living room as she stood and picked her way through a large pile of ironing. Cheryl would stop by and try to engage her father in conversation. Even Cheryl, Virginia thought, seemed jealous of Pierson's affection for his mother. Her son always seemed fine.

As Virginia Pierson's mind wandered, she found herself thinking back to so many situations in which they were together. Festive occasions, tragic ones. How he would often surprise his mother in the mornings before work and stop by for coffee. And as she did, her thoughts turned to a funeral she and her son attended together for the father of a close friend. It was January 1984—not long after Pierson's fortieth birthday party. Cathleen was so ill that day she remained at home. Pierson and his mother headed to the funeral alone. The two were seated in Pierson's car. James Pierson was driving. They were talking about this and that, the way they always did—talk was easy between the two of them—when suddenly he turned to his mother and asked her a question that she would find impossible to forget.

"Does insanity run in our family?" he had asked.

"No, of course not," she had replied, never asking her son why. But now, looking back on it, Virginia Pierson would say, it was obvious. He must have known even then that Cheryl at the young age of fourteen was deranged.

It was a Tuesday night in November. Marilyn Adams and her family sat around the kitchen table, that familiar table with its blue-flowered vinyl tablecloth and matching blue, scented candles. The telephone was ringing as Marilyn prepared a pot of coffee. The television set was on as it always was to watch the six o'clock news when a familiar face appeared across the television screen. The room fell silent.

It was a picture of Sean. He was being interviewed on camera in jail by a popular New York City anchorman. Kimmie, Marilyn's twenty-year-old daughter, turned up the volume. She pulled a chair inches from the screen. Virginia Pierson and Marilyn Adams sat at the table. JoAnn flitted around the room like a trapped fly.

"I feel guilty for not feeling guilty," Sean was saying as a picture of James Pierson's corpse came onto the screen. "I personally feel he deserved to die."

Marilyn Adams and Virginia Pierson were exhausted from the publicity. They wanted to get on with things. Now that Cheryl was in jail, they hoped all the media attention would go away. No matter how many times they sat through the details of the murder plot, it was as if they were hearing about it for the first time, as if they were revisiting the scene of an accident they could still somehow stop.

The program continued. No one spoke, and when it was done Virginia Pierson went to her bedroom to cry. Marilyn, unleashing her rage as much at her family's situation as the program, started shouting. She picked up the telephone and began dialing the number of the NBC newsroom. When someone answered, she demanded to speak to the anchorman and she was told he would have to call her back. Marilyn hung up and resumed shouting.

JoAnn, who in the interim had taken a seat at one end of the dining room table, was now hunched over a Mickey Mouse coloring book. She looked up and studied her aunt. She watched the woman for a moment and then stood. She walked over to where Marilyn was seated and, standing behind her, began stroking her head and shoulders the way Cheryl so often had done when things were going bad for her father.

* * *

JoAnn Pierson at ten years old had been through more tragedy than most experience in a lifetime. Yet to meet her is to meet a pretty, poised, intelligent little girl, who is bubbly in demeanor and outgoing in style. She was the one, James Pierson had always said, who had most reminded him of himself. Tough. Proud. The only one of his children who, when he smacked her hard across the face, did not cry. He liked that about JoAnn, that "she could take it." At the time she was born, she was "Mommy's little girl." She liked that her father thought her special, that she could make her daddy proud.

"I'm mad for what Cheryl did," JoAnn said sadly. "But I love her because she's my sister."

JoAnn would never visit her sister Cheryl in jail nor once talk to her by telephone. It was not only that she did not want to, but Marilyn would constantly say that "jail is not place for a little girl." JoAnn would agree and add that she believed her sister "deserved to be punished."

JoAnn was nostalgic. She wished that she could go back in time. The year would be 1982. It was the happiest time in her life. It was her fifth birthday. She remembered the party. Her mother was healthy then. Her father seemed happy. Everyone did. She missed Christmas too, how she would wake up the entire house, how she loved the surprises, all the fun. JoAnn said she missed those times. She wished she could go back to the way things were before. She missed her father. She missed Cheryl.

"What do you miss about her?" she was asked.

JoAnn's eyes clouded over. She was silent for a long time. It was the first and only time pain was visible on her face.

"I just miss her," she finally said sadly.

"Will you forgive her?" a friend asked.

"I don't know," she said.

"When will you know?"

"Soon," she replied, as if she had given it a lot of thought.

"What will it take?"

"The truth," she said, "For her to tell me the truth."

"Because you think she's lied to you until now."

"Yep."

"And because you don't think anyone knows the truth except Cheryl."

"Yep," she said, pausing for a moment. "And my father . . . and God."

"But what if what she's told you is the truth?"

JoAnn was silent again. She looked off in the distance.

"Then I'm going to have to learn to live with it," JoAnn said with determination, the same determination James Pierson had always admired.

Ed Jablonski had moved on to other things. A newlywed was murdered Christmas Eve by her husband. A nurse was accused of killing at least twelve patients at a Long Island hospital.

He was happy to have the Pierson case behind him.

"I didn't like wearing the black hat," Ed Jablonski said, adding he had never prosecuted a case where all the mail he received was against what he was doing. Like so many involved with the case, the Pierson case had become an important part of his life. There were still things that gnawed away at him. He was sorry not to have been able to send Robert Cuccio to jail. Tactically, he said, he needed the youth's testimony against Cheryl and Sean. Additionally, his case against Cuccio was weak because it would have been totally contingent upon the cooperation of James Pierson Jr. Sean Pica would have pleaded the Fifth and refused to testify on the grounds of self-incrimination. But all in all, Jablonski said, looking back on things, he was sorry there had not been a trial. Jablonski, after all, always relished a good courtroom battle.

"I looked forward to cross-examining Pica," he would say. "I wanted to have him explain about the money and why did he go and buy jewelry. I would have been interested in questioning Cheryl. It would have been a challenge. Because if I had done it the wrong way, it would have invoked a tremendous amount of sympathy for her. But had I done it the right way, right in front of their eyes . . ."

He stopped himself. Cheryl Pierson, he said, was not the girl everyone thought she was.

Rob and Cheryl had had their ups and downs as romances often do. Still, as she whiled away her time in jail, the only subject that ever seemed to make her smile was that of her love for Rob. Just as she had fantasized about his asking her to go steady at her Sweet Sixteen, so too she dreamed about his proposal of marriage, their wedding.

They had known each other now not quite two years, and most of that time was wrapped up in plans for the murder and its aftermath. He was the first boy Cheryl would say she ever loved.

Still, there were others who thought their relationship strange. Even before her niece's arrest, Marilyn Adams had commented to friends how rough Rob seemed to treat Cheryl. At the funeral, she would recall, he grabbed her by the neck in such a painful hold Marilyn had to ask him to stop. Ed Jablonski would recall Cheryl's brother telling police how Rob often punched Cheryl when they were kidding around. In her letter to Judge Sherman, Kim Adams spoke of how frequently she saw Rob hit her cousin.

"They would fool around and tickle each other and punch each other and stuff," JoAnn Pierson would recall of her sister's relationship with Rob. This characterization sounded hauntingly familiar, reminiscent of the relationship Cheryl's parents had a young lovers and later the relationship Cheryl had had with her father.

"Cheryl would almost provoke the wrestling, the rough play as an excuse to be able to punch him when she was angry," Dr. Oitzinger would say of Cheryl's relationship with Rob. "That is how her father showed his affection to her. That was the beginning of the sex play."

But that Cheryl and Rob were in love no one would doubt. Rob was devoted. Every day he demonstrated his feelings by making the long trip to visit Cheryl in jail, not unlike the long trip James Pierson had made daily to the hospital to visit his wife, Cathleen. For every day that Cheryl was in jail Rob tied a ribbon on the oak tree across from his parents' house. He said it time and again: The only thing he wanted, the only thing he cared about, was for his Cheryl to be free.

It is hard not to try to imagine how different things might have been had Cathleen Pierson never become ill. It is hard, too, not to think about what would have happened if Cheryl had never been seated next to a boy named Sean Pica, had never heard about a woman named Beverly Wallace, had only told someone else about what was happening to her.

Selden, like so many small American towns, is a place where being normal is expected, where children are told that they should respect their elders, where people like James Pierson install expensive security devices to be safe from the violence of strangers, where danger is thought to come from outside. It is the kind of place in which people see themselves in each other, perhaps like all of us, deriving comfort from the familiar, the predictable, the known. Not unlike a mirror image, what they see in their neighbors is who they are.

It was Dr. Oitzinger, Cheryl's therapist, who said that Cheryl had trouble differentiating between what was real and what was not. To Cheryl, anything that people did not know simply was not true. It was an intricate defense mechanism she developed, her way

of coping with daily life, to be able to deny something
even as it was happening before her eyes. Dr. Oitzinger might have been describing the community in
which Cheryl lived.

The shock, in the end, was not that James Pierson
had sexually abused his daughter, but how many people suspected it and found it too frightening to confront. They preferred not to know, not to ask, and,
because of that, found it surprisingly easy to deny.
Because they did not want to believe something terrible was going on, they decided it simply wasn't—just
as Cheryl, finding her father bleeding in the driveway,
decided he must have slipped. What an extraordinary
psychological moment. Not wanting to face that she
was responsible for her father's death, Cheryl decided
even as she stood over her father's body that she
wasn't. Her vision was clouded with the same powerful denial as so many of her father, who had watched
her stroke her father's chest, who had seen the two of
them in bed. They, too, did not want to face what was
all too painfully clear. They did not want to take the
responsibility, voice the suspicion, say it out loud.

Sadly, the only time Cheryl would speak was when
she had already contracted a killer. The only time her
neighbors would break their silence was at Cheryl's
hearing when it was already too late: too late for James
Pierson, too late for Sean Pica, too late for Cheryl,
too late for so many whose lives were devastated by
yet another act of violence.

Child rearing is a private matter. It is about as private as any there is, and that privacy allows the illu-
sion of normalcy to continue, masked by birthday
parties and Christmas dinners, by family outings and
smiling portraits prominently placed on living room
walls. It is the American dream in many ways, this
''happy family'' with picture-perfect lives; the lives
that mirror the sweet, simple Norman Rockwell scenes
so many who live in Selden put on display; the lives
that cut to the core of so many cherished American

principles—privacy, parental control, discipline, trust. But the disturbing truth is beneath the surface in Selden, as in so many other places, how many others were either physically or sexually abused, how many other lives were wrecked by family violence, how many other secrets extended back generations. Cheryl's mother. Sean's mother. Sean's stepfather. Cheryl's great-grandmother. Cheryl's uncle. Cheryl's cousin. The policeman who arrested Cheryl. The adopted brother of Cheryl's boyfriend. Cheryl's good friend from around the block. No one said a word. They thought they were alone.

People learn about love, about intimacy, about honesty from their parents, the ones they are closest to. And behind every one of these tales of family violence is the story of an adult who was abused as a child and never told anyone either, then grew up and went on to do what was most familiar to them: They abused and neglected their own children. Cheryl was devastated to learn that her mother was aware of what was happening to her and was unable to stop it. But clearly, for many reasons, Cathleen Pierson could not give to Cheryl the childhood she herself never had. The violence was all too familiar, the secrecy normal, the silence expected.

It was on January 9, 1984—just two days after James Pierson's fortieth birthday party—that *Something About Amelia*, a television movie about a girl being sexually abused by her father, was shown on network television. Cheryl's mother wasn't feeling well, and they watched the program together in the living room on the couch. At one point Alberta Kosser walked in, and they all watched as Amelia and her problem family went for therapy. When it ended, Cheryl shut the television off and kept quiet. So did her mother. "If you have a problem, come to Daddy," James Pierson had told his children. He never told them what to do if Daddy was the problem.

Judge Harvey W. Sherman was troubled by the Pierson case. What he could never understand, even once it was over, was why Cheryl never told anyone. "It would have been so easy," he had said. But to ask Cheryl Pierson why she could not speak is to ask why a woman being raped cannot scream. There is no easy answer. Cheryl's scream was silent. Cheryl wanted to keep her already fragile family together as much as she wanted the abuse to stop. She wanted the abuse to end as much as she wanted to believe it was not true. She felt to blame. She felt ashamed, guilty, afraid, confused, ambivalent, torn. This was her father. She knew how violent he could be. She wanted to please him. She needed his approval. She trusted him. To speak up was to admit to herself, to the world, that there was something desperately wrong. Just as it was for so many of her neighbors. They did not want to speak. They did not want to face themselves.

It is comforting to think that if Cheryl, like Amelia, had only told someone, something could have been done. But to blithely believe that there was a way out is as much of a deception as denying that the abuse ever took place. The uncomfortable truth is that while murder certainly was not the answer, Cheryl's telling someone may not have been either. James Pierson, after all, was a man to whom family and appearances were everything. It is hard to imagine he would have been like the father on the television program: going into therapy, apologizing for his ways. James Pierson loved his daughter. But he was also a man who punched his daughter in the face after she sent a Valentine to someone else, a man who slept with a rifle under his bed, a man who struck his dying wife when she confronted him with what she knew, a man who held a gun to the temple of a friend when he was the butt of a practical joke. What would James Pierson have done? We will never know.

James Pierson's murder shocked just about everyone in Selden. Who he was, how he led his life, what he had been through with his wife, how strong and devoted he had been, how dedicated a father was not what anyone associated with being gunned down in a driveway. The coldblooded violence sent a chill throughout the community to everyone except for the youngsters involved. To them, it was a clinical execution in every way. Cheryl wanted details of the slaying. Rob was impressed with Sean's marksmanship. Sean was paid.

It was Dr. Oitzinger who spoke during the hearing of Cheryl's ability to remove herself from painful experiences; how Cheryl, like so many youngsters who grow up in homes amid violence learn the psychological tricks of "depersonalization" and "numbing" in order to cope. Sean's psychiatrists, too, described how he learned to sit and helplessly watch amid building rage as his mother was beaten. Why then should it be a surprise that Cheryl and Sean, who daily removed themselves psychically from what they saw, were able to distance themselves so easily from a murder. To them, it was hauntingly matter-of-fact, shockingly commonplace.

"I really didn't think much about it," Sean said. "I just did it. I felt good it was off my back. I didn't have to worry about it not more."

"I would have liked to see what happened," Cheryl said, "If he looked. If he knew. I wonder if he died right away. If he didn't, if he knew why he got shot. It's weird not knowing."

No, James Pierson was not the family man everyone thought he was. Sean Pica was not the hardworking Eagle Scout, who seemed so easygoing and content. Cheryl Pierson was not the sweet, vulnerable little girl so many wanted to believe. How could she have been?

The case of Cheryl Pierson is troubling because it has no easy lessons. It is factually messy and rife with ambiguity. To study it is to emerge bleary-eyed from all the blurred lines, the distorted images. The only thing clear is that when Sean Pica fired those shots that early icy morning and killed a man he had never met in a community that was content to belive that everything was find, he shattered the silence of generations.

With good behavior and the time she had served following her arrest, Cheryl was to be released from jail 106 days—three and one half months—after she first arrived. It had snowed all weekend long, but that Tuesday morning, for the first time in days, the sky was clear. Cheryl's brother and boyfriend had been planning her release for weeks. Their surprise: a white stretch limousine, just like the one Cheryl always dreamed about. Long before dawn it pulled up to the Suffolk County jail with stocked bar, television, sun roof, and all: the white bird that would whisk Cheryl away to freedom.

The sky was still dark when Cheryl emerged from the prison door, absolutely radiant. Much thinner than she had been in court, blusher on her cheeks, just a hint of eyeshadow and pink lipstick, she wore a white sweatshirt with her name and two large hearts, a tiny cross around her neck. She held Rob's hand.

"I'm just glad it's over," she said breathlessly, looking out at the group of reporters who had gathered in the darkness. "It was rough but I made it."

She was beaming.

With that, she and Rob Cuccio joined Cheryl's brother and a neighborhood friend in the backseat. Their shrieks of joy could be heard from one end of the parking lot to the other. The sun had come out. The four youths stood up through the sun roof of the limousine and waved. Cheryl made a victory sign with her fist. All four youths were smiling. It was a strange image. The cameras followed the group.

"A happy picture," Tina Cuccio said, inviting photographers onto her lawn as Cheryl cut down a yellow ribbon and held it victoriously over her head.

"Well, we made it," Cheryl said, beaming.

That afternoon Rob asked Cheryl to marry him just

as she had always envisioned. He got down on one knee and presented her with a one-carat marquise-shaped diamond ring. They posed for photographers. The next day the newspaper headlines read:

"Wedding Bells Ring for Cheryl!"

"Ribbons and Ring for Happy Cheryl."

"Former Cheerleader Cheryl Pierson, 18, of Selden, New York, Whoops It Up . . ."

The front pages were filled with the tidy, picture-perfect ending to Cheryl Pierson's story.

It was a tough winter on Long Island. More snow fell than anyone in recent years could remember. Virginia Pierson's hearing was permanently impaired from her stroke. JoAnn Pierson had begun to have problems in school. Marilyn Adams went back to college to study psychology and English. Vincent Pica, Sean's youngest brother, had gone to live with his father. Life went on.

Meanwhile, in an upstate jail, Sean got into a fight and was transferred to a facility much farther north. His friends and family continued to write. Diana Gabb broke off the engagement after she met another boy. She returned the ring she had receive to Sean's mother. Visitors were sparse because the jail was so far.

Virginia Pierson spent much of the time looking through old photographs. The birthdays and the Valentine's Day dinners, the anniversaries and the Thanksgivings. She kept them all in a shoebox under her bed. She particularly loved the shot of James Pierson as a little boy, all frecklefaced and impish, the one in choir robes. She now held in her hand the photograph of a girl her son knew before he met Cathleen and mused how different things might have been. Then she fell upon a photograph of Cheryl.

"All I want to do is wrap my arms around her and tell her I love her," Virginia Pierson said, her voice filled with pain. "God help me, I want to kill her."

Cheryl's life was now a whirlwind of wedding plans,

engagement parties, bridal registry, a place to live. She and Rob went to a resort in upstate New York with heart-shaped beds and sunken bathtubs. Tina Cuccio was helping Cheryl pick out stemware and dishes. She had given her new daughter-in-law-to-be some fancy lingerie and a bottle of cologne. The couple registered at Fortunoff's in Westbury for a crystal pattern called Windswept. They debated whether to buy furniture off the floor at Sear's or to wait the six weeks and special order. A wedding date was planned for October.

"I want to be the best wife and mother," Cheryl said solemnly. "And have a family of my own."

Holy Sepulchre cemetery was quiet. The snow was beginning to melt. There was still no inscription on the tomb of James Pierson. The flowers someone had left for Christmas now had wilted; the red ribbons were still in place but frayed. But James Pierson had left behind a message. He had been a sentimental man; a man who often quoted the inscriptions on greeting cards, a man who always spoke about wanting to walk his daughter down the aisle. Indeed perhaps it was for Cheryl that his words were intended. They were the words he had chosen for the tombstone of his wife. He had them framed by a heart and flourished with a rose. In part comforting, in part forgiving, in part a haunting threat, they were the words, the only words, James Pierson left behind.

"Love Is Forever."

# Update 1989

Cheryl Pierson and Robert Cuccio were married on Oct. 9, 1988. At last report, they were living quietly on Long Island not far from Selden. Cheryl was working in an office as a word processor; Rob was driving a truck. Cheryl had virtually no contact with her sister, JoAnn, now 12, who continued to live with her Aunt Marilyn and grandmother. Cheryl saw her brother Jimmy once, at Christmas. After a brief time in California, Jimmy had returned to Long Island to live. Alberta Kosser and others in Selden had a difficult year following Cheryl's incarceration. Mike Kosser developed lung cancer and died four days before Cheryl's wedding. Kenny and Cathy Zimlinghaus separated. Sean remained in prison and was not expected to be eligible for parole until 1996.

## About the Author

Dena Kleiman is an award-winning reporter for *The New York Times*. She lives in New York City.